GW00362858

LIVING and RETIRING ABROAD

uestion:
When one of the world's great financial organisations – managing in excess of US$110 billion for over 44 million clients, and earning more from its investments than any other insurance company in the world – creates an offshore investment service . . .
. . . introduces a range of major offshore expatriate investment accounts . . .
. . . offers a unique charging structure that pays for itself and used 100% of invested capital from the outset . . .
. . . builds in exceptional flexibility, control and tax advantages . . .
. . . and sets up in one of the world's best regulated offshore financial centres . . .
. . . what should you be doing about it?
nswer:
If you're an expatriate investor, call your financial adviser.
If you're a financial adviser, call us.
Albany International
ALBANY INTERNATIONAL ASSURANCE LIMITED
St. Mary's, The Parade, Castletown, Isle of Man, British Isles.
Telephone: 0624 823262. Telefax: 0624 822560. Telex: 629889 ALINTL-G.
A member of LAUTRO
ALBANY INTERNATIONAL ASSURANCE LIMITED
A MEMBER OF THE METROPOLITAN LIFE GROUP
FUNDS MANAGED WITH ADVICE FROM MERCURY ASSET MANAGEMENT PLC
Please send me details of Albany International investment accounts:
Name:
Company:
Address:
Tel:

The Daily Telegraph Guide

LIVING and RETIRING ABROAD

THIRD EDITION

Michael Furnell

To my wife Barbara and my daughter Gillian, for all the happiness they have given me. Also to my long serving secretaries Jackie and Jean.

The Author

Michael Furnell has 40 years' experience in property journalism, and has a weekly property column in the *Sunday Telegraph*. He is the author of two property books, and editor of the journal *Homes Overseas*.

First published in Great Britain in 1986 by
Kogan Page Limited, 120 Pentonville Road,
London N1 9JN.
Second edition 1988
Third edition 1989

British Cataloguing in Publication Data
Furnell, Michael
Living and retiring abroad. – 3rd ed.
1. Overseas retirement. – For British
personnel 2. Overseas medicine
I. Title
646.7'9

ISBN 1-85091-715-9

Printed and bound in Great Britain by
A Wheaton & Co Limited

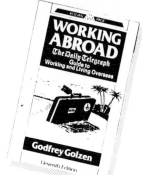

Contents

Index of Advertisers

Introduction

It is with much pleasure that I write this introduction to the third edition of *Living and Retiring Abroad*, for this title is an indication of the continuing interest of British people in acquiring a home in the sun.

Spain, Portugal and France, in that order, remain the most popular countries for ownership of holiday and retirement homes in southern Europe and in the first two of these locations it is not unusual now for over 50 per cent of builders' clients to emanate from the UK.

France is experiencing new interest in Normandy and Brittany which in a few years will be easily accessible by car via the Channel tunnel. In the south of the country the formerly exclusive Riviera is within reach of the less wealthy, following the activities of developers who are offering modest flats west of Cannes on the coast or a short distance inland on a leaseback contract.

Two of the larger Mediterranean islands have made a comeback. Malta now positively encourages foreigners to retire to the island and to purchase residential properties following a change of government and new policies.

Cyprus continues to grow as an extremely popular tourist centre and has an abundance of new hotels, apartments and villa developments in the Greek sector; but the Northern territory, occupied by Turkish troops, does not at present have the same attraction from a residential or vacation point of view.

Tiny Andorra continues to handle admirably an influx of new residents who enjoy mountain living, while Switzerland and Austria have found it necessary to impose restrictions on non-nationals who want to buy real estate, in order to protect their own people from being priced out of home ownership.

Title problems and property purchase procedures are being simplified in Greece and the acquisition of homes throughout the country is possible except in designated border areas of the mainland and some of the islands close to Turkey, where restrictions are imposed on foreigners for national security reasons.

Italy is another country where British people formerly experienced problems in property purchase, but there are now more agents specialising in local property so additional information and offers are available. Umbria and Tuscany to the north of Rome provide some exceptional opportunities to convert old agricultural buildings and small abandoned, mainly hilltop, villages into attractive modern-style living accommodation, although planning requirements often restrict the propositions to construction or repair within the existing fabric.

I have been forecasting for some time that the Mediterranean coastline of Turkey would be the next popular location for homes in the sun. Tourism is gaining popularity at a rapid rate among British people, and also other Europeans, and already evident are pioneers among selling organisations proposing to market homes in Turkey. Turkey is keen to join the European Community and is planning the development of more hotels, facilities for visitors and improved communications.

At present British nationals are the most prolific purchasers of residential property in most countries of southern Europe. They have exceptional finance facilities with short- and long-term loans from banks, building societies and insurance companies. Some loan sources are prepared to accept as security a substantial UK-based house, while others will grant loans on the basis of the overseas property being purchased. A surprising number of cash purchasers also exist. Many of these have realised the substantial equity tied up in their family homes and used the proceeds to buy a smaller more manageable UK house plus a place in the sun.

Caution should be the watchword in any property transaction and this is even more necessary when buying a home in a foreign country. It is vital therefore to obtain adequate legal and financial advice from experts before signing any documents or paying over substantial sums of money to unknown third parties. Fortunately, there is a growing number of legal advisers with international experience who have offices in the UK. These are generally branches of established lawyers from abroad or well-established firms of British solicitors who have special departments devoted to advising clients on the purchase of real estate in various European countries. A number of firms are listed elsewhere in this book (pages 375-6).

It is 24 years since I produced the first issue of the monthly *Homes Overseas* magazine. I have edited every issue over this period and travelled extensively to view holiday and retirement homes in resorts around the Mediterranean and elsewhere. My experience tells me that ownership of a home in the sun is a very worthwhile proposition provided the correct procedures are adopted right from the start.

I hope that this book will help many families and individuals to acquire their 'dream home' without unnecessary hassle.

Michael Furnell

Part 1
Before You Go

Chapter 1

Keeping the Family Happy

You are approaching retirement; the family has grown up and left home; you are both in reasonably good health or could benefit from living in a warmer climate; you will have sufficient income from pensions and investments to live reasonably comfortably in the foreseeable future and you enjoy a challenge. So you plan to start a new life when you finally cease committing yourself to the daily routine of earning a living and the strain of a life-long career.

There are many older couples in these circumstances who seriously consider cutting ties with their motherland and starting a new life in another country. Often they have enjoyed a succession of family holidays in southern Europe or have travelled further afield, to the American continent perhaps, as their family commitments grew less. Possibly business travel has enabled one or both parties to visit places across on the other side of the world. All these experiences have helped them to form opinions about their most favoured locations for a life of leisure without boredom.

The first essential is to narrow down the choice to perhaps just one or two countries where they both feel they would be happy to set up a new home. Sometimes the children and grandchildren are horrified at the thought of grandparents deserting them and going off to a remote location where they will never be seen again, so accessibility is often an important factor in the choice of location.

The next step should be a more detailed exploration of the facilities and attractions of the selected area(s) in the chosen country. This should entail several quick visits to likely locations for preliminary impressions, followed by a stay of at least a month in the most promising area. The visit should be timed to coincide with the off-peak season when the holiday-makers have gone home and some of the amenities have closed for the winter. Popular resorts full of lively families in summer can look very different in the cooler months of January and February and the climate may not be so attractive. But if you are going to live there permanently you will have to experience all seasons and the winter climate might not suit you. Don't be afraid to undertake two or three forays before making your final decision. (*See also* Chapter 14.)

Having found your 'ideal' spot, the next step will be to decide if you want to live all year round in an apartment block or a villa. Apartments are often built close to the sea and may be a little exposed to cool winds in the winter, yet you may feel more secure in a building surrounded by other inhabitants. Remember however, there could be a noise problem, or the majority of owners may only use their accommodation for summer holidays with perhaps an occasional visit in the off-peak season, say in December over Christmas. Thus the building might be almost empty for half the year.

Detached villas generally appeal to retirees because they have more private, spacious accommodation, and a garden for relaxation and exercise. But pueblo-style developments and town houses are becoming more popular, particularly in Spain where land costs are increasingly expensive. This style of living is more neighbourly than residing in isolation and attracts the more gregarious.

Remote country cottages are not suitable for the most frail or those suffering from medical disabilities, because they may be too far from shopping facilities, doctors or public transport.

In regions which attract tourism, living costs may be more expensive but social activities should be easier to enjoy and access to international airports could be much more satisfactory.

Having completed your research and selected your destination, you are ready to proceed with arranging your new life. But what *will* the family say?

They may well be apprehensive about you living in a foreign country, hundreds (or thousands) of miles away from them. How will you cope on your own and will you really like living among strangers?

On the other hand, they may welcome your wise decision to live in a less severe and varied climate where you should enjoy improved health and the challenge of starting a new life, instead of gradually vegetating in your old family home which has grown too large for normal needs, too expensive to maintain and requiring an unnecessary amount of work to keep it clean.

With parents living permanently abroad the family has the opportunity of spending part or all of the summer holidays with them in their new home or renting a nearby property. Furthermore, with ever improving international communications, parents can return to England occasionally for short holidays with the family at, say, Christmas or Easter. So the problem of family ties may not be such a difficult one to solve as originally envisaged.

In larger countries popular with expatriates there are often bridge clubs, garden societies and regular gatherings for English-speaking nationals. In some places there are British churches of various denominations which help new residents to meet each other.

If you are a TV addict it is now possible to receive your favourite British programmes via satellite TV in some European countries. It is also easy to keep in touch with life in the UK via the excellent news and cultural programmes broadcast by the BBC World Service.

Chapter 2

Tax and Financial Planning

Bill Blevins, David Franks and Robert Maas
Investment and tax specialists of Blackstone Franks, Chartered Accountants

UK residence

The emigrant and expatriate are usually hoping to cease to be both 'resident' and 'ordinarily resident' in the UK, to avoid UK income tax and capital gains tax on their worldwide income and capital gains. To succeed, one has to understand the meaning of the terms 'resident' and 'ordinarily resident'. Ordinary residence is explained on pages 24-5, and residence is explained below.

Resident in the UK has a very wide meaning. A tax year starts on 6 April and ends on the following 5 April. As a general rule, an individual will be resident in the UK in a particular tax year if:

1. he lives in the UK for more than six months in that year; or
2. he lives in the UK for more than three months on average over four consecutive tax years; or
3. he visits the UK even for just a few minutes, and has accommodation in the UK 'available' for his use.

The word 'available' does not necessarily mean that the individual owns residential accommodation, nor does it imply a legal right of occupation. Merely having a place set aside for his use (eg, a bedroom in someone's home) could be sufficient. A house which you own, but which is commercially let, is not 'available' accommodation. Not using available accommodation on a particular visit is irrelevant. Simply setting foot in the UK can trigger residence for tax purposes.

The above rules may be overridden by double taxation agreements where the individual is resident both in the UK and in another country.

There is an exception where an individual is engaged overseas full time in a trade, profession, vocation, office, or employment, provided that no part of its duties are carried out in the UK (with minor exceptions in the case of company employees). Such an individual will be non-resident, even though he has a property available to him in the UK. This exception covers a person working in a self-employed capacity so long as the activities are genuinely full time, ie the number of hours worked are similar to those of a national of the country of residence with a full-time business or employment.

It is important to note that such an individual must either (1) be working full time in a trade, profession or vocation and *no part* of the trade must be carried on in the UK; or (2) be working full time in employment overseas and any duties performed in the UK are *merely incidental* to the overseas duties. In such a case, having available accommodation will *not* be a factor in determining resident status.

A husband and wife are looked at separately. Thus it is possible for the husband to be non-resident while his wife is a UK resident. For example, if the husband is in genuine full-time employment overseas he will be regarded as non-resident. On the other hand, his wife, if she is not employed overseas, will be a UK resident and therefore liable to tax on her income worldwide (even though she is living with him), if the couple have the use of the family property in the UK and she spends a few minutes in the UK.

The diagram opposite will help you through the maze of rules on residence. However, it must be stressed that the residence rules are not precisely defined and your individual circumstances always need to be considered. In particular, if you plan your life so as to keep marginally within (1) and (2) above, or so as to remain outside the UK for a single tax year and a day or two on either side, there is a significant risk that the Revenue could successfully challenge your anticipated non-resident status.

The residence maze

To help you work out whether or not you are likely to be resident in the UK in a tax year, follow the maze overleaf.

The date of non-residence

By concession, you are normally regarded as becoming non-resident the day after you leave the UK, even though this may be in the middle of a tax year. As explained earlier, a tax year starts on 6 April and ends the following 5 April. This concession applies for both income tax and capital gains tax.

Technically, however, your UK residence extends for the *entire* tax year, ending 5 April after you leave the UK. The Inland Revenue can refuse to apply the concession if they consider that you have timed your departure, or entered into a transaction, specifically to avoid capital gains tax. It can therefore be dangerous, for

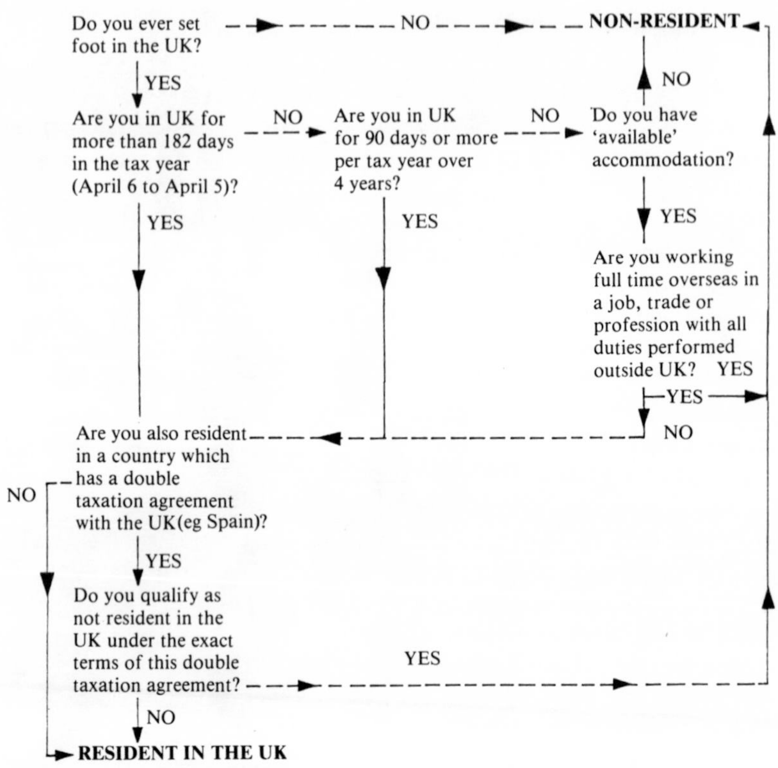

example, to realise an enormous capital gain on shares or property or on a business soon after you leave the country. It is safer to sell your assets in the tax year *following* your departure from the UK.

Ordinary residence

The UK recognises two forms of residence: residence and ordinary residence. This is a distinction made by few other countries. Accordingly, double taxation agreements do not cover the ordinary residence rules.

Ordinarily resident is not defined in the Taxes Act, but is generally understood to denote the status of someone who is usually resident as opposed to extraordinarily or casually resident for one tax year only. You will normally be ordinarily resident in the UK if you spend more than three months in the UK on average over four tax years. This concept is very important for capital gains tax the UK to be free from UK capital gains tax. You have only to be not resident to avoid UK income tax on income other than UK income.

Usually, the Inland Revenue accept that if you are not resident in the UK for three *complete* and *consecutive* tax years, you are not ordinarily resident from 6 April following your departure from the UK. By concession, they might regard the date of commencement of not ordinarily resident to be the date of departure.

You can obtain provisional clearance as being not ordinarily resident if you produce evidence to show that your departure from the UK will be for at least three years. (In other words, your intention to leave the UK permanently is important.) Such evidence would include the disposal of UK accommodation and the availability of a permanent home overseas. The provisional clearance will usually have effect from the day after you leave the UK. You can lose your provisional clearance if you return to the UK before three complete tax years have elapsed.

If you cannot provide such evidence, the Revenue will wait until after the three complete tax years have passed and then decide, based on what has happened. The clearance, if given, can be effective from the tax year after you left the UK.

The three-year period mentioned above is an arbitrary period deemed by the Inland Revenue to be sufficient to decide whether or not you have made a 'distinct break' from the UK.

Finally, remember that even if you obtain provisional tax clearance, if you return within the three-year period you will forfeit the exemption. It does not matter why you returned; returning because of the illness of a loved one will not be a reason for avoiding residence status. There is no compassionate exemption from tax. In such a case, the existence of available accommodation can lead to someone being classed as not resident but ordinarily resident in the UK, and hence liable to UK capital gains tax. So retaining a home could lead to a large tax liability.

If you have a full-time job overseas, the position is less clear, but it is often better not to have any accommodation available in the UK if there is a large UK capital gains tax liability at stake. Professional advice should be sought.

Proposed changes to residence rules

The Inland Revenue would like to change the residence rules, and these changes might be made law in the Budget of 1989.

For intending emigrants, the rules will make life easier.

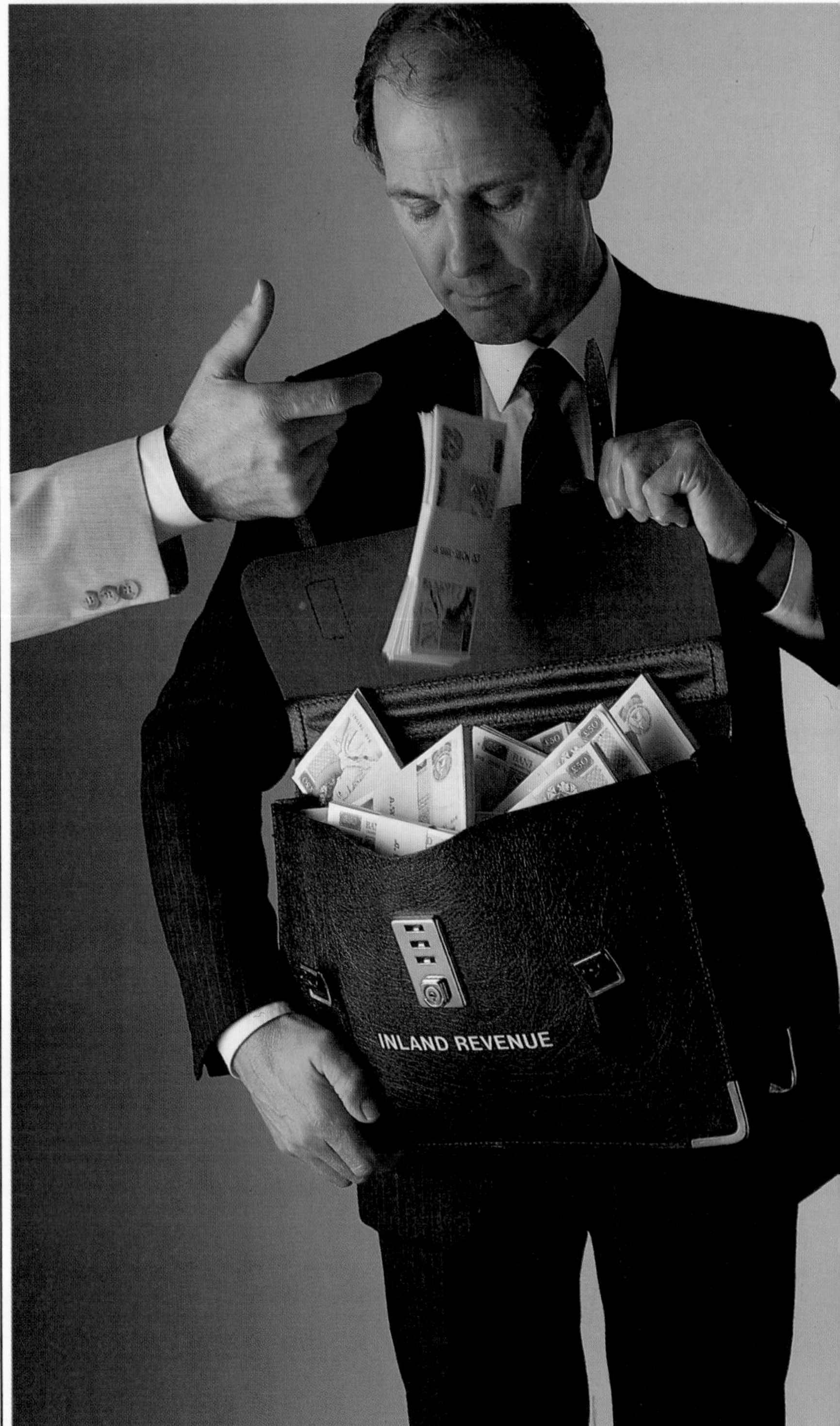
INLAND REVENUE

Are you continuing a great British tradition overseas?

One of the most beneficial aspects of working overseas is that you don't have to face those UK-sized tax bills.

However, we estimate that over 85% of British expatriates who have yet to seek advice are parting with more tax than is necessary.

Clearly a more comprehensive approach to personal tax planning is called for. And that is precisely what we offer.

We were the first clearing bank to organise a total financial service for 'expats.'

Our specialists are very well acquainted with every topic from obtaining income tax repayments to the consequences of a sudden return home.

They're also constantly reviewing the legislation, ensuring that all their information is right up to the minute.

Once we've helped put your tax affairs in order, you'll be looking for a prudent place to keep the extra cash. (Without, of course, tying it up long-term.)

Lloyds Bank offers a choice.

The High Interest Cheque Account, Extra Interest Account, foreign currency accounts and term accounts.

In addition, you can benefit from a wealth of experience in investment.

Unit trusts are just one option, tax-efficient offshore funds being of particular interest to those living or working abroad.

And as a safeguard, we have arranged an insurance programme designed exclusively for 'expats.'

It is tailor made to encompass everything from personal belongings to health care.

For further details, just fill in the coupon below.

The sooner you get in touch with us, the less contact you'll have with the taxman.

To: John Crittenden, Manager, Expatriate Services, Lloyds Bank Trust Company (Isle of Man) Ltd , PO Box 111, United House, 14-16 Nelson Street, Douglas, Isle of Man.

Please send details of your services for Expatriates.

NAME____________________

ADDRESS____________________

____

____________________ LWA2

I am/am not a customer of Lloyds Bank.

THE THOROUGHBRED BANK.

Lloyds Bank Plc is a member of IMRO. Lloyds Bank Plc, 71 Lombard Street, London EC3P 3BS.

1. You will not have to bother about 'available accommodation' as in future it will be ignored. Thus you can spend time in the UK in your own house and *not* be classed as resident.
2. In determining what is a day in the UK, all days of travel will be included (ie both the day of arrival and the day of departure will be treated as days in the UK).
3. If in any tax year you spend more than 183 days in the UK, you will be UK tax resident.
4. If you spend less than 30 days in the UK you will *not* be resident for that tax year.
5. If you spend between 30 and 183 days in the UK, the residence for that year will be calculated by using the following formula:

   number of days in tax year
   plus 1/3 × number of days in preceding tax year
   plus 1/6 × number of days in next preceding tax year.

   If the total is under 183 days, the individual will not be tax resident.

This change in the rules is staggering. Here is an example, supposing Mr A has a house in the UK and spends the following time in the UK.

Example

Before Year 1	fully resident in UK for 365 days a year
Year 1 – leaves UK	25 days in UK
Year 2	110 days in UK
Year 3	136 days in UK
Year 4	118 days in UK

Under the present rule, Mr A would be resident in *each* of the tax years above. Under the new rules, he will be non-resident in each of these years. The calculations proving this are:

		Days in UK	
Year 1 – this year	=	25	
preceding year 1/3 × 365	=	121	
next preceding year 1/6 × 365	=	61	
		207	not resident

While the total exceeds 183 days, he is none the less non-resident because the number of days in the UK in Year 1 is under 30.

			Days in UK	
Year 2 –	this year	=	110	
	preceding year 1/3 × 25	=	9	
	next preceding year 1/6 × 365	=	61	
			180	(under 183 days – not resident)
Year 3 –	this year	=	136	
	preceding year 1/3 × 110	=	37	
	next preceding year 1/6 × 25	=	5	
			178	(under 183 days – not resident)
Year 4 –	this year	=	118	
	preceding year 1/3 × 136	=	45	
	next preceding year 1/6 × 110	=	19	
			182	(under 183 days – not resident)

Indeed, once a pattern has been established, on average Mr A could spend 120 days a year in the UK and *not* be UK resident, as the following numbers demonstrate:

this year	=	120	
1/3 × last year = 1/3 × 120	=	40	
1/6 × previous year = 1/6 × 120	=	20	
Total		180	(under 183 days – not resident)

Thus if Mr A's pattern was

lives in villa in Spain	180 days
lives in house in UK	120 days
elsewhere (eg USA, yacht)	63 days
	363 days

Mr A would not be resident anywhere in the world. He would not be resident in the UK because of the new formula. He is non-resident in Spain (as you have to be there for more than 183 days). The USA has similar rules to the proposed UK ones, so he would not be resident there either.

Remember how you felt when

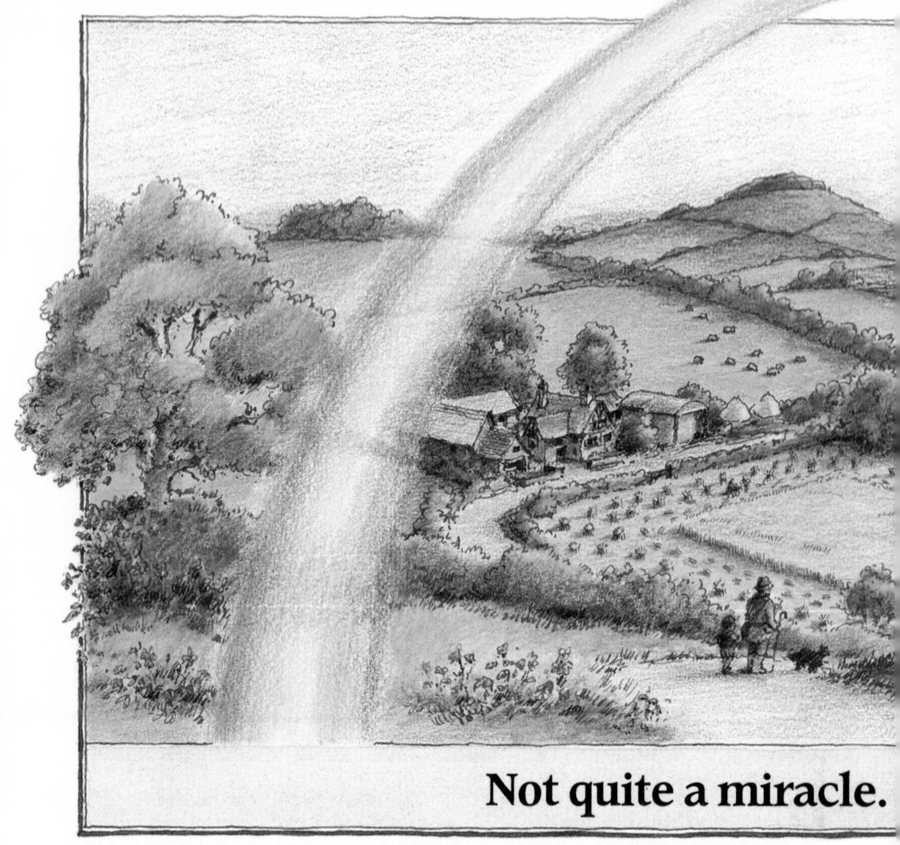

Not quite a miracle.

Enchanted. And, even when you found out that it wasn't really magic, but simply the result of rather special circumstances, it didn't make the rainbow any less enthralling.

Now, Eagle Star International has something to capture the most grown-up imaginations. It's called the Offshore Rainbow Bond, and it's simple as ABC. It means you can share in the profits of the world's major stock markets yet keep your funds offshore. So if you're working away from home, or you've retired abroad – or simply want to invest offshore – you can have all the offshore advantages you'd like with the security of a major financial services group, established in 1807, to give you the peace of mind you need.

It may be that you've already heard of Rainbow Funds – Eagle Star's risk related range of managed investments especially designed for UK investors. Since their launch in 1985 Rainbow Funds have been outstanding performers in their field.

Offshore Rainbow Bonds offer exactly the same unique investment opportunities, with Funds that span the whole spectrum of individual choice: you decide how adventurous you'd like your money to be, not us.

But the rewards from Offshore Rainbow Bonds (remember, investment values can go down as well as up) are kept safe and sound in a tax-effective environment, free from exchange controls, where they can outshine even their UK cousins.

Offshore Rainbow Bonds from

Membership of Lautro applied for.

'ou saw your first rainbow?

ıst the next best thing.

ɩeems too good to be true? So, perhaps, did your first rainbow. Find out that this is no
t of fancy by filling in the end of the rainbow.

Eagle Star
INTERNATIONAL

ry House, Prospect Hill,
ouglas, Isle of Man.
Tel: 0624 20601.
Fax: 0624 20558.

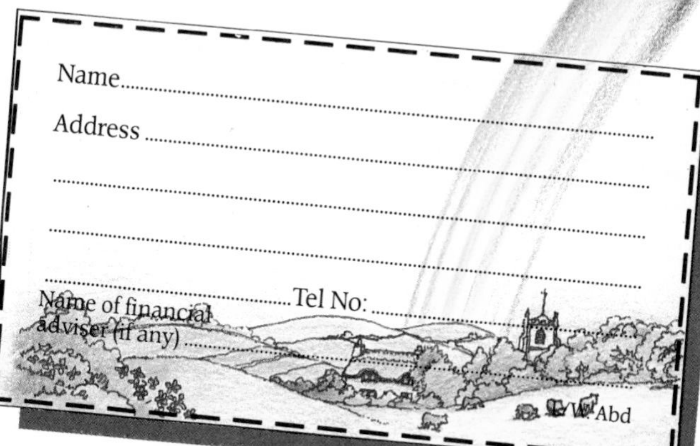

Name..
Address ....
....
....
.....................................Tel No: ....
Name of financial adviser (if any) ....

agle Star

First the bad news...

History has an unfortunate way of repeating itself. Norton Warburg, Exchange Securities of Warwick, McDonald Wheeler, Barlow Clowes...

Time and again, unfortunate investors have handed their money over to nice plausible salesmen, many of whom, through ignorance or inexperience, had no idea of the dubious nature of the companies whose products they were selling.

Sadly, it will probably continue: many companies and individuals advising expatriates remain uncontrolled by any recognised authority in the UK.

Most are honest and many are competent, but how can you tell?

There are two points Mr A must watch:

1. The tax year in Spain (and in most other countries) is from 1 January to 31 December, unlike the UK which is from 6 April to 5 April.
2. The new rules for the UK are not yet law; they are just proposals at the time of writing.

'How do they know where I am resident?'

We are often asked how the tax men of the world can find out whether or not you are resident in their country, and how they can then tax you. There are many points to be aware of.

In most countries it is your responsibility to make yourself known to the tax authorities if you are tax resident. If you are caught not declaring your tax residence, you can be fined, or even gaoled. In Spain, for example, the fine can be six times the tax, plus interest, plus a gaol sentence.

There is usually a huge amount of information which is automatically passed to your new country's tax authority. This might include yacht registration, becoming a company director, buying a property, receiving bank interest. Often you need a tax reference number just to open a bank account. Under a new agreement being supported by all members of the OECD, each member state will *automatically* pass information to the other, and help collect the other country's tax debt. So if you move from the UK to Spain, for example, your UK tax inspector might in the future be required to send full details of your assets, tax history, etc, to the Spanish tax man. Note that at the time of writing this agreement has not yet been ratified or implemented. However, even now most double tax treaties enable information to be passed to the other country, but not automatically.

Many non-residents totally confuse tax residence with two other kinds of residence – immigration and exchange control. The definitions of tax residence, immigration residence and exchange control residence are normally completely different.

Being non-resident for exchange control or immigration purposes has nothing to do with your tax residence. Your tax residence is determined by completely different rules, and therefore you must make no assumptions, but take good professional advice in order to understand your position.

It is no good saying to the tax man in country A that you are resident in country B unless it is true. He will immediately ask for your tax identification number in country B, so that he can make contact to check out your story.

As you wonder how they can tell where you have been for the last 183 days (or whatever) as your passport is never stamped, think about the massive trail of paperwork which you leave behind you – telephone bills, electricity bills, bank statements, credit cards, parking fines, correspondence with professional advisers or files with doctors/dentists, etc. All stand by to give evidence of your whereabouts on a daily basis. Airline manifests are not sacrosanct. In Spain recently American Express were forced to disclose to the tax authorities the names of all holders of their Gold Card. Most tax men have power to obtain this kind of information direct from third parties. Computers are phenomenal at storing and retrieving information easily.

Try firing your gardener, or divorcing your wife, upsetting a neighbour, or falling out with a business partner. These people are well known for shopping 'ghosts' (individuals who are tax resident in a country but never declare themselves). In many countries, eg Spain, there exists a system of 'denunciation' where individuals may be rewarded for passing information on to the tax or rating authorities.

Most reasonably sophisticated tax authorities have the right to interview you, and possibly your spouse. Quite often the onus of proof can be placed on the taxpayer rather than the tax inspector.

Moreover, if they have not asked the right questions during your lifetime, you may find that when your death certificate is filed an inspector of taxes becomes interested as to how you managed to die in his country when you do not have a tax file number! You, of course, are not too interested at this point. But your wife may find that your estate disappears into paying large back taxes, penalties and interest.

Finally, if you are caught, your assets can be frozen in your country, making you bankrupt and, under new OECD rules being introduced, your tax debts can be chased into other OECD countries.

Take good professional advice to avoid tax legally – there is no need to go the illegal route.

Avoiding capital gains tax – non residence: the general rules

This section sets out the UK capital gains tax position for someone going to live *anywhere* outside the UK.

ADVERTISEMENT FEATURE

"AFTER 1992"

WHAT OTHER CHOICE THAN SWISS SECRECY TO GUARANTEE THE PRIVACY OF YOUR INVESTMENT

The planned integration of financial services throughout the EEC in 1992 should leave Switzerland's status as the only truly secure place remaining to guarantee absolute privacy for your investments.

Switzerland has always been a place of security/refuge during a crisis, surviving wars and revolutions. How secure Swiss secrecy really is, has been questioned recently by numerous cases involving the freezing of foreign asssets. But the ground rules have always stipulated that criminality override secrecy and as long as an offence is illegal **In** Switzerland, the banks will have to disclose evidence. As a matter of fact political and foreign exchange offence has not, in the past, constituted a reason to repudiate confidentiality and not even fiscal offence, except when fraud, as defined by Swiss law, can be proven to have taken place.

Swiss secrecy especially Swiss banking secrecy is **not** a cynical attempt to secure customers for the banks, but it is a reflection of deeply-held values. Those who indiscriminately criticise all banks secrecy heavens fail to distinguish between Swiss financial institutions, which predicate **secrecy In principle** and offshore heaven institutions which use secrecy solely to attract customers. Swiss institutions as well as portfolio managers and investment advisers are more responsible in applying secrecy than other financial centres. Panama or other tax heavens such as Cayman Islands and Channel Islands, will attempt to resist economic pressure from the USA or the EEC countries, but Switzerland can and will do so. Integration of the EEC financial services means free transfer of capital from any EEC country to another. In order to create a unified market for financial services embracing 320 million people, the EEC must eliminate all remaining capital controls, harmonise taxes and regulations which discriminate against other member status, which will permit to sell financial products freely across the border. How to control these moves? One can expect that new taxes, especially withholding taxes, will be introduced on financial products and services. Exchange of tax information could be established, so the privacy of investors will be threatened. Economi̊cal pressure, if not "blackmail", based on the reciprocity system could arise and so even Switzerland's banking system could be damaged.

Let us suppose you have some cash that you consider as none of the tax collector's business in the EEC or elsewhere. Where can you place it for maximum benefit and privacy? Well again, most Americans and just about every European, not to mention Middle Easterners as well as Far Easterners, would without hesitation select a Swiss life insurance policy. Tax exempt, hard currency, guaranteed basic yield, assured profit sharing dividend, utmost discretion, possibility of exchange rate gain, comprehensive risk protection, guaranteed flexibility for subsequent increase in investment. No fuss credit facilities, complementary tax investment opportunities, estate planning, portability negotiability.

It is also important to expect that even Swiss financial services and products offered through Swiss organisations based within the EEC will be subjected to the same EEC rules and regulations, including (I.E.) withholding tax.

So a dual investment system will emerge, in order to protect privacy and tax-free investment.

Therefore, an individual investor will continue to seek traditional protection of the Swiss secrecy and confidentiality in Switzerland.

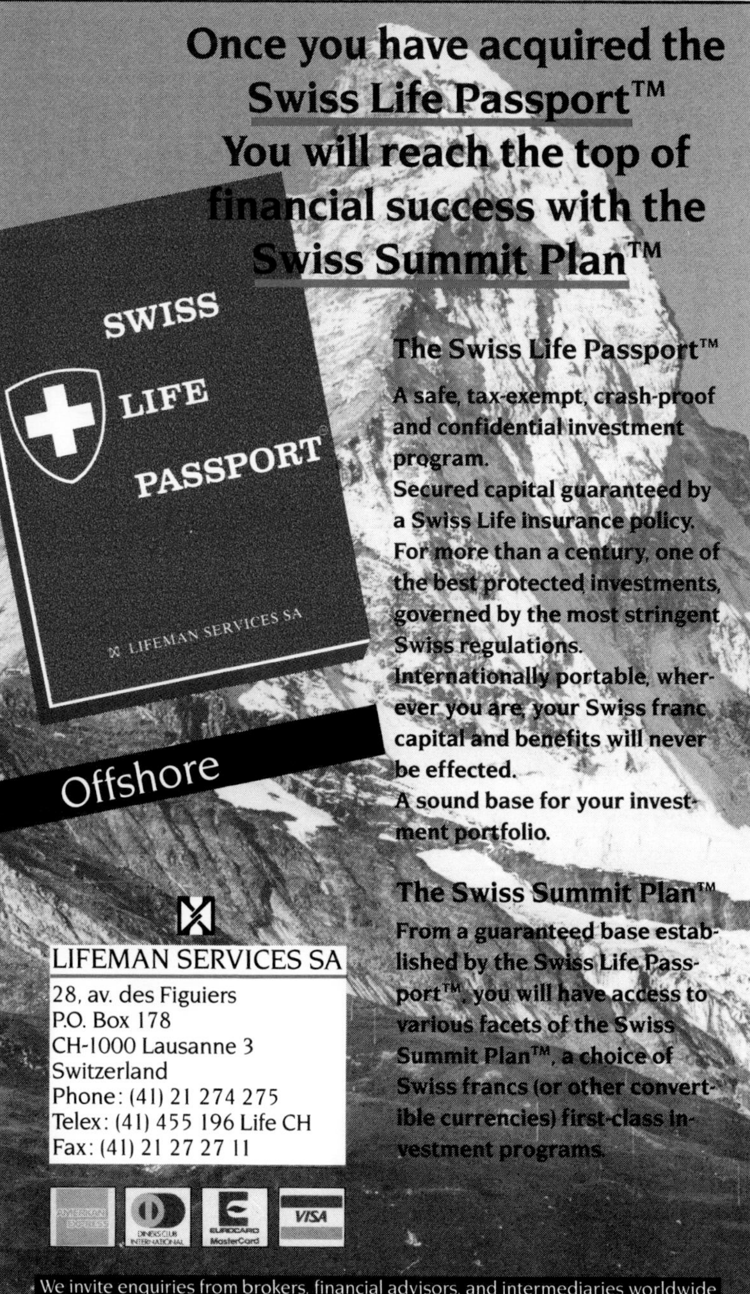
Once you have acquired the
Swiss Life Passport™
You will reach the top of
financial success with the
Swiss Summit Plan™
SWISS
LIFE
PASSPORT
LIFEMAN SERVICES SA
Offshore
The Swiss Life Passport™
A safe, tax-exempt, crash-proof and confidential investment program.
Secured capital guaranteed by a Swiss Life insurance policy.
For more than a century, one of the best protected investments, governed by the most stringent Swiss regulations.
Internationally portable, wherever you are, your Swiss franc capital and benefits will never be effected.
A sound base for your investment portfolio.
The Swiss Summit Plan™
From a guaranteed base established by the Swiss Life Passport™, you will have access to various facets of the Swiss Summit Plan™, a choice of Swiss francs (or other convertible currencies) first-class investment programs.
LIFEMAN SERVICES SA
28, av. des Figuiers
P.O. Box 178
CH-1000 Lausanne 3
Switzerland
Phone: (41) 21 274 275
Telex: (41) 455 196 Life CH
Fax: (41) 21 27 27 11
VISA
We invite enquiries from brokers, financial advisors, and intermediaries worldwide

The definitions of 'resident' and 'ordinarily resident' are to be found on pages 21-5. For UK domiciled individuals:

For UK domiciled	*Capital gains tax liability*
Resident	UK capital gains tax due on all assets throughout the world.
Non-resident and not ordinarily resident	*Not liable* even if the assets are located in the UK (unless assets used for a trade in the UK; see page 42.

By concession, an individual leaving the UK is treated as non-resident the day after he has left the UK. This concession can be refused if the Revenue thinks tax has been deliberately avoided. It is therefore safer to realise capital gains in the tax year *after* you have left the UK (ie the year starting 6 April after you have left).

Notice that the effective date a capital gain is realised is on the making of a contract, which in some cases can even be before a formal unconditional exchange of contracts, not on completion. A verbal agreement has been held to constitute an enforceable contract. 'Arrangements' made to sell an asset while in the UK, even though they are not legally enforceable, have been held to have been the effective date of disposal. Remember also that the Inland Revenue has the right to see all correspondence, file notes, memos, etc, leading up to a contract, and they often request such documents from you, your accountant, your solicitor, the purchaser and even from the purchaser's solicitor.

If you realise a capital gain in the tax year during which you leave the UK and before the date you leave, the gain is definitely liable to UK capital gains tax, subject to the annual exemption and the other exemptions listed on pages 66-7.

To avoid UK capital gains tax, you have to be not resident and not ordinarily resident. Returning within three tax years of leaving will normally forfeit the exemption from capital gains tax. You need to be non-resident for three complete tax years.

There is a possible exception: if you have a full-time job overseas, and you are absent for a complete tax year, the Revenue's normal practice is to treat you as both not resident and not ordinarily resident in that year. However, you must have a genuine job full time overseas, and this is a concession which can be withdrawn by the Inland Revenue if they believe it is applied mainly to save tax. Furthermore, it was introduced for income tax purposes and you should be wary of relying on it if you intend to realise a large capital gain.

Assets used in a trade: the general rule

If you own an asset used in a UK trade and the asset is situated in the UK, even if you become not resident and not ordinarily resident, you will remain liable for capital gains tax.

Example

Mr and Mrs Lowes owned a successful freehold nursing home which they operated as a partnership. They left the UK in February 1988, leaving a manager in charge of the home. In May 1988, the manager agreed to buy the nursing home, giving the Lowes a capital gain of £430,000. Unfortunately, Mr and Mrs Lowes remain liable for UK capital gains tax, even though they are both not resident and not ordinarily resident.

The reason why they are liable is that section 12 of the Capital Gains Tax Act 1979 continues to tax a gain made on:

- assets situated in the UK; and
- where those assets are used in a trade. This includes business premises, work in progress, or goodwill; and
- where the trade is conducted through a branch or agency in the UK.

Thus a partner disposing of an interest in assets used in the UK partnership would remain liable to UK capital gains tax. Even then, you should note that the capital gains tax is only chargeable in respect of a *trade*, not a profession. Unfortunately, there is no definition of a profession. It appears that training and examinations are an important test, and some code of professional honour. The courts have suggested that a journalist, editor, auctioneer, barrister and actress all exercise a profession, but not an insurance broker or stockbroker. However, this is not clear.

It is also worth pointing out that letting a UK property, held as an investment, is *not* a trade, and therefore not liable to be taxed by this trap. Even disposals of short-term holiday lettings, regarded as a trade for some sections of the Taxes Act, are not caught by section 12 of the Capital Gains Tax Act.

If you cannot avoid the tax based on any of the above points, there are some other tax planning hints set out below.

Tax planning

Mr and Mrs Lowes could have avoided UK capital gains tax by one of two methods.

(a) *Incorporation.* If the business had been incorporated, the property could have been transferred to the new company or left in their own names and let (at a market rent) to the company. In either case, the sale of the shares and/or the nursing home freehold would have been free of UK capital gains tax if sold in the tax year after leaving the UK, provided that the Lowes remained both not resident and not ordinarily resident.

(b) *Renting the freehold.* An alternative way would have been for the Lowes to let the nursing home to the manager. He would sign a lease, paying a market rent. Later, having left the UK, established non-residence and non-ordinary residence, they could have sold the rental property to him free of UK capital gains tax.

There is one word of caution about such tax planning. There have been several tax cases (and one in particular called *Furniss* v *Dawson*) which enable the Revenue to ignore a series of transactions which have no real commercial purpose, other than the avoidance of tax. They can impose tax as if they have not occurred.

Avoiding both UK capital gains tax and the overseas tax

We have explained some methods of avoiding UK capital gains tax, but clever avoidance of UK tax could end up becoming a case of 'out of the frying pan and into the fire'. You also have to avoid paying tax on your gain in your new country.

There are several ways of achieving this; for example, by being a fiscal nomad for a few months. Alternatively, you can make your capital gains disposal while in a period when you are living in the new country *but* neither resident there nor in the UK. Another plan makes use of the fact that some countries treat the individual as making notional disposal and reacquisition at market value of all assets at the time when he becomes, or ceases to be, resident there. Professional advice should be sought to ensure all taxes are properly avoided.

Letting your home – tax deductible costs

If you decide to continue to own your UK house but to let it, you will continue to be liable to UK tax on the rental income even if you are not resident and not ordinarily resident in the UK. The UK includes England, Northern Ireland, Scotland and Wales.

The following costs can usually be deducted against the income:

general and water rates where paid by the landlord;
agent's fees;
legal fees relating to the letting (including VAT);
repairs and redecorations;
postage and telephone costs directly relating to the letting;
wear and tear;
other services (electricity, gas, TV paid by the landlord);
insurance;
inventory fees;
ground rent;
valuation fees for insurance purposes;
gardening costs or window cleaner, if imposed on the landlord by the lease;
accountancy fees;
interest costs;
VAT charged.

Rent receivable

The income is *not* the rent paid; it is the rent due under the terms of the lease in any tax year (6 April to 5 April). No adjustment is to be made for pre-paid rent. The accounts must always be drawn up for the year to 5 April (although, in practice, the Inland Revenue do not always insist on this). Only if it can be shown that unpaid rent due is irrecoverable, after all reasonable steps have been taken to recover it, can the income be reduced to take account of unpaid rent.

Deducting interest

Interest on a loan is deductible against the rental income if:

- the loan was used only to purchase or improve the property;
- the property is let at a commercial rent, not at a low rent to a friend or relative;
- it is let for at least 26 weeks in a 52-week period which includes the interest payment date and is either available for letting or under repair for the remainder of the period;
- in most cases, the interest is paid to a UK bank, not an overseas one; and
- the interest is payable on a loan not an overdraft.

If these conditions are met, there is *no limit* on the loan, unlike the £30,000 limit applied to your home mortgage when you live

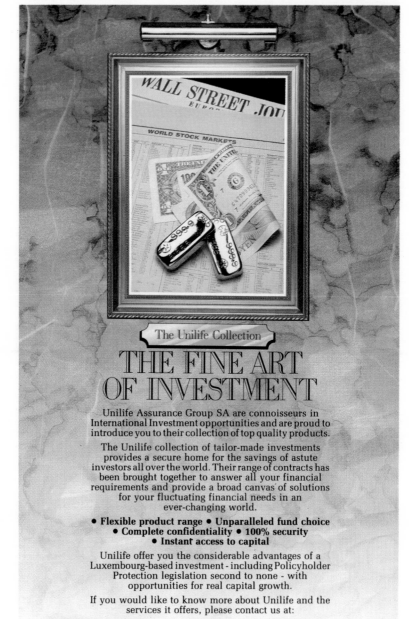

there. However, relief for the interest can be given only against UK rental income. It cannot be claimed against any other UK income.

UK capital gains tax – your own home

If you sell the property in a tax year in which you are both not resident and not ordinarily resident, there is no UK capital gains tax due. If you are planning to return to the UK and have a potential UK capital gains tax liability on your house, you may be better off selling it in the tax year *before* you return when you are not resident and not ordinarily resident. That way, you will avoid UK capital gains tax.

Provided a house has been your only or main residence at some time, the last two years of ownership are always exempt from capital gains tax.

There are many other rules about avoiding capital gains tax on a principal private residence (your own home) which are rather complex, but worth setting out in detail as this is often a key point for the working expatriate. Note that the rules for interest relief (MIRAS, etc) and capital gains tax exemption are entirely separate.

More than one residence

It must be borne in mind that you can have two residences available to you without owning them both. A home which you rent counts as a residence. An overseas flat or house, whether owned or rented, is also a residence.

If you own (or have available) more than one residence, you can elect which property should be regarded as the principal private residence for the capital gains tax exemption. Such an election, which must be in writing, cannot apply for a period starting earlier than two years prior to the election. The election can be varied at any time by giving a fresh notice, but again the variation cannot apply to any period over two years before the date of the new election. If no election is made, the Inspector of Taxes will choose, on the basis of what appears to him on his examination of the facts to be the main residence at the time. A second property which you let to bona fide tenants (or keep available for letting) is not treated as being available to you.

Time limit for election

The Revenue consider that the time limit for making the election is two years from the date the second residence first becomes available. Most people doubt this interpretation of the legislation and in practice elections are often accepted outside this limit (but not to operate more than two years retrospectively). The Revenue have stated that, where the taxpayer's interest in one of the properties has 'no more than a negligible capital value in the open market' and the taxpayer was unaware that an election could be made, they will extend the time limit to a reasonable time after the individual first becomes aware that he is entitled to make an election. They will then treat it as having effect from the date on which he acquired the second residence (Inland Revenue Extra-Statutory Concession D21). This concession is intended to cover the position where one of the properties is rented and the taxpayer did not realise that it constitutes a residence.

Husband and wife

A husband and wife can only have one main residence between them while they are living together. Where a private residence election affects both (eg joint ownership) it must be given by both.

The capital gains computation

If you let your house (or leave it unoccupied) and sell it in a tax year when you are resident (or ordinarily resident) in the UK, you may have a capital gains tax liability for the period let (or unoccupied). The amount of the gain which remains free of capital gains tax is:

$$\text{Total gain} \times \frac{\text{Number of weeks owned as principal private residence}}{\text{Number of weeks owned}}$$

Remember that the number of weeks which count as your owning it as a principal private residence always includes:

- the last 24 months, even if let;
- all weeks prior to 6 April 1965, even if let.

Periods of absence

In the above calculation, certain periods of absence can also count as being periods when the house is your principal private residence, even though factually it was not (eg it can even be let).

These periods of absence are:

1. Any period (or periods) not exceeding three years; *plus*
2. Any period where you worked overseas as an employee and all the duties were performed overseas. There is no time limit.

Note that if the husband works but the wife does not, she would still be eligible for relief for her part ownership as long as she is living with the husband. Note that this exemption does not apply if you are self-employed, nor does it apply if *any* of the duties were performed in the UK, however incidental they might be; *plus*

3. Up to four years where your job in the UK requires you to live elsewhere (this usually means more than 100 miles away).

There are several major traps in obtaining any of the above three periods of relief. You must meet each of the following three conditions:

1. The house must be your main residence *before* the start of the period of absence; *and*
2. It must be your main residence at some time *subsequent* to the period of absence. This means that you must re-occupy the house before you sell it. There is no legal limit on the minimum time the house must be occupied, and some say that even one week is sufficient, so long as you have no other residence available. The Inland Revenue have stated that they believe the minimum period is three months, but their view has not been tested in the courts. There is one exception to having to re-occupy before you sell. The Inland Revenue have granted a concession where you are forced by your job to live elsewhere in the UK on your return; *and*
3. You must have no other residence eligible for relief during the periods of absence. Of course, while overseas you are bound to have your overseas house available for your use as a residence. In practice, the Inland Revenue tend to ignore this, though there is no guarantee that they will continue to adopt this approach. It is therefore advisable to submit a written election to the Inland Revenue within two years of going overseas that your UK home is to be treated as your principal private residence. If you do not make the election, the Inland Revenue could claim that your overseas home is your main residence, and hence you will fail to meet this condition.

Buying while overseas

An expatriate who buys a UK house while he is overseas would not have met the rule of using the house both *before* and after a period of absence as his principal private residence. While there may be relief for interest purposes, there is no relief for capital gains tax purposes. Instead, the expatriate should consider selling the house in the tax year *before* he returns, while he is both not resident and not ordinarily resident, when he is exempt from all capital gains tax. By concession, if you work full time overseas, the Revenue will regard you as both not resident and not ordinarily resident until the day you return to the UK, in which case it appears unnecessary to sell the house in the tax year before you return; selling before you return, even in the same tax year, would be sufficient. However, if possible you should not rely too heavily on this concession as it can always be withdrawn.

Avoiding capital gains tax and keeping the house

As an alternative to selling to a third party in the tax year before return, you could transfer it to a trust for yourself and your wife's benefit. The transfer into the trust will be tax free if the requirements of not resident and not ordinarily resident are met, and any subsequent disposal by the trust will also be tax free if the property is occupied by you under the terms of the trust.

Alternatively, the property could be transferred on return into a trust with a 'hold over' relief election signed to avoid paying any capital gains tax immediately. If the trustees benefit from the private residence exemption (which they can do if the property has been used by the beneficiary under the terms of trust as his only or main residence throughout the period of the trustees' ownership), no capital gains tax is payable on the eventual disposal. Professional advice should be taken in these areas.

Working abroad and MIRAS

Keeping a house in the UK will not in itself affect your UK tax residence status. You may still even be able to continue with your MIRAS relief.

Since 6 April 1983 (or in some cases even earlier) mortgage interest on house loans may be paid after deduction of tax at the basic rate, for the income tax year in which the payment becomes due, if the interest is 'relevant loan interest' paid by you being a 'qualifying borrower' to a 'qualifying lender'.

1. 'Relevant loan interest' is interest paid and payable in the UK to a 'qualifying lender' and it is interest on loans for the purchase of a residence including a residential caravan or houseboat in the UK which when the interest is paid is used wholly, or to a substantial extent, as the only or main residence of the borrower. Before 5 April 1988 relief was also available for the purchase of a residence for a dependent relative or separated or former spouse and for home improvements. Interest relief will continue for such loans until they are repaid *or* replaced.

SO YOU'RE THINKING OF MOVING OVERSEAS!

Moving overseas, for either business or retirement reasons, is usually an exciting experience. Most people are well prepared for the pleasant aspects, for example an outdoor lifestyle, changes in food and language.

The aim of The Bachmann Group, a leading trust and financial services organisation based in Guernsey, is to ensure that its clients are equally well prepared to meet the fiscal and legal consequences of their moves.

Bachmann consider that the trend of people and industry moving from the traditional industrial centres, which were located close to raw material sources, to areas where people would choose to live, will continue to develop in Europe. However, unlike the USA where such movements have taken place within the one country, movements in Europe have the complication of crossing national frontiers.

Based in Guernsey, but with offices in Spain and Portugal and a worldwide network of professional consultants, Bachmann are well placed to advise such clients. Advice is readily available on all property ownership matters (including finance and insurance), taxation, wills and trusts, investments and banking. Ideally, Bachmann prefer to start talking with clients as soon as the clients begin to consider a move.

TAXATION

From a taxation viewpoint, it is equally important to plan the consequences of leaving a country as it is to plan the entry into another, particularly if valuable assets are being realised. Whilst taxation should never be the only reason for moving from one country to another, such moves do open up many tax saving opportunities.

PROPERTY

Bachmann will also advise on the most appropriate structure for acquiring overseas property. This will frequently be through an offshore company. In addition finance can be arranged for the purchase of overseas property through a unique scheme operated in conjunction with a major UK clearing bank. Loans are available over twenty years, with interest charged at 2% over LIBOR, in all major currencies. These loans are available to finance stage payments, and there is no penalty for early repayment.

TRUSTS

Many countries have succession laws and inheritance tax rules which are complex and confusing to the new immigrant. Bachmann advise on trusts and wills to ensure maximum flexibility and long term security.

INVESTMENTS

Long term security and growth is also the basis on which Bachmann's investment department operates, with the objective of providing a highly personal service to clients in the management of their portfolios. A global strategy is applied to ensure that risk and profit opportunity are spread through all major markets.

BANKING

Through a fellow subsidiary, Bachmann provide a high quality, personal banking service for expatriate clients, including current, deposit and loan accounts in all currencies. The combination of these services enable clients to receive advice and ongoing management of all their financial affairs from one source.

THE BACHMANN GROUP

OVERSEAS PROPERTY SERVICES

Bachmann & Co Ltd, P.O. Box 175,
Frances House, Sir William Place,
St. Peter Port, Guernsey,
Channel Islands.
Telephone 0481 23573
Facsimile 0481 711353
Telex 4191637 BACFID G

2. 'Qualifying borrower' is any individual who pays 'relevant loan interest'. There is an exception to this. If you or your husband or wife receive(s) earnings that are exempt from UK tax, eg certain Crown and Foreign Office appointments, neither of you can qualify for MIRAS. There are very few tax exempt occupations.
3. A 'qualifying lender' includes a building society, a local authority, the Bank of England, an insurance company authorised to carry on long-term business (eg life assurance) in the UK, a trustee savings bank, an existing lender under the mortgage option scheme, and any recognised bank or licensed deposit-taking institution authorised by the Treasury.

MIRAS (Mortgage Interest Relief At Source) enables you to reduce your mortgage interest payments by the basic rate of tax (25 per cent, post 1988 Budget). It is limited to interest on the first £30,000 of a loan to buy your principal private residence. Even though you, as an expatriate, are no longer living in the UK and may have no UK income, you can still obtain MIRAS relief because of an Inland Revenue concession.

Where you are required by reason of your employment to move from your home to another place, either in the UK or abroad, for a period not expected to exceed four years, any property being bought with the aid of a mortgage, which was being used as your only or main residence *before* you went away, will still be treated as such, provided that it can reasonably be expected to be so again on your return. It is *not* sufficient to claim the first four years of an expected five-year absence. The maximum period is four years, but if there is a further temporary absence *after* the property has been re-occupied for a minimum period of three months, the four-year test will apply to the year of absence *without* regard to the previous absence.

If you are already working abroad and buy a property in the UK in the course of a leave period *and* use that property as an only or main residence for a period of not less than three months *before* your return to the place of your overseas employment, you will be regarded as satisfying the condition that the property was used as your only or main residence before you went away.

If you let your property while you are away at a commercial rent, the benefit of the concession may be claimed where appropriate, if this is more favourable than a claim for relief against letting income.

If you go abroad but leave your family in your UK house, MIRAS relief will not be subject to the above-mentioned four-year time limit.

The poll tax

The poll tax starts in Scotland from 1 April 1989 and in England and Wales on 1 April 1990. It is due to replace domestic rates. There are a number of exempt individuals, and full-time students need only pay 20 per cent of the total charge. The charge will vary enormously depending on the local authority. A Camden resident can expect a bill of £782 per adult, while if you live in Croydon it will be about £158 per adult.

The charge is payable on any unoccupied property by the owner, unless it is let on a lease for more than six months, in which case the tenant is liable. For people with second homes in the UK, the local authority can charge up to twice the usual amount. Anyone over the age of 18 (including live-in staff, such as nannies) must register and pay the tax.

UK personal allowances

The main personal allowances are:

	1987-88	*1988-89*
Married person	£3795	£4095
Single person	2425	2605

	1987-88	*1987-88*	*1988-89*	*1988-89*
Age allowance	*Single*	*Married*	*Single*	*Married*
65 or over	£2960	£4675	£3180	£5035
80 or over	3070	4845	3310	5205

Age allowance is reduced by two-thirds for income over £10,600 for 1988-89 (£9800 for 1987-88).

Wife's earned income relief is £2605 for 1988-89 (£2425 for 1987-88).

A non-resident may claim personal allowance on what is effectively a proportionate basis. For example, if a married man has £10,000 of UK income and £20,000 of overseas income (total worldwide income being £30,000), he would be entitled to one-third of the £4095 married person's allowance. Claiming this allowance will generate a tax saving of £1023 if he pays UK tax at 25 per cent and more if his UK income brings him into the higher rates of tax.

This tax saving can be improved following a case brought against the Inland Revenue in 1984 by a man called Addison. Where the overseas investment income belongs to the non-resident's wife, it can be left out of account altogether. There is

no restriction similar to this one for personal allowances on allowable loan interest or on the benefit of the higher rate tax bands.

It is important to note that the overseas income is not itself taxed. It is merely taken into account to determine what tax is payable on any UK income. None the less, because many taxpayers are reluctant to disclose this information to the UK Inland Revenue, this allowance is often not claimed. If the Revenue are aware of the extent of your overseas income, this may make it more difficult to convince them that you have changed your residence or domicile status.

This restriction over the personal allowance is often thought to be unfair, especially for those who have retired on a government pension. Their pension is fully liable to UK tax – wherever they live – but their personal allowance can be restricted if they have overseas income. One way around this is to let the wife have all the overseas income, and follow the path trodden by Mr Addison mentioned above.

Many people have not bothered to claim the personal allowances because it has meant declaring their worldwide income to the UK authorities and since the allowance is often so derisory the effort is not worth while. This is all going to change from 6 April 1989, and will enable expatriates to obtain a much larger tax allowance. The changes are:

- there will be no restriction on claiming personal allowances, and thus no need to declare your worldwide income;
- both husband and wife will be eligible for the allowance, and can each make separate claims.

If an expatriate has a UK bank deposit account or 'non-resident' UK building society account, the interest is tax free by virtue of an extra-statutory concession known as B3. However, such interest is taken into account when personal allowances are claimed in the UK against UK income. It is advisable to keep such deposit accounts outside the UK (eg in the Channel Islands) to avoid UK tax.

UK pensions

UK pensions paid to a non-resident are liable to UK tax unless the pensioner is exempted by a double tax agreement or the pension is paid out under one of the following schemes:

1. India, Pakistan, Burma and colonial schemes;

2. Pension funds for former public service employees of overseas territories;
3. The Central African Pension Fund;
4. The Overseas Service Pension Fund;
5. Pension funds set up for overseas employees of UK employers.

Most double taxation agreements tax pensions only in the country in which you are resident, with the exception of pensions paid out of public funds in the UK, which remain taxable in the UK. Public funds include pensions paid to former servants of the Crown, and pensions paid for services rendered to a local authority in the UK. Such public fund pensions may be free of UK tax under the double taxation agreement if the pensioner is a national of the other country.

If your pension is going to be liable to UK income tax or foreign tax, it is normally better to elect to take a tax-free lump sum and to reduce the level of pension liable to tax.

If you are moving to an EC country, there are flexible agreements over pension and many other social security benefits. UK social security pensions are payable in your new EC country including cost of living increases, though these will be related to the British cost of living index. There is a leaflet (SA29) produced by the DSS which discusses some of these points (for address, see page 382).

In addition, the UK has agreements with non-EC countries, primarily covering retirement pensions.

UK dividends

Dividends from UK companies constitute taxable income. However, they carry with them a tax credit which covers the shareholder's liability to basic rate tax.

For example, a £100 dividend can be expressed as follows:

Dividend	*Tax Credit*
£100	£33.33

The figures used are for the 1988-89 UK tax year, and the tax credit is 25 per cent of the aggregate sum. This 25 per cent tax rate is the basic rate of tax in the UK.

Under many double taxation agreements, it is possible to claim a refund or part of the tax credit. The refund may amount to 10 per cent of the dividend plus tax credit, leaving a 15 per cent effective UK tax rate. Credit is given in the foreign country for the 15 per cent tax paid in the UK.

If you control 10 per cent of the company (either directly or indirectly), the tax refund may be increased to 15 per cent leaving only a 10 per cent UK tax rate.

It is possible for a UK company to enter into an arrangement with the UK Inspector of Foreign Dividends to pay in effect the tax refund to non-resident shareholders covered by a double tax agreement without their needing to make a formal claim. Many companies are unwilling to take on the increased administration and the liability to pay the Revenue any tax refunded to which it has subsequently been discovered the shareholder was not entitled.

UK interest (banks and building societies)

Normal 'onshore' building society and bank accounts are not suitable for United Kingdom expatriates. Many societies and banks advertise 'international accounts', suggesting that interest payments may be made gross without risk of UK income tax. At first sight, these appear highly attractive when compared to the returns available on high interest money market bank accounts. In fact, such income is liable to UK tax, but by concession the Inland Revenue often do not charge such tax if you are non-resident for the entire tax year and do not claim a tax repayment in respect of any other UK income that has suffered tax by deduction at source. Where other UK income arises in the UK, the tax may be easier to collect. For example, where a non-resident is in receipt of a government pension, there may be less reluctance on the part of the Inland Revenue to apply the concession. Many building society depositors who are living outside the United Kingdom have found that an assessment has been raised in these circumstances. This assessment may be dropped where the depositor can provide evidence that the income has been declared in his new country of residence. If the interest is taxed overseas, the UK tax rate may be reduced to 12 per cent (with tax credit given overseas).

In addition, if the non-resident is not domiciled in the UK, he would be putting his capital at risk unnecessarily to a charge to UK inheritance tax. Finally, interest in the UK suffers tax deduction at source (called composite rate tax) and it is thus always preferable for a non-resident to invest in gross funds outside the UK.

UK gilts

Gilts are publicly quoted stocks backed fully by the British government. The name gilt comes from the original certificates which were issued with gilded edges. At no time has a British government failed to meet any of its funded debt obligations whether in the nature of capital or income. But do not be fooled into thinking that gilts are always safe. If you have to sell before maturity, you can lose a lot of money. How much you lose or gain depends on what has happened to interest rates since you purchased your stock.

When you buy a gilt, you are lending the government money at a guaranteed interest rate (called the 'coupon'). Repayment is normally due at a specified date, so you can work out exactly how much you will receive and when, although the government has the right to repay some stocks at any time over a three- to five-year period. Rates of return are often higher than from a bank or building society, and the guarantee is stronger – the government is less likely to go bankrupt than Barclays Bank or Abbey National.

UK tax position

Interest on gilts is liable to UK income tax and the majority have tax deducted at source. However, there are a number of gilts on which there is no tax due either on income or capital gain if you are not resident in the UK. It will be up to you to prove your non-resident status, though. It is not enough simply to provide a foreign address; you may have to give details of your tax reference number and district in the overseas country. In order to obtain approval, you should obtain Form A1 from the Inspector of Foreign Dividends, Lynwood Road, Thames Ditton, Surrey KT7 0DP. Unless you have already been cleared as non-resident, expect some searching questions about your long-term plans, duration of visits, location of home, and so on.

The list of gilt stocks which are free of tax to residents abroad may be obtained from the Bank of England, Threadneedle Street, London EC2R 8AH.

Seventeen ways to avoid UK inheritance tax

1. Giving it away tax free

If you give away no more than £110,000, there is no inheritance tax (IHT) to pay. After seven years, you can give a further £110,000 (and so on every seven years and one day). Both husband and wife each have their own £110,000 limit. In addition, each year you (and your wife) can give away £3000. Thus over a period of seven years and one day you can give away:

	Husband	*Wife*	*Total*
2 × £110,000	220,000	220,000	£440,000
8 × £3000	24,000	24,000	£48,000
	244,000	244,000	£488,000

2. Giving away 'in consideration of marriage'

Each parent can give away an additional £5000 to a child or £2500 to a grandchild and £1000 to anyone else on the recipient's marriage. The rules are very strict and professional advice on how to do it should be taken, in advance of the marriage.

3. Normal income expenditure

Regular amounts can be gifted as 'normal expenditure out of income' representing perhaps as much as 10-50 per cent of annual income *free of IHT*. Careful use of this exemption can significantly reduce, even eliminate, your IHT problem.

4. Unlimited lifetime transfers to individuals or trusts

You can give *unlimited* amounts to any other individual during your lifetime or to most trusts (but not discretionary trusts). The gift could be money, or shares in a company, or any other asset. Provided that the recipient is a UK resident, capital gains tax can be avoided by signing a holdover relief election, though there may be none to pay if the donor is both not resident and not ordinarily resident. In the event of the donor dying within seven years, there will be IHT to pay but at reduced rates. If he dies within three years of the gift, there is no tax reduction. These trusts can be very useful for giving wealth to grandchildren under the age of 25.

5. Avoid 'reservation'

Gifts 'with reservation' will not be exempt from tax under 4. above. The gift must be given absolutely. A gift where the donor enjoys any interest or rights is not acceptable. Thus the gift of a house, with rights for the donor to reside, is not an absolute gift, nor is the gift of shares with the right to an exceptional salary from the company. So avoid giving anything which has reservation of interest. This is a very technical area. It is possible to carve out for oneself a right to reside in the house prior to making the gift. Professional advice should be sought before attempting such a gift.

6. 50 per cent discount

Even if you are going to pay the tax, if you give away *before* your death, the tax rates are halved (maximum 30 per cent instead of 60 per cent). If you die within three years of the gift, the rates are more.

7. Keep the back door open

You could give away any amounts into a discretionary trust, where you are *not* a beneficiary, but other relatives, including your wife, are the named beneficiaries. You could remain as the controller of the assets in trust (called the trustee). A series of trusts is recommended for technical reasons. As long as your gifts are within the limits set out in 1. above, there will be no IHT due. Careful draughtsmanship and planning are required in this area. Your wife can also establish a similar series of trusts.

8. Life insurance

Life insurance can be a surprisingly cheap way of covering any eventual IHT bill. For example, if your estate was worth £330,000, you and your wife were aged 50, and you left all your assets to her on your death, the IHT payable at the second death would be £88,000. For an annual outlay of about £900 per annum, a tax free benefit under trust of over £90,000 can be obtained, and indeed is projected to be worth over £220,000 on the death at age 85 of the survivor.

Alternatively, at 65 you could invest £25,000 in a last survivor investment bond (under trust) with life cover of a sum assured at second death of just under £100,000.

These costs can be reduced considerably by purchasing term life insurance which provides cover for a fixed number of years only. You choose how long. During the time you pay regular premiums, if you die, the policy pays out a fixed amount. If you survive to the end of the term, you receive nothing back and premiums cease.

9. Equalising estates

If the husband's estate is worth £500,000, the IHT payable is £156,000, leaving £344,000 as the net estate. If estates are equalised between husband and wife and each wills their estate to children/grandchildren/relatives, the IHT payable is reduced to approximately £112,000, saving £44,000.

10. Residential property

If a donor gifts a property and continues to stay in it, or even visit it if for other than short periods, the gift is treated under the 'reservation' rules, unless a commercial rent is paid.

Various solutions are possible. If a leasehold can be created on a freehold property, it is likely (but not certain) that the gift of freehold will be outside the donor's estate. Once the leasehold has expired, the donor would have to vacate the property or pay a commercial rent.

If a property can be sold and the proceeds gifted, the beneficiary could purchase a new property and allow the donor to live there rent free. Capital gains tax could be avoided subsequently if the beneficiary is not ordinarily resident or is eligible for 'dependent relative relief'.

11. Company shares, business assets and woodlands

Private company (ie close company) shares are eligible for a special 50 per cent business relief, ie the value is reduced by 50 per cent (or 30 per cent) for IHT purposes, for a controlling interest (which is defined as a shareholding of at least 25 per cent for this purpose) or 30 per cent for a lesser interest. Another way to reduce the value is to form another company (owned by the ultimate beneficiaries) and build this new company up in preference to the existing one. Assets used in Lloyd's underwriting or in any other business you carry on are also eligible for 50 per cent reduction.

Certain other property used by a private company or a partnership is also eligible for business relief at the reduced rate of 30 per cent. Similar rules apply to agricultural property but the rate is increased to 50 per cent if there is vacant possession. Woodlands can also qualify for the 50 per cent relief with, in addition, the timber being left out of account until it is sold.

12. Single premium bonds

An investment bond can be a useful way to reduce your estate yet retain an income. The beneficiary of the bond is a child or grandchild instead of the investor. Inheritance tax may be payable at the time of buying the bond, but inheritance tax is avoided on any growth in value of the bond.

Alternatively, a trust can be established and an interest free loan made to the trustees who then use the loan to purchase an investment bond. 'Income' can be taken in the form of loan repayments. No IHT is payable on the loan and the trust fund, with the exception of any outstanding loan, remains outside the settlor's estate.

13. Giving away shares in newly formed companies

Making gifts of assets likely to appreciate is an effective way of reducing your estate. The gift is valued at the date it is gifted, not the subsequent value. Giving away shares in a newly formed company to trusts for your children's benefit can make sense.

14. Giving away when cheap

One of the few benefits of 1987's stock market crash was that it reduced values for IHT purposes. Gifts are therefore valued at a lower level.

15. Generation skipping

If your own children are already wealthy, pass your estate on to your grandchildren instead. This skips a generation and reduces the likely IHT on your children's death.

16. Writing in trust

Life insurances and death benefits from pension schemes may form part of your estate for IHT purposes. You can set up the policy to pay the benefits direct to your children, in which case they do *not* attract IHT. If you are concerned that your wife, should she survive you, should receive the benefit, it is advisable that you write the policy benefits in trust for your children, unless your wife survives you by 30 days, in which case she receives the benefit.

17. Interest free loans

An interest free loan is *not* a gift as long as:

- the loan is documented; and
- the loan is repayable on demand or at very short notice.

Such loans can be used to purchase assets from the donor. Professional advice should be sought before granting such loans.

Working abroad – UK tax

If you work abroad and live abroad for a period of less than one year, you will normally remain liable in full to UK tax.

If you work abroad for a period of at least 365 days (regardless of whether or not this covers a complete tax year), you will be exempt from UK tax on those earnings. This is regardless of your residence status in the UK. The performance of some duties in the UK will not cause this relief to be lost as long as they are merely incidental.

However, the Inland Revenue take a harsh line on the meaning of 'merely incidental duties' and the more senior the employee, the harder it is to establish that UK duties are 'merely incidental'. Visiting the UK to report to your boss is usually regarded as incidental. Attending a board meeting, however, is not regarded as incidental by the Inland Revenue. The Revenue will look at the *quality of the duties* undertaken in the UK rather than the time spent on them to determine whether or not they are merely incidental.

This relief is not given to the self-employed, only to the employed, but some tax planning points for the self-employed are set out below.

There is a trap, however. To achieve your 365 days of continuous employment abroad, you cannot during that period:

- spend more than 62 days continuously in the UK for any reason;
- spend days in the UK which in aggregate exceed one-sixth of the length of the total period under consideration.

Note in particular that just avoiding spending more than 62 days in the UK is not the rule. You must also avoid the 'one-sixth' rule.

A day will be considered to be a day of absence if you are outside the UK at midnight. If your flight leaves the UK at 11 pm in the evening, that is normally regarded as an entire day spent abroad, although there is no legislative basis for this and it is accordingly unwise to rely on it. If you return from abroad at 11 pm, even after a hard day's work, the legislation provides that this must nevertheless be taken as a day in the UK.

The one-sixth limit is very rigidly applied. An unplanned or unexpected visit to the UK can spell disaster in trying to establish the 365-day minimum period. Careful planning is required, as shown in the following example:

	Date	*Days abroad*	*Days in UK*	*Total days*
Leaves UK for Spain	12.8.87			
Returns to UK for Christmas	15.12.87	125		125
Leaves UK for Spain	20.1.88		36	161
Returns to UK for grandfather's funeral	7.2.88	18		179
Leaves UK for Spain	10.2.88		3	182
Returns to UK	10.12.88	304		486

The number of days spent in the UK between two periods of absence cannot exceed one-sixth of the total number of days in the period under consideration. In the above example, the individual spends 486 days from the time he leaves to work in Spain to the end of his assignment. On returning to the UK on 7 February 1988, there is a total period of 179 days. One-sixth of 179 is 30, but he has spent more than this in the UK as he was here for 36 days. Thus, the period from 12 August 1987 to 20 January 1988 is *not* a qualifying one. The calculation now starts again on 20 January 1988. He spends 18 days abroad, then three days in the UK, and finally 304 days abroad before returning permanently. Since this is a total of 325 days and is less than the required 365, the entire period of 486 days does not count as exempt from UK tax. Instead, UK tax is payable in full, even though this taxpayer has been on an overseas assignment which lasted about 16 months.

National Insurance contributions

Social security and pension schemes

The system of UK social security, known as National Insurance, is administered by the Department of Social Security (DSS) through a network of local offices around the country and specialist offices.

Wherever you or your employer have any overseas involvement your National Insurance contribution position can become very complicated. All such matters are the responsibility of the DSS Overseas Branch whose address is given on page 382.

Chapter 3

Learn a Language

Please learn the native language of the country where you intend to settle, even if you are of retirement age. Surely it is just good manners to speak even a few halting words of the language of your host country when you go to live there permanently or even just to spend long vacations?

If you take this advice you will enjoy the many benefits of closer contact with your neighbours, in business relations or with tradespeople. They will all appreciate your efforts to communicate with them in their language and in most cases will go out of their way to help you, not only to learn the right words, but also assisting you to solve any domestic problems while shopping, visiting banks and post offices or dealing with officialdom.

There are many different methods of learning a language and if you persevere your efforts will be rewarded.

Before you go to live abroad, a year or two in advance why not take a series of evening classes at a local college of further education or enrol for a 'crash course' at one of the many language colleges either publicly funded or privately organised?

Other sources of spare-time language education include the Linguaphone system which offers a wide variety of courses using tapes, together with books containing exercises and further tuition. It is one of the longest-established organisations specialising in teaching foreign languages, and is based at the Linguaphone Institute Ltd, Silwood Park, Ascot, Berkshire SL5 7PY. It has a range of 30 languages and has helped over 5 million people to learn a second language. This organisation currently operates in 101 countries with over 300 courses.

Using audio cassettes supplemented by an excellent series of books, the courses are designed for students who want to learn in their own time and place. Some can speak quite fluently in just three months while others take six months or more. An advisory service is available free of charge and a panel of qualified language experts are able to answer students' linguistic or general study questions.

Videos continue to grow in popularity as a means of communication and entertainment. Among the video language courses is 'Hello World' which has been produced by the Response Language Learning Foundation. Courses are available in Spanish, French, Italian, German or English on VHS, Betamax and V2000 formats and comprise 10 lessons together with a specially prepared textbook.

It is widely accepted that the technique of learning by imitation is one of the most successful methods of education. Video encourages participation by the student, who can work peacefully at home, and as a result, retain a stronger interest in the subject than by studying from books alone.

The 'Hello World' course is set in familiar situations such as the airport, passport office, customs department, restaurants and hotels and thus provides the student with vocabulary which will be useful immediately on arrival at a foreign destination. The course is marketed by Videoview, 68-70 Wardour Street, London W1V 3HP, and costs £14.95 plus postage. It is also obtainable from selected video stockists.

Hugo's cassette language courses are also very suitable for study at home. The system is based on a two-pronged attack to learning a foreign language, namely:

1. Subliminal absorption
2. Conscious analytical study.

The tutors consider that item 1 above should come first, for a child, when first born, only hears the sounds of the language, which in due course it understands. Later it uses the sounds for self-expression and finally it studies the language analytically.

The two elements of the course are a combination of audio and visual; there is a book to read and a tape for listening. The relevant chapter of the book can be studied in a concentrated session of, say, an hour and the tape should be heard in a relaxed situation to assist absorption. The tape can also be played as a background to other tasks such as driving to work, washing, shaving and so on.

The course can be purchased complete with tape and book from some bookshops, price £31.95. It is also available direct from Hugo's Language Books, Old Station Yard, Marlesford, Near Woodbridge, Suffolk IT13 0AG. Courses are available in Spanish, French, German, Italian, Dutch, Portuguese and Swedish.

Linguarama Ltd of 53 Pall Mall, London SW1Y 5JH offers individual face-to-face instruction in many different languages.

Intensive or part-time tuition is available with teachers who are native to the country of the language being taught. Study can be in the UK, France, Spain or Italy. For details and terms, contact David Thompson at the above address.

Knowledge of a foreign language has other practical advantages, especially if you need to communicate with local authorities such as the police. If you are stopped by a traffic patrolman for an alleged infringement of the law, such as speeding in, say, southern Europe, it is very difficult to plead your innocence if the officer cannot speak your language and you are unable to understand his. In this sort of situation you may well decide to pay the fixed penalty rather than become more deeply involved; if you can speak the local language you may save yourself a fine.

If your home is burgled and you need to report the event to the upholders of law and order, you may find it necessary to pay the not inconsiderable cost of an interpreter to explain all the details to the police. A basic knowledge of the local language could avoid this problem.

Chapter 4

Taking Your Pets With You

Many families are very fond of their pets, particularly cats and dogs, and are loth to leave them behind when they go to live abroad. Import regulations vary from one European country to another and a summary of these rules is given below.

Do remember, however, that if you take a cat or dog to a place outside the British Isles and then want to bring it back, it becomes an imported animal so far as the Rabies Act 1974 is concerned and will have to undergo a period of quarantine.

France

No import permit is required, but dogs and cats not intended for sale in France have to be accompanied in transit, or met at the port of entry by the owner. You will be expected to verify that the animal is not for sale. A maximum of three animals, one of which may be a puppy, is permitted; all must be at least three months old.

Health certification, in French and English, from a local veterinary inspector of the Ministry of Agriculture, Fisheries and Food (Rabies Branch, MAFF, Hook Rise South, Surbiton, Surrey KT6 7NF) is required and it must be issued not more than five days before export, stating that the animal is in good health.

An export certificate from the Ministry of Agriculture is also required stating that Great Britain has been free from rabies for three years and that the animal has been domiciled in this country for over six months. This certificate also has to be issued within five days of export.

Where dogs and cats are intended for sale, there is no restriction on the number of animals which may be imported into France but they must all be at least three months old. Prior authorisation is necessary from the French Ministry of Agriculture and this is obtained by the importer, who must be the owner of an officially approved establishment. Applications in quadruplicate should be submitted through the Director General for Veterinary Services of the area where the importer's establishment is located.

These are sent to: Direction de la Qualité, Bureau des Echanges Internationaux, 175 rue de Chevaleret, 75646 Paris, Cedex 13.

Dogs are required to be inoculated annually against rabies in France and the number of the inoculation certificate is tattooed on each animal's ear.

Greece

A permit is not required for the importation of a dog or cat into Greece from Great Britain.

Certificates, however, are required to accompany the animal; these are as follows:

1. A health certificate issued by a local veterinary inspector of the Ministry of Agriculture, stating species and breed of the animal and that it has been examined and found to be in good health and free from any signs and symptoms of contagious or infectious diseases. The certificate is valid for a period of 20 days from the date of issue.
2. For dogs only, a vaccination certificate indicating that the animal has been vaccinated against rabies not less than 15 days and not more than 12 months prior to importation.
3. It is not necessary to have a dog under three months of age vaccinated against rabies before importation into Greece provided the animal is presented for vaccination on reaching the appropriate age after entry.

Certificates have to be presented to the Greek Consulate in London for legalisation.

Italy

The Italian authorities do not require an import permit for cats or dogs, but the animals must be accompanied by documentation as follows.

Animals accompanied by travellers

A bilingual (Italian and English) certificate of health is required from the local veterinary inspector of the Ministry of Agriculture, indicating that the animal was examined on the day of issue of the certificate and found to be free of any clinical signs of disease and that the animal has been vaccinated against rabies not less than 20 days and no more than 11 months prior to the date of issue of the certificate.

Accompanied animals which have not been vaccinated against

rabies, but were vaccinated outside the qualifying period mentioned above, can be imported into Italy provided they have a veterinary examination at the point of entry into the country.

Unaccompanied animals

A bilingual certificate of health from a local veterinary inspector of the Ministry of Agriculture is required stating that the animal was examined on the day of issue of the certificate and found to be free of any clinical signs of disease and that the animal had been vaccinated against rabies not less than 20 days and no more than 11 months prior to the date of issue of the health certificate.

Also required is a certificate issued by the Ministry indicating that no cases of rabies had occurred for at least the last six months in the locality from which the animal originates. Animals must also undergo a final examination by an Italian veterinary officer at the point of entry and found to be disease free in order to qualify for admission into Italy.

Dogs and cats under 12 weeks old need not be vaccinated against rabies before export, but must have certificates and undergo examination as indicated above.

Portugal

An import permit is required for dogs and cats entering Portugal, together with certificates as follows: a health certificate issued not more than 14 days prior to export by a local veterinary inspector of the Ministry of Agriculture stating that the animals are free of signs of contagious or infectious diseases including distemper and rabies. Also required is the Ministry of Agriculture's export certificate declaring that rabies has not existed in any of the districts from which the animal originates and that it has remained in the area of origin for six months prior to the date of shipment or birth.

A health certificate has to be sent to the Ministry at Surbiton for authentication and this then has to be forwarded to the Portuguese Embassy in London for legalisation. A fee is charged for this service.

Dogs have to be kept in the home under the supervision of the animal health services on arrival in Portugal. The period of restriction may be specified on the import permit or by the animal health services. All dogs in Portugal over four months of age must be vaccinated against rabies; this is undertaken during the period of quarantine and must be repeated annually.

Spain

Animals exported for commercial purposes only to Spain require import permits, but all cats and dogs destined for Spain require the following certificates: a certificate of health in duplicate is required from a veterinary inspector authorised by the Ministry of Agriculture indicating that the animal is healthy and has no signs of contagious or infectious diseases and is not suspected of suffering from rabies. The certificate has to be issued not more than two days prior to the animal leaving Great Britain.

Vaccination against rabies is not required for animals under two months of age, or for those that are native to Great Britain and are domestic pets. Other animals which are aged three months or more which have been imported to Great Britain from a country which has not been rabies free within the last six months must be vaccinated not more than 12 months, or less than one month, before importation into Spain. Where vaccination is required a certificate by a local veterinary inspector stating that the dog or cat has been vaccinated is necessary. When this is not available the animal will be quarantined for 20 days and then, providing there are no sickness symptoms, it may be vaccinated and a certificate issued. An export certificate issued by the Ministry of Agriculture is required which states that no disease to which the species is liable, and which is compulsorily notifiable under the Animal Health Act 1981, has existed at the address where the animal has normally been kept over the past two years.

All certificates must be legalised by the Spanish Consulate General in London.

Chapter 5

Education Overseas

Parents who go abroad for business reasons or retirement when their children are still of school age often arrange for their offspring to continue their education at a boarding school in the UK, so that they see them only during the holidays or at half-term.

This is a pity because it tends to break up the family and can be very expensive. What is more, it is not really necessary as there are excellent English-speaking establishments in most European countries where pupils learn not only the subjects normally studied in Britain, but also a wider curriculum which introduces them to the international scene.

Very young children who commence their education in a foreign country also have the opportunity of mixing naturally with local youngsters and soon become bilingual. (Some even become fluent in three languages if their parents are of different nationalities and the country where they reside speaks a third tongue.)

A long-established advisory service for UK education is offered by Gabbitas, Truman & Thring of 6-8 Sackville Street, Piccadilly, London W1X 2BR. This includes free impartial advice on the selection of independent schools throughout the UK. A careers counselling service is available on a fee-charging basis and a full guardianship service is offered in the UK for children whose parents live abroad.

The firm publishes annually an 800-page book listing schools in the UK and abroad. It costs £8.50 plus £2 postage and can be obtained from the above address.

A brief selection of schools in Europe for English-speaking children is given below.

Cyprus

Nicosia

American Academy, 3A, M Parides Street, PO Box 1967, Nicosia; tel: 021 62886.
Secondary school for girls and boys.

Ecole St Joseph, PO Box 1546, Nicosia; tel: 021 63338.
Secondary school for girls only.

English School, PO Box 3575, Nicosia; tel: 021 22274.
Secondary day school for boys and girls.

Falkon School, PO Box 3640, Nicosia; tel: 021 24781.
Secondary school for boys and girls.

GC School of Careers, PO Box 5276, Nicosia; tel: 021 48187.
Secondary school for boys and girls.

Grammar School, Anthoupolis Area, PO Box 2262, Nicosia; tel: 021 21744.
Secondary school for boys and girls; also a junior school.

Junior School, PO Box 3903, Nicosia; tel: 021 43855.
Junior school for boys and girls.

Terra Santa College, PO Box 1546, Nicosia; tel: 021 21100.
Secondary school for boys and girls.

Limassol

Limassol Grammar School (Foley's), Homer Street, Ayios Nicolaos, Limassol; tel: 051 54191.
Secondary school for boys and girls.

The Logos School of English Education, Nikocleous Street, PO Box 1075, Limassol; tel: 051 73650.
Secondary school for boys and girls.

Private Grammar School (Gregoriou), PO Box 1340, Limassol; tel: 051 52141.
Secondary school for boys and girls.

St Mary's School, Grivas Digenis Avenue, Limassol; tel: 051 62481.
Primary school for boys and girls.

Larnaca

American Academy, Afxentiou Avenue, PO Box 112, Larnaca; tel: 041 52046.
Secondary school for boys and girls.

St Joseph, Mich. Parides Square, Larnaca; tel: 041 52449.
Secondary school for girls.

Paphos

Anglo-American International School, 24-26 Hellas Avenue, Paphos; tel: 061 322236.
Primary and secondary school for boys and girls, 5-18 years.

France

American School of Paris, 41 rue Pasteur, 92210 Saint Cloud, Paris.
Boys and girls, 5-18 years.

British School of Paris, 38 Quai de l'Ecluse, 78290 Croissy-sur-Seine, Paris.
Boys and girls, 4½-18 years.

International School of Paris, 96 rue du Ranelagh, 75016 Paris.
Boys and girls, 4-14 years.

Marymount School, 72 Boulevard de la Saussaye, 92200 Neuilly-sur-Seine.
Boys and girls, 3-14 years.

Greece

Athens College, PO Box 5, Psychio, Athens.
Boys and girls, grades 1-6. Boys only, grades 7-13.

Italy

International School of Naples, Mostra d'Oltremore, 80125 Naples.
Boys and girls, 4½-17 years.

St George's English School, Via Cassia, Km16, 00123 Rome.
Boys and girls, 5-18 years.

Malta

Verdala School, Cottonera, Malta.
Boys and girls, 5-18 years.

The Netherlands

British School of Amsterdam, Jekerstraat 86, 1078 MG Amsterdam.
Boys and girls, 3-12 years.

British School in the Netherlands, Tapijtweg 10, 2597KH The Hague (junior school); Jan van Hooflaan 3, 2252BC Voorschoten.
Boys and girls, 3½-18 years.

Portugal

Prince Henry International School, Vale do Lobo, Almansil, Algarve.
Boys and girls, 3-16 years.

Algarve International School, Porches, near Lagoa, Algarve.
Boys and girls, 5-16 years. Centre in southern Portugal for London University GCE examinations.

Barlavento English School, Espiche 8600, Lagos, Algarve.
Boys and girls, kindergarten.

American International School, Apartado 10, Carnaxide 2795, Linda-a-Velha, Lisbon.
Boys and girls, 5-17 years.

St Julian's School, Quinta Nova, Carcavelos, 2775 Parede (about 10 miles from Lisbon).
Boys and girls, 3½-18 years.

St Anthony's International Primary School, Avenida de Portugal 11, 2765 Estoril.
Boys and girls up to 12 years of age.

Casa dos Santos Infant School, Quinta do Relógio, 2710 Sintra.
Nursery school for boys and girls 1-6 years.

St George's School, Vila Conçalves, Quinta dos Loureiras, Estrada Nacional, 2750 Cascais.
Boys and girls, 4-13 years.

Nursery Class, Rua da Arriaga 39, 1200 Lisbon.
Boys and girls, 3-6 years.

St Dominic's College, Rua Outeiro da Polima, 2780 Arneiro.
Catholic school for boys and girls, 4-16 years.

O Pincho Kindergarten, Quinta de S Joao, Rebelva, Carcavelos.
Boys and girls, 2-6 years.

Spain

A large number of British schools have been established in Spain and most of these are members of the National Association of British Schools in Spain, Arga 9, Madrid 2. A list of establishments in major resort areas is given below but further information can be obtained from the Association's address given above.

Costa del Sol

Calpe College, San Pedro de Alcantara, Marbella, 4½-17 years.

Sunny View School, Apartado 175, Cerro del Toril, Torremolinos.
Co-educational, 4-18 years.

Marbella College, 15 Villa Marina, Carretera de Cadiz 174, Marbella. College of higher education.

Swan School, Villa Capricho 1, Marbella, 3-15 years.

English College, Apartado 318, Benalmadena Costa, 5-18 years.

St Anthony's College, Apartado 119, Los Boliches, Fuengirola, 3-18 years.

English International College, Urbanizacion Ricmar, Ctra. de Cadiz, Km 196, Marbella, Malaga, 3-18 years.

Costa Blanca

Beverly Hills School, Beverly Hills 4, San Rafael, Alfaz Del Pi, Alicante, 2½-16 years.

Sierra Bernia School, La Caneta San Rafael, Alfaz del Pi, Alicante, 4-18 years.

Edge Hill College, Ctra. Benidorm-La Nurcia Km53, La Nurcia, Alicante, 5-11 years.

Barcelona

Anglo-American School, Paseo de Garbi 152, Casteldelfels, Barcelona, 3-18 years.

Kensington School, Carretera de Esplugas 86 bis, Barcelona, 5-17 years.

Madrid

English Montessori School, Calle Triona 65, Madrid, 4-11 years.

International Primary School, Madre Carmen de Niño Jesus 3, Madrid, 2½-11 years.

King's College, Paseo de los Andes S/N, Urb. Sato de Vinuelos, Carretera de Colmenter Viejo, Madrid, 3-18 years.

Hastings School, Puerto de la Habona 204, Madrid, 4-11 years.

Numont PNEU, Parma 16, Madrid, 3-11 years.

Runnymede College, British Secondary School, Arga 9, Madrid, 11-18 years.

St Anne's School, Jaroma 9, Madrid, 3-14 years.

St Michael's Preparatory School, Avenida Comandante Franco 8, Madrid, 3-11 years.

Kensington School, Avenida de Bulares, Pazuelo de Alarcon, Madrid, 3-17 years.

Canary Islands

British Yeoward School, Parque Taoro, Puerto de la Cruz, Tenerife, 3-16 years.

Colegio Hispano-Britanico, Corijo de los Caserones San Antonio, Tias, Las Palmas, Grand Canary, 3-16 years.

British School of Grand Canary, PO Box 11, Tarifa Alta, Las Palmas, 4-16 years.

Wingate School, Mirador de la Unbritas 10, Cabo Blanco, Arona, Tenerife, 3-11 years.

Balearic Islands

American School of Majorca, Portals Nous, Majorca, 4-18 years.

Baleares International School, San Augustín, Palma, Majorca, 5-19 years.

King's College, Juan de Saridakis 64, Palma, Majorca, 3-16 years.

Bellver International College, José Costa Ferrer 10, Cala Mayor, Palma, Majorca, 4-16 years.

Morna Valley School, Santa Eulalia del Rio, Apartado 95, Ibiza, 3-18 years.

Switzerland

Aiglon College, 1885 Chesiares Villas.
Boys and girls, 11-18 years.

International School of Berne, Mattenstrasse 3,
3073 Gumlegen bei Bern.
Boys and girls, 5-18 years.

Turkey

International Community School, Robert College,
Arnavutkoy PKI, Istanbul.
Boys and girls, 4-15 years.

Chapter 6

Health Benefits and Insurance

Greece, Spain and Portugal are now members of the EC and pensioners living in any of the EC countries are entitled to claim medical and health facilities that are available to nationals of the country concerned.

Benefits include free dental treatment, sickness benefit, free medicine and drugs. Widows' benefits are also payable on the death of a husband. Generally speaking, the benefits are available to pensioners who were, at some time during their working life, employed in any of the twelve EC countries, but there are exceptions.

Those drawing their pensions from the Department of Social Security at Newcastle upon Tyne should receive a copy of Form 121 whereon the Newcastle authorities certify the pensioner's entitlement and this is sent to the appropriate social security authority in the country of residence.

Pensioners, or younger members of the family who stay temporarily in an EC member state, can obtain full medical and hospital treatment, if taken ill in that country, but they must obtain Form E111 before they leave home and give it to the appropriate health authority in the country where they are staying.

A series of leaflets which give information for nationals of each member state moving permanently, or temporarily, to another member state, can be obtained free from: The Office for Official Publications of the European Community, PO Box 1003, Luxembourg.

More information about individual countries is provided in Part 4.

Although these free medical benefits are available, delays in obtaining treatment in hospitals and consulting doctors can be lengthy, as in the UK. Also hospital wards often lack the desired privacy when a patient is seriously ill.

It is therefore highly recommended that those living permanently in an overseas country should subscribe to a private medical insurance scheme. The well-known UK schemes, BUPA and PPP, can provide health cover for members residing abroad.

A worldwide private health insurance plan for expatriates in retirement abroad is also available from Exeter Hospital Aid Society of Exeter, Devon. This organisation is a registered friendly society and a member of the International Federation of Voluntary Health Societies.

The Society widened its scale of operations in the early 1960s with the aim of giving lifetime protection against the high cost of medical treatment abroad and members are guaranteed the right to renew cover every year throughout their life, irrespective of their claims record.

As treatment charges vary from one country to another, the scheme gives subscribers a choice of several scales of benefit covering either average costs or a super scale for areas where charges are higher. The hospital accommodation benefit within each scale can be increased by buying extra accommodation units.

The scales cover a wide selection of treatments in addition to hospital costs. Claims may be submitted in respect of convalescence, private health checks, body scans, private outpatient treatment, qualified nursing at home, surgical appliances and so on.

Details of annual subscriptions can be obtained from Exeter Hospital Aid Society, 5-7 Palace Gate, Exeter, Devon EX1 1UE.

Chapter 7

Recreation and Self-employment

If you are going to retire to a sunny country overseas you really should make some plans in advance as to how you propose to occupy your time when you no longer have to travel daily to your place of employment.

Having spent perhaps 40 years or more earning your living, it will feel very strange to be without specific duty targets to achieve or jobs to be done. Just the thought of being able to please yourself as to how you spend each day may at first seem very attractive. But beware – after a few weeks of lying in the sun or reading books, watching television or even taking a little exercise with a gentle round of golf, the lack of a definite target to achieve will for most people soon become boring and disconcerting.

In the early months, you will no doubt find little jobs to do around the home and make excursions to local towns to discover the best shops or markets for everyday needs. Then, if you are a car owner, journeys to resorts or places of interest can be enjoyed.

Owners of villas with gardens large or small will be able to while away the time with horticultural pottering, which may ultimately develop into a hobby of absorbing interest, providing not only exercise but also an end result in the form of sweet-smelling flowers to decorate the house, fresh vegetables for the kitchen or luscious fruit for immediate consumption and freezing for future use. Certainly tilling the soil can be a productive pastime for the able-bodied.

Not everyone was born with green fingers so what other hobbies or pleasurable tasks can be considered? (*See also* Chapter 9.)

Recreation

If you are a golfer and live in southern Spain, Portugal or France, you will find there are many opportunities to indulge in your favourite sport throughout the year. In Spain, on the Costa del Sol, the demand for a round of golf is so intense that it is sometimes necessary to wait several hours before you can get on the course.

Membership and green fees are often expensive, but the liquid refreshments dispensed at the 19th hole are cheaper than in England, so unless your spouse also participates in the sport, take care that she does not become a golf widow and you an alcoholic.

Bowls is growing in popularity for old and young alike. In England outdoor rinks have always been noteworthy for immaculate green turf. In the south of Europe artificial surfaces were used initially because of the warm, dry climate but hard-wearing grass is now also being planted to provide a natural surface. Bowls clubs in Spain and elsewhere are popular with Britons as meeting places and provide opportunities for gentle, yet challenging, exercise throughout most of the year.

Tennis, of course, is another popular outdoor sport which is tackled by some senior citizens who enjoy more active exercise. There are numerous clubs and tennis centres along the Mediterranean coastline and there is even a cricket club at La Manga in Spain.

All these sporting activities provide opportunities for socialising with fellow nationals and also mixing with citizens from many other nations. In addition, there are clubs devoted to bridge, whist, art, philately, local history, music, theatricals, the cinema and a host of other subjects.

However, not everyone wants to spend every day on the club circuit, so let us consider some other ideas.

Those who want to make themselves useful to their fellow citizens can become involved in philanthropic organisations. Areas covered include child welfare, animal care, nursing the elderly and infirm, helping the sick by visiting or shopping for them, and partaking in emergency services for fellow expatriates who are injured in accidents or suddenly bereaved.

Employment

If you aim to achieve some remunerative self-employment in retirement make sure you undertake some research into the opportunities available before you complete your plans to emigrate. Remember, in some countries, retired foreigners are not permitted to work for payment.

Can you write a good story or report? If so, you might be able to start a part-time career as a journalist. You need to specialise in a particular subject if possible or write short stories. The early stages can be tough with many rejections, but with perseverance, you may have the pleasure of seeing your name in type.

Submit your manuscript to a local English-language magazine or to a travel or specialist publication in the UK. Don't forget to type the article neatly with double spacing between lines and send an International Reply Coupon to cover return postage if you want your manuscript back.

First efforts should be submitted to the smaller circulation journals, many of whom will use freelance contributions and may take the trouble to read unsolicited contributions. The mass circulation magazines and newspapers generally employ staff journalists or use well-established specialist writers.

The rewards from freelance writing may be small, but the satisfaction of being accepted is great and you should also enjoy the research part of the project which can occupy many an hour that would otherwise be wasted, but do try to make some contacts among publishers and editors before you leave the UK.

Those with a hectare or more of land around their villa could invest in the production of citrus fruit, cultivation of vines or growing avocados (remember that three years elapse from planting avocados before any crops materialise). These could all produce pocket money from sales to neighbours or local shops.

Philately is an intriguing hobby and can also be a useful spare-time business, operated from home. Some capital will be needed to invest in stock, but if a specialisation is carefully chosen, it need not involve thousands of pounds.

Kiloware is an interesting sideline. This involves the accumulation of stamps from friends' and business houses' daily post, both local and international. The stamps are cut from envelopes, taking care not to damage them, and left on the backing paper. They are then sorted into country classifications or accumulated as mixed lots and sold by weight to stamp dealers or collectors who specialise in this area. British stamps and mixed lots realise the lowest prices, but good returns can be obtained with stamps from small countries or remote islands.

Contacts with firms which receive a high quantity of overseas mail are essential if you are to make a success of this trade. Sometimes these organisations are prepared to give stamps from their mail free to a regular contact. In other cases a small charge may be made for the privilege.

If you live in a country which issues half a dozen or more commemorative sets of stamps each year, there may be scope for you to prepare and service first-day covers for individual collectors or dealers. This involves designing and printing special envelopes for each set, sticking the newly issued stamps on to the envelopes and taking them to a post office to have the stamps carefully cancelled with a postmark bearing the date of the day of issue. The envelopes then sell for a premium over the face value of the stamps.

Depending on your skills and language facility, part- or full-time work may be found in offices which require secretarial services or garages which employ mechanics or hire car staff; travel couriers are often required, there are opportunities as sales staff for estate agents and launderettes may need supervisors. But remember, most countries now have work permit regulations and these may apply to the above occupations. If you fail to observe the rules you could be expelled from the country you have chosen as your retirement spot.

When you are retired, take care not to burden yourself with too many tasks so that you have no time for relaxation or mixing with neighbours and family. It takes many years to earn a pension and you should aim to live long enough to enjoy a slower pace of life. But do not be completely idle, for some constructive interests are essential for most of us when a career no longer dominates all else.

Part 2
Moving Out, Settling In and Coming Back

Chapter 8

Moving Overseas

Moving house can be a traumatic experience at the best of times. At worst, with careless planning and trying to cut costs, it can be a disaster!

Before the actual move there are always weeks of preparation; bringing down old boxes from the loft and poring over their contents to see if they are worth keeping; clearing out the garage and throwing away the odd bits of wood and junk that you were keeping in case they proved useful – ask any remover, we've all got much more in our homes than we think.

So imagine the additional problems facing a householder who is moving abroad. He (or usually she) has to go through the family's possessions and ruthlessly pare them down to manageable proportions for packing into a container for shipping or air freighting to perhaps the other side of the world.

Difficult decisions have to be made such as whether to take the three-piece suite and dining room table/chairs or to buy new ones once you are settled in your new home. How do prices compare? Who to ask?

Invaluable help can be provided by a reputable international remover who will be able to advise you as to what is best left behind and replaced at destination and what should be taken to save expense or because of supply difficulties and so on. It costs nothing to invite a remover to survey your household goods and personal effects and to provide an estimate of the removal costs – and it could save you a lot of time and energy.

The first main danger which people can suffer is sending their possessions through a freight forwarding agent who only delivers as far as the port of entry of the destination country. This means you will have to arrange customs clearance and also find someone to transfer your belongings from the port to your new home or, if that is not ready, into store. And without knowledgeable help, finding proper local storage facilities is no easy task in a strange country.

Second, a surprising number of people rely on a remover with no financial or other backing who nevertheless quotes extremely attractive prices. Unfortunately, this lack of financial base has often in the past meant the remover going bankrupt and being unable to carry out the move for which he was contracted.

In this case, the hapless customer, who will already have paid the first remover, will have to pay yet again for someone else to complete the move. Regrettably, the chance of redress is so limited as not to be worth considering.

Both these circumstances can be avoided if you choose a contractor from among the Overseas Group members of the British Association of Removers (BAR). All international member companies have links throughout the world with equally reputable removers, through their international trade association, the Federation of International Furniture Removers (FIDI).

Membership of FIDI means a contractor can arrange a door-to-door international removal, working with a reliable and knowledgeable firm in the destination country who will deal with the formalities relating to customs clearance and (if pets are involved) quarantine regulations, store the consignment as long as necessary and finally deliver it to your new address.

While these relationships offer a comforting level of expertise, the BAR Overseas Group also provides tangible security, through its guarantee of the financial soundness of its members. Its BAR-IMMI advance payment scheme provides a written guarantee that, should a member company fail to fulfil its commitments to a customer, the removal will be completed at no extra cost or the money refunded.

So people moving overseas who use a BAR Overseas Group member need have no fear of settling in their new home with only the clothes they stand up in while the rest of their belongings are stranded in Britain – something which has happened to many people using non-BAR Overseas Group members which have gone out of business.

In addition, a qualified remover can also guide you through the minefield of documentation relating to import/export licences and customs regulations.

Electrical appliances may not be compatible with voltages in your destination country and your TV will probably not be suitable. If you are moving to a warmer climate, you will definitely need a larger fridge/freezer so, unless you have recently bought a new one, the freezer, or fridge, is not worth taking. Many houses have built-in furniture, so you may not need your wardrobes either.

On the other hand, there are some items which cost less in

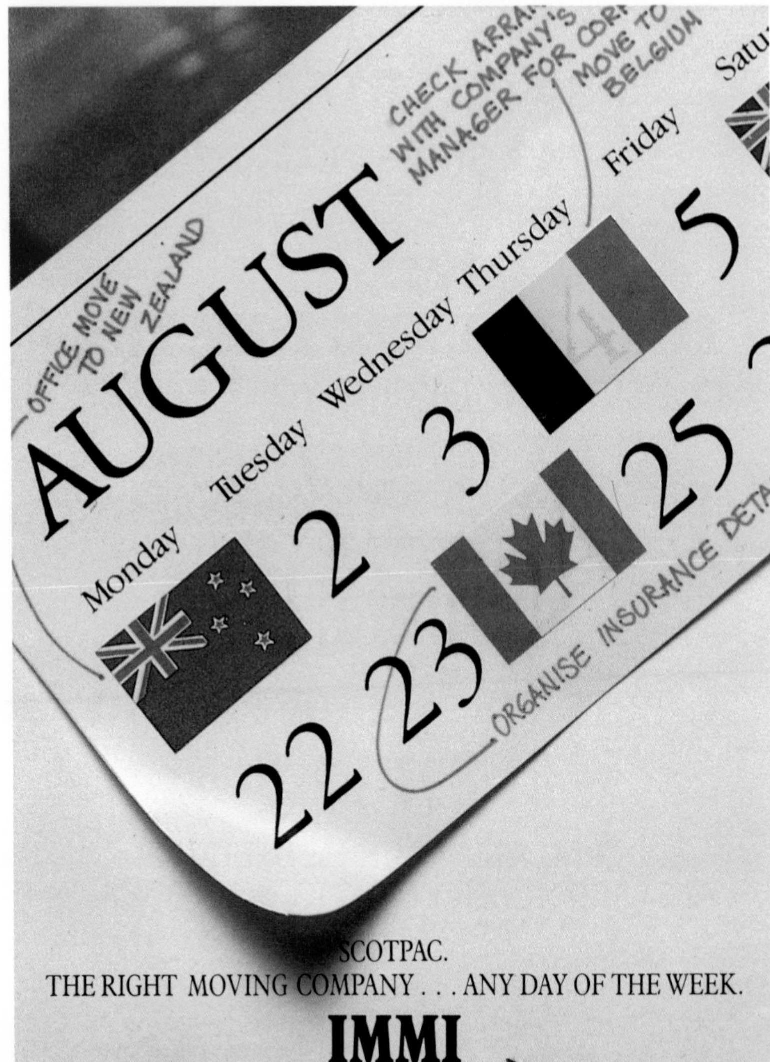
AUGUST
Monday
Tuesday
Wednesday
Thursday
Friday
2
3
5
22
23
25
OFFICE MOVE TO NEW ZEALAND
WITH COMPANY'S
MANAGER FOR
MOVE TO BELGIUM
ORGANISE INSURANCE
SCOTPAC.
THE RIGHT MOVING COMPANY . . . ANY DAY OF THE WEEK.
IMMI
ADVANCE PAYMENT GUARANTEE

Britain than elsewhere and it may be worth buying these before you go. Under the government's personal export scheme, people who are emigrating or who intend spending at least 12 months out of the country are allowed to buy certain goods free of VAT charges. Your remover will be able to give you details of this.

Take good carpets, high-quality furniture and fine china/glass if you wish, and remember some articles of winter clothing. Even in warmer climes, the evenings can be chilly.

Take your tool kit too, as tools are difficult and costly to replace wherever you live. But think twice about taking cane furniture as this is viewed with grave suspicion in most countries. As a precaution the quarantine authorities may decide to have the furniture fumigated at your expense, and the cost is high.

English books are often expensive in foreign countries, so you may wish to take, not only your present collection, but some for future reading and reference.

Special provision usually has to be made for pets and cars. In some countries, both may be banned; in others (such as the USA) the car will have to comply with exhaust emission legislation.

Finally, do not forget to make a complete inventory of everything to be moved and to give your remover a copy. Any discrepancy between the list and the contents of your consignment could result in customs officials delaying clearance – and although there may be the temptation to slip a few 'extras' in, don't try it; customs searches are rigorous and the penalties severe.

For more hints about moving abroad, a free leaflet is available by sending a stamped and self-addressed envelope (preferably 9 x 4 in) to the British Association of Removers, 3 Churchill Court, 58 Station Road, North Harrow, Middlesex. There is also an easy-to-use audio-visual programme available free of charge to local associations which gives complete advice on how to go about a removal.

Removal checklist

Don't forget to arrange a UK contact address and to tell the following organisations that you are moving abroad:

Your bank

Income Tax Office. Notify the Inland Revenue giving the exact date of departure.

National Insurance/DSS. For benefits, allowances, pension. Send your full name, date of birth, full National Insurance number, details of country to which you are moving and duration of your stay to the DSS Overseas Branch, Newcastle upon Tyne NE98 1YX.

Vehicle licence. If you are taking your vehicle abroad for longer than a year this is regarded as a 'permanent export'. In this case you should return your existing (new style) registration document to the Vehicle Licensing Centre, Swansea SA99 1AB, filling in the 'permanent export' section. Alternatively, you can apply to your local Vehicle Licensing Office for the necessary forms.

Driving licence. You will probably want to retain your British driving licence. Many countries recognise it as valid and a list of those which do not is available from the AA.

International driving licence. An international driving licence is obtainable from the AA (even if you are not a member) and is valid for one year. The licence is not valid in the country where it is issued so you must obtain it before leaving the UK. Most countries require residents to hold a local driving licence so check whether this is the case on taking up your new residence.

Motor insurance. Notify your insurers of the date of your departure – your insurance should be cancelled from that date and you should obtain a refund for the rest of the insurance period. Ask your insurance company for a letter outlining your no-claim record to show to your new insurer.

Life and other insurances. Notify the companies concerned or your insurance broker if you use one.

Dentist. Let him know you are moving, as a matter of courtesy; it will save him posting useless check-up reminders.

Private health insurance. Notify subscriber records department.

Gas. If you use it, notify your local gas showroom giving at least *48 hours'* notice. They will give you a standard form to fill in with details of the move and any current hire-purchase agreements. If appliances are to be removed they require as much notice as possible to arrange an appointment; there is a disconnection charge.

Electricity. Notify your local district office or showroom at least *48 hours* before moving. Otherwise arrangements are much the same as for gas.

Water. The local water board should also be notified at least *48 hours* before the move. Drain tanks and pipes if the house is to remain empty in winter.

Telephone. Notify your local telephone sales office as shown in the front of your directory at least *seven days* before the move.

Rates. If you are a ratepayer, notify the town hall.

Libraries. Return books and give in tickets to be cancelled.

Professional advisers. Solicitors, accountants, stockbrokers, insurance brokers, etc. Make sure they have a forwarding address.

Stocks and shares. Write to the company registrar at the address on the last annual report or share certificates.

Organisations and clubs. Any business, civic, social, cultural, sports or automobile club of which you are a member. For the AA write to Membership Subscription and Records, PO Box 50, Basingstoke, Hampshire and for the RAC write to RAC House, Lansdowne Road, East Croydon, Surrey.

Credit card companies. Advise them that you are leaving the country.

HP companies. Notify the office where repayments are made. You will need to settle your account.

Local business accounts. Department stores, newsagents, dairy, baker, chemist, dry cleaner, laundry, motor service station.

Publications. Cancel postal subscriptions to newsagents, magazines, professional and trade journals, books and record clubs, etc.

National Health Service. Return your NHS card to the Family Practitioners' Committee for your area, giving your date of departure, or hand in the card to the immigration officer at your point of departure.

Pension schemes. If you have a 'frozen' or paid-up pension from a previous employer be sure to notify the pension trust of your new address.

TV. If you have a rented set, make arrangements to return it.

Post Office. Notify day of departure and UK contact address as letters can be forwarded for a fee.

Personal Giro. The Post Office have a special SAE for this.

Premium Bonds. Anything rather than join the sad list of unclaimed prizes! Contact Bonds and Stocks Office, Lytham St Annes, Lancashire FY0 1YN, to check the current position, because in a few countries, Premium Bond holdings may contravene their lottery laws.

Save As You Earn and National Savings Certificates. It is important to notify any permanent change of address, particularly for index-linked retirement issue certificates and SAYE contracts. Advise the National Savings Certificate Office, Durham DH99 1NS, quoting the contract number(s).

National Savings Bank. Notify at Glasgow G58 1SB.

Your landlord. If you are a tenant, give the appropriate notice to quit.

Your tenants. If you are a landlord that UK address you've organised will be needed.

Your employer. Give new address details, or a contact address, in writing.

Schools. Try to give your children's schools a term's notice that they will be leaving. If you wish your children's education to be continued in Britain contact your local Education Authority or the Department of Education and Science, Elizabeth House, York Road, London SE1 7PH, for advice.

Make sure your *removers* have any temporary contact address and phone numbers for you, both in the UK and abroad, so that they can get in touch with you when the need arises. It is also useful for them if you can tell them when you expect to arrive in your new country.

Reproduced by courtesy of Pickfords Ltd.

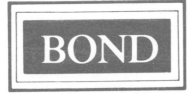

Taking a car abroad

After a virtual lifetime of driving on the left, British people still tend to prefer right-hand drive or automatic and will therefore consider buying their car here and taking it with them. First check at the embassy of the country you propose to live in that private car imports are permitted.

Probably the best way to plan this is to make a list of what you will want your car to do. You will no longer be using it to commute, so there will be less stopping and starting; the road surfaces may be less good than those you are used to, so you may consider taking a good second-hand car rather than a brand new one. You will not then be so worried about driving through very narrow streets. In some places drivers actually park by shunting the cars ahead and behind!

In the Channel Islands small old cars are fine if your budget is tight. The road network will limit the amount of driving you are likely to do and a good used car can be bought from a reputable dealer with a guarantee.

If you are used to driving a large, comfortable car in this country, when you retire abroad you may feel happier with a new, luxurious, well-appointed small car rather than a very old model. If you buy a new car in the UK before going abroad, you can use it here for six months, run it in and have your first service before you take it overseas.

Check the servicing facilities in the area where you plan to live. It would be unwise to take a car abroad if the nearest dealer service is 70 miles away. This factor may well limit your choice.

A big car will be expensive with petrol and difficult to park. If you will be living in an apartment and there is no garage, the car will usually be left in the street, and possibly for long periods at that. Consider carefully the security of your car and what you may have in it. Choose a model with locking wheel nuts and high-quality locks so it is hard to get into without smashing the windows. Radio thefts are prevalent in some countries; therefore you may wish to consider a demountable radio.

Should you decide to take a small car to a hot country, always buy one with a sun roof because the smaller cars carry no air conditioning.

People retiring to Spain will often choose diesel cars because the fuel is half the price of petrol and easily available. Lead-free petrol is now available in many countries and you should check

TRAVEL IN COMFORT

DON'T FEEL THE PINCH

PARK LANE EXPORT
TAKE A NEW BMW ABROAD AND LEAVE THE TAX BEHIND

As the sole official BMW export department in the UK, Park Lane Export are the only people qualified to advise on the eligibility and advantages of a new tax free BMW.

Our experienced export specialists will ensure the efficient operation of complex export procedures which could prove to be a minefield to the inexperienced.

Park Lane Export can provide all required specifications, left or right hand drive and can arrange insurance and shipping to any final destination.

To discover whether you are eligible for a tax free BMW, contact our export specialists on 01-629 9277.

Park Lane Export
Tourist and NATO Sales
56 Park Lane, London W1Y 3DA
Telephone: 01-629 9277
Telex: 261360

whether your engine will take this quality. Some engines need minor adaptation.

If you plan to put small pieces of furniture in the car for your move abroad, a hatchback is easier. On the other hand, an economical way of organising a move to the Continent is to hire a transit van, load it up with your furniture, and drive it there, returning with the empty van to pick up your own car, and any remaining luggage.

Personal export of new cars

Those who wish to buy a new car and use it in the UK before they go abroad to live can take advantage of a special scheme which allows the purchase without payment of VAT or car tax. Motor cycles and motor caravans can also be purchased under the scheme. UK citizens who use the scheme may have the use of the vehicle in this country for up to six months before it is exported.

Form VAT 410, obtainable from UK manufacturers and foreign manufacturers' sole selling agents approved by Customs and Excise to operate the scheme, must be completed and returned to the manufacturer or agent. Customs and Excise will need to approve the application, after which the vehicle can be delivered to you. It is wise to allow plenty of time for the procedure. Only the applicant may take delivery of the vehicle, and there are restrictions on who can drive it while it is still in the UK. It must not be disposed of in any way before it is exported.

The vehicle may be taken abroad temporarily before the export date shown on the documents, but must be declared to customs on its return to the UK, and the documentation produced. If the car is not exported by the due date for any reason (even if it is stolen or damaged), then VAT and car tax will become payable on its value when new, so it is vital to insure it for its full value as soon as it is delivered to you.

It is worth making shipping arrangements well in advance of the due export date, to avoid last-minute problems which could involve you in payment of VAT and car tax. These payments will also be levied if the car is brought back into the UK within six months of the export date on the documents.

Details of the scheme are explained in Notice 705, available from your local Customs and Excise Office.

It is possible to take delivery of a new car outside the UK free of VAT and car tax if you do not want to use it before you go abroad to live; this is a direct export and the manufacturer or sole selling

626

Whatever the country there's only one way to travel.
THE COROLLA
THE MR2
THE CARINA
THE SUPRA
THE SPACE CRUISER
THE CAMRY
To discover the only way to travel post this coupon to:
Toyota Tax-Free Sales, The Quadrangle, Station Road, Redhill, Surrey RH1 1PX.
Or phone Redhill (0737) 68585.
I am interested in a tax-free deal on:
Name
LRA
Address
Country of Destination
Tel Work
Tel Home
Supra
Celica
Corolla
Tercel 4WD
Carina
Camry
Space Cruiser
Land Cruiser
THE BEST TAX-FREE DEAL.
TOYOTA

agent of a foreign manufacturer in the UK will be able to supply full information.

Taking your existing car abroad

If you take the car you own at present abroad for longer than 12 months, this is regarded as a permanent export and the procedure is described in leaflet V526, obtainable from your local Vehicle Licensing Office.

The following procedure applies to exports from England, Scotland, Wales and the Isles of Scilly only, not to Northern Ireland or the Isle of Man, where cars are registered separately.

Complete section 2 on the back of the Vehicle Registration Document, entering the proposed date of export, and send the document to your local Vehicle Licensing Office or to the Driver and Vehicle Licensing Centre. This should be done well in advance of your departure.

You will receive back a Certificate of Export (V561) which in effect confirms your vehicle registration.

A different procedure applies in Northern Ireland as vehicles are registered locally; it is necessary to register and license a car taken *to* Northern Ireland permanently as soon as the current British tax disc expires, if not before. The Certificate of Export mentioned above will still be necessary.

Motoring services in Europe

The International Touring Alliance has its headquarters in Geneva, and driving clubs throughout Europe are affiliated to it, including the Automobile Association. These clubs provide a wide range of services to each other's members travelling abroad, so membership of one is worthwhile.

Austria
Osterreichischer Automobil Motorrad and Touring Club (OAMTC)

Belgium
Touring Club Royal de Belgique (TCB)

Cyprus
Cyprus Automobile Association (CAA)

France
Association Française des Automobilistes (AFA). (The Automobile Association has a Continental Emergency Centre at Boulogne-sur-Mer.)

Germany (Federal Republic)
Allgemeine Deutscher Automobile Club (ADAC)

Greece
Automobile and Touring Club of Greece (ELPA)

Italy
Automobile Club d'Italia (ACI)

Luxembourg
Automobile Club du Grand-Duché de Luxembourg (ACL)

Netherlands
Koninklijke Nederlandse Toeristenbond (ANWB)

Portugal
Automovel Club de Portugal (ACP)

Spain
Real Automovil Club de España (RACE)

Switzerland
Touring Club Suisse (TCS)

Turkey
Turkiye Turing Ve Otomobil Kurumu

Chapter 9

Settling In

After the excitement of the move and the traumas of starting a new life in a foreign country, a period of calm ought to be enjoyed while settling down in your newly acquired villa or apartment.

Unless you are very experienced in uprooting your family and shifting them to an entirely new environment you are almost certain to have a few problems to solve before you really are accepted as a 'local' by your neighbours in your adopted country, so here are a few tips on the subject of settling in.

Documentation

Most countries require the completion of some documentation by new residents from overseas. It may be as simple as having an up-to-date British passport, so make sure that yours has at least one year to run before it expires in order to give yourself a breathing space prior to having it renewed by the local British Consul or the passport office in Britain. The one-year passport which can be obtained from post offices in Britain is not a satisfactory document for emigrants as its life is too short and it is not always acceptable by overseas authorities.

If you already hold a pink driving licence issued in the UK and endorsed 'European Communities model', you do not need to obtain any other licence to drive a car in any EC country.

The International Driving Licence issued by the AA or RAC contains translations in nine languages plus an identity photograph of the holder. This impresses officialdom in some countries, particularly if you are stopped by the police, but many nations now require new residents to apply for a local driving licence. This may involve the completion of a simple form and the payment of a fee, but in some instances it is necessary to pass a driving test and to repass that test on achieving the age of three score years and ten or some other arbitrary figure.

Residence permits are required in many countries and before these are issued, certain qualifications need to be fulfilled. These may take the form of satisfactory certificates from the police or legal bodies in your homeland regarding social or crime-free behaviour. Bank certificates are also often necessary to prove that you have sufficient income and/or capital to sustain an appropriate standard of living, so that you will not become a burden to your host country.

Take care regarding technical terms used in some countries. For instance a *permanencia* is not a permanent permit to reside in Spain but temporary permission to remain in Spain for a further 90 days after the first 90 days granted to tourists has expired. A *residencia* is a permit to reside in Spain and it lasts for five years for EC nationals and can be renewed for a further five years.

If you are hoping to take up some form of employment in your new home country, examine the laws regarding work permits. In areas of high unemployment these are often very hard to obtain and permission to work in your own business which you are planning to set up is sometimes required. Professional people like doctors, lawyers and accountants may need to be accepted into membership of the local professional guild before being permitted to practise their particular skill and foreigners do not always find it easy to qualify, particularly if the profession is already over-staffed.

In EC countries mobility of labour should be unrestricted but this ideal situation has not yet been achieved throughout the Community.

Remember, it is never worthwhile, in the long run, to flout regulations; if you are caught, a large fine can be imposed or you may be banned from living in the country of your choice.

The fees charged by local consultants such as the *gestor* (business agent) or *abogado* (lawyer) in Spain are generally money well spent when dealing with officialdom, for it is much better to solve any problem first time round.

Finances

Before departing for your new home make sure that you have settled your financial affairs and that your income will be sufficient for your requirements. The cost of living in countries with a temperate climate can be lower than in northern Europe as far less has to be spent on home heating and warm clothing. But food is more expensive if you insist on eating familiar brand names imported from the UK or America.

In planning your finances do ensure that you have a reasonable reserve fund to cover unexpected or unplanned expenditure on setting up home, for it is impossible to anticipate each and every need for a new life-style.

Where to shop

Countries with an outdoor way of life mostly have regular weekly markets in the main square or some other convenient location in each town and many villages.

These are the places where you can learn to shop for fruit, vegetables and other products and get good value for money, but you do need some linguistic ability if you are going to have any meaningful conversation with the local traders.

Supermarkets abound in towns with a sizeable local or tourist population. These establishments may be a little more expensive than the markets, but they do stock prepacked products, all individually priced, which means that you can serve yourself to packs that suit your requirements and know immediately how much they cost.

Although you will miss familiar foods, local products are often just as satisfactory and fruit and vegetables are particularly good value. Fish caught fresh from the sea is much tastier than frozen slabs of produce whose origins are far distant from the area of consumption. Meat producers are also more skilled in marketing cuts of joints, chops and other meat products than in former years. Even British-type sausages can be found in some shops.

Specialised shops covering ironmongery, shoes, clothes, pharmaceutical products and many other household requirements demand a little more courage for shoppers unskilled in the local tongue, but practice makes perfect and if you do not make the effort to use these establishments, you will never make progress in shopping and some of the staff may be able to talk your language!

It is well worth while taking advice from local people when planning the purchase of luxury items such as leather goods and jewellery as they should know the shops which offer the best value.

Local relationships

If you are ever to become accepted by your neighbours you must endeavour to mix and talk with them, irrespective of whether they are of the same nationality as yourself.

The apparent inability of British people, particularly those from the large towns and cities, to mix and meet with neighbours must be overcome when living abroad, otherwise new residents will find it almost impossible to establish the friendships which are so essential to a happy life of retirement in a new environment away from familiar places and people. Loneliness must be avoided if at all possible.

Much can be learned from those who have lived in a particular area for a number of years or a lifetime.

Domesticity

Running a house in a strange country can produce problems for the housekeeper. Different types of food, new styles of catering, a much warmer climate, strange shops with unfamiliar product brands can all produce periods of uncertainty during the first months of residing in a different country. It is during this period that men should show a greater interest in the household routine by trying to assist with daily chores and even shopping, to the detriment, if necessary, of work in the garden or even giving up a round of golf!

Hobbies and sports

Retired people should have interests that not only entertain them but also, if possible, produce some useful end results. (*See also* Chapter 7.)

Woodwork or photography, painting or model making, needlework or floral decoration, sewing or music are just a few suggestions for acquiring or improving useful skills which will help to pass the time, all year round.

In the summer everyone can enjoy walking, gardening, bird watching and nature studies in the open air. Those able to participate in sport will find opportunities for lawn bowls, swimming, archery, tennis and riding plus extensive opportunities for golf in an ideal climate.

Many of these activities have their own clubs which enable members to mix and meet.

Voluntary work

In every country there are opportunities for voluntary welfare work among the young and the old and also looking after the welfare of animals. This can be a most rewarding full- or part-time occupation and the need is great, particularly with local underprivileged children and the elderly who are often housebound and lonely. For them a regular weekly visit to do some shopping or just to have a chat is a kindness which is much appreciated. All able-bodied people should keep an eye on those who are physically handicapped or elderly, and frequent visits will help to allay their fears of being taken ill with nobody near to help them.

Organisations of expatriates often establish a service through their members to undertake this valuable welfare work and this should receive willing support from those who are capable of looking after others as well as themselves.

Clubs and social organisations

In almost every location where there are a number of expatriates living in fairly close proximity, clubs covering a wide variety of activities become established.

These range from simple lunch clubs for males, females or both sexes, where a wide variety of topics can be discussed and differing opinions aired over a meal and a glass of wine or other refreshment. From this a debating club might emerge, or specialised clubs covering subjects such as gardening, music, chess, bridge, darts, amateur dramatics, film societies and table tennis to mention but a few.

Apartment blocks in Spain generally have a Community of Owners, so that individuals can have a say in the management of the communal facilities, public parks, or gardens, and the expenditure on external maintenance, caretaking staff, refuse disposal and so on. These regular gatherings of owners provide an opportunity to meet other owners in the development, which might not occur in the normal way where there are a large number of units in the scheme.

A word of warning about owners' meetings – sometimes there are individuals who are determined not to agree with the majority views on any particular subject and they can cause considerable dissension among other residents which may lead to unpleasant situations. An effort to reach agreement would make life so much more pleasant.

Exploration

Please do not settle too permanently in your new home, for there are almost certainly many sights to be seen and territory explored within easy reach of your base.

Every retiree who is active in mind and body should take the opportunity of visiting all the noteworthy historical monuments and modern 'wonders of the world' within, say, 30 miles of their home, so as to be aware of local attractions and knowledgeable about the history, flora and fauna of the territory where they live. This will make life much more interesting and it is to be hoped that the knowledge acquired can be passed on to newcomers who are ignorant of the local attractions.

Many of the foregoing remarks have been devoted to urging expatriates to get out and about and to help not only themselves, but others less fortunate. However, a word of warning – do not overdo these activities or undertake too many obligations which will make them all onerous. Just take life steadily so you enjoy the daily round without getting too tired or exhausted. If you do this you will have greater enjoyment from all your activities.

Appointments and punctuality

Do remember that you need a degree of patience when dealing with those who have a Latin or Mediterranean temperament. In business or even domestic life you may have considered punctuality to be vital, but those fortunate enough to live a more placid, easygoing life do not consider this trait to be of such great importance.

If you reside in, say, Portugal or Spain, you will soon discover that a meeting planned at 10 am may not take place until noon, or even the following day. No discourtesy is intended for 'there is always tomorrow for things not done today'. A charming philosophy if you can get away with it and one that gradually becomes acceptable when you get to know your contacts better.

Chapter 10

Furnishing and Decorating Your Home

Use local products wherever possible; this is a good general rule when choosing furniture for a home overseas. It ensures that your belongings look right in their new environment and also saves transporting heavy items of equipment from Britain to the new location, an exercise that can be very expensive.

If you are establishing a new home or are adapting the efforts of someone else, it is a great challenge to achieve a sympathetic scheme which will not only appeal to you but also be attractive to visitors for years to come.

Most new homes in southern Europe are liberally supplied with built-in cupboards in the bedrooms, so large Victorian-style wardrobes and chests of drawers are superfluous and that may mean disposing of Granny's heirlooms before you leave Britain. A chair and a dressing table plus a double bed or two singles are all that will be required in the sleeping quarters. Fitted bedheads with small cupboards are often included as a useful fitment by builders of the more expensive homes.

So far as bedding is concerned, duvets are the ideal answer, for they simplify bed-making and are both cool in summer and cosy in winter. The feather-filled varieties are considered best, but man-made fibre fillings are also acceptable. On double beds some prefer two individual duvets while others find the largest sizes are preferable.

Spare covers for duvets, undersheets and pillow cases should always be purchased so that they may be laundered regularly, as with traditional bedding. A wide variety of patterns and plain covers is available; some have co-ordinating designs which match curtains and wallpaper.

Bedroom floors are generally of marble or tiles in the warmer climates so the only floor coverings that need to be purchased are bedside rugs and these are available in many colours and finishes, ranging from woven squares to sheepskins.

Windows, even if external shutters are supplied, will look more attractive if they have colourful cotton curtains. Venetian or louvre blinds can be purchased in a wide range of materials and colours. The old metal slats, formerly used for Venetian blinds, are rarely incorporated these days. Picture windows are often installed in living rooms if there is an outstanding view from the property, but bedroom windows tend to be small to keep out the sun and heat of the summer and to admit the minimum of light.

For other parts of the house Brussels and Persian short-piled carpets are often used – also bonded and tufted types using man-made fibres with a short pile. Sisal and rush matting are alternatives.

The living area of a villa or apartment will require a dining table with four or six chairs, armchairs and perhaps a settee which will convert into a single or double bed, for use by unexpected visitors. A couple of coffee tables are always useful and a television set is presumably essential; these are often supplied with their own stand or legs. (As mentioned before, don't make the mistake of bringing your old TV set from the UK as it is unlikely to work in an overseas country without an expensive conversion.)

If you are a bibliophile then bookcases will be an important part of your furnishing plan and a compact desk is always useful for correspondence – also for storing bills and documents.

Hi-fi equipment is an important item in many households and unless your home is large enough to provide space for a study or den, then room will also have to be found in the lounge.

Pine furniture is handsome and appropriate for the Mediterranean climate and bamboo is also extensively used. In Spain wrought iron is popular for bedheads, balconies and as a framework to some lounge furniture.

Don't forget that outdoor living is one of the many advantages of residing in a warm climate, so if you have a balcony or patio, make sure you acquire sun-beds, folding easy chairs, a metal or plastic table and a sun umbrella to provide that extra touch of comfort. If your leisure area is large enough you might also install a bar and a barbecue.

Two washrooms are often provided in modern homes. The larger one will almost certainly be equipped with a bath (often shorter than the standard five-foot-sixer found in most British homes) plus shower attachment, basin, WC pan and a bidet. Coloured suites are frequently supplied and walls are generally half or fully tiled. The only additional equipment needed is a dirty-linen chest, chair and medicine cabinet with mirror.

The second bathroom is generally much smaller and simply equipped with shower cabinet, basin and WC. There is generally insufficient room for any additional equipment.

Before making any purchases for the kitchen, check with the vendor which items of equipment are included in the purchase price. Items such as sink unit, worktops and storage cupboards, shelves and built-in cooker and refrigerator are generally supplied as standard. Some enterprising builders also provide washing machines, spin driers, refrigerators, freezers and even dishwashers as part of the package.

If you are furnishing a holiday home it is best to purchase all your supplies from local shops and some developers are prepared to arrange for a complete package to be supplied at a discount price by a local firm. The only snag with this scheme is that practically every home on an estate has a similar internal appearance.

Those retiring to a property in the sun invariably like to bring a few items of furniture or knick-knacks of sentimental value from the old home and to supplement these with local purchases. Furniture shops in most Continental countries offer a wide selection of modern designs, but if you prefer a few old-fashioned items, a visit to the local second-hand or antique establishment can be worth while.

Electrical equipment is best purchased locally as it will then comply with the appropriate voltage and safety requirements.

Décor should receive careful attention. In a small home an integrated look can be a good idea to give the impression of more space. Link colour or pattern between rooms by having the same colours for walls or floors throughout, but have different-coloured accessories for each room.

It is not essential to use pale colours because you are living in a warm climate. A burst of vivid colour such as red can provide a striking effect, while plain strong colours are often used to create attractive schemes and can accentuate special architectural features.

Bright colours tend to appear more vivid in a sunny climate, so use them in moderation. For a cooling effect green, blue and violet shades are appropriate in strong tones. Black and white added to a colour scheme help to define patterns more clearly. For an eye-catching theme use black furniture against a vivid green or plain white background.

Personal tastes should be reflected in general décor, but remember that the chosen colours create a mood that may be restful or stimulating.

Furnishing a new home can be an exciting time for some and rather a bore for others, but is a task which repays both care and attention, for you are likely to have to live with the results of your efforts for a long time.

If you are well-off then of course you can employ a specialist consultant to undertake the work for you. A substantial fee will probably be required, but at least you will have someone else to blame if you do not like the result!

Chapter 11

Gardening in Southern Europe

Plan the garden for your new home in Spain, France or Portugal with some care and try to complete your deliberations well in advance of your occupation of the property.

Of course, if you are buying an apartment your task is greatly simplified for you will probably only have to tackle a few flower troughs on the balcony.

On some modern developments the balconies have built-in troughs with automatic watering systems so you simply obtain some trailing geraniums and a few exotic plants and in less than six months your horticultural tasks are solved and you need do little more than cut off dead flower heads and prune back the prolific growth occasionally before the plants take over the entire verandah.

Some upper-floor apartments have roof gardens which give much more scope for the amateur botanist and it is not uncommon to see small fruit trees under intensive cultivation in these locations as well as a multitude of annual and biennial plants which make a very colourful display throughout most months of the year.

Ground-floor apartments do sometimes have a small 'sitting out' garden in place of a patio or a balcony. Here it is perhaps best to plant a major part of the garden with a coarse quality grass which will withstand the long days of dry weather. Roses are hardy and grow well in many soils, particularly those of a heavy texture. Other favourites in a small garden include mimosa, bougainvillaea, oleander, wistaria, hibiscus, and poinsettias with their brilliant red or pale yellow-green leaves.

If your villa is on a plot of say 800 sq m or more, you may want to incorporate a swimming or plunge pool within your boundaries, in which case it is advisable to plant hedges in order to provide some protection from winds and to add privacy to the 'sports' area. However, try to avoid the cultivation of trees or shrubs which produce a heavy leaf-fall in the autumn, otherwise you will spend too much time cleaning the pool or trying to keep the surroundings neat and tidy.

Remember, too, that pools do require constant and regular attention if they are to be kept in a usable condition. Clear sparkling water looks attractive and inviting at all times, but areas of water with a green tinge, with slimy corners or loads of debris floating on the surface are not only objectionable to look at, but can also be a health hazard.

Sadly, we all grow older and less agile as the years pass by, so plan your garden with easy maintenance very much in mind and do not create a masterpiece now which may become an onerous burden in a few years, simply because you have become less capable of manual work.

Choose your plants, bushes and trees wisely and remember that most of the Mediterranean countries enjoy long periods of drought when the garden needs watering to keep stock growing. Lawns, for instance, can be a burden, and a natural garden with stones and rocks interplanted with favoured species of hardy specimens that will withstand dry sunny conditions is much more likely to bring success and satisfaction.

Citrus trees such as oranges and lemons make attractive displays in strategic positions and contrast well with a few cacti, yuccas, agaves and succulents which can be cultivated without too many problems as they are not water-hungry.

Palms, once they are established, give a regal air to almost any plot; tall cypresses add a soothing colour to arid land as they are evergreen; a patch of bamboo can also be attractive.

Mature umbrella pines are impressive but make sure they are not too close to the villa, for their roots may affect drainpipes. Olive trees, pines and ancient locust-bean trees are other worthwhile additions to the garden.

In contrast to the dampness of the climate in the UK where weeds grow in abundance, these horticultural pests do not thrive as well in the warmer climates and so are less of a nuisance to the keen gardener.

Gardens in the south of Europe have their own special small wildlife such as lizards which scuttle in and out of the rocks and stones; tiny grass snakes and geckos are also a familiar sight, as are toads and frogs which suddenly appear after a shower of rain.

Keen gardeners are sure to enjoy their hobby in these temperate climates and even the half-hearted efforts of the not-so-keen naturalist should become more enjoyable when snow, frost and days of heavy rain do not have to be faced persistently for up to six months in the year, as in Britain.

Chapter 12

Coming Back to the UK

The biggest single event which causes emigrants to return to their native country is the death of one partner, when the survivor feels that he or she just cannot cope with life alone in another country.

Elderly people come to realise they are less able to care and cater for themselves with the passage of time and they feel that they would prefer to reside near the family and old friends in their declining years.

The third factor that makes people decide to give up the 'new life' and return to their former living conditions is the discovery that they are not really happy in a strange environment with all its contributory features such as different weather conditions, unfamiliar food, new traditions and ways of life, or just a deep dissatisfaction with the property purchased in the sun, or with one's neighbours.

There is no disgrace in admitting defeat and returning home, but there are certain factors which must be considered in advance of any plans to move. These include the following.

Sale of the overseas property

For the best results, appoint a well-established, legally constituted estate agent to sell your home. He will value it for you and undertake the marketing. In many areas a speedy sale can be effected if the price is right, but remember agents' commissions are much higher on the Continent compared with the UK. Ascertain the agent's terms before giving instructions to sell and don't be surprised if you are quoted commission figures of between 5 and 10 per cent of the purchase price.

Once appointed, let the agent get on with the sales campaign, but make sure that you keep the house neat and tidy at all times, so that it will look its best to any unexpected prospective buyers, no matter what time they call.

Grant a sole agency for a limited period whenever possible and leave the agent to appoint a sub-agency if this is thought desirable. In this case a commission-sharing arrangement will be worked out between the two firms.

Next, ascertain the current regulations regarding the repatriation of the sales proceeds and any capital gains. Make sure that permission will be granted to remit the money received from the sale back to the UK. Generally this is allowed, provided you can produce evidence that foreign currency was imported to pay for the property in the first place.

An alternative is to sell the property to a non-resident of the country where it is located and have the proceeds remitted to your normal UK bank. This procedure works quite well and obviates the necessity for long-winded applications which need to be approved by officialdom. The change of ownership must, of course, be registered at the local Land Registry; also local legal fees and tax will have to be paid.

Check up on current procedures for pension and other receipts. Give the bank and other officials adequate time to make the appropriate arrangements.

Taxation

On returning to the UK after a number of years abroad, your status for taxation purposes will probably change quite dramatically and it is essential to seek full advice from an accountant or tax expert.

Exchange control

Restrictions on the export of capital are imposed by a number of countries. If you have substantial capital invested in shares or a local bank account, check the procedures and restrictions (if any) about the repatriation of your funds. A comprehensive review should be undertaken of all investments, with the aid of expert advice.

It is sensible to re-examine testamentary provisions on return to the UK, particularly if a will has been drawn up in a foreign country. Don't forget to advise relations, friends, business contacts and insurance companies of your new address on returning to the UK. Work through the removal checklist on pages 95-9 in case it applies to your move back.

Chapter 13

The End

Death comes to us all eventually so it is wise to have made some plans in advance if you are living in a foreign country, and the following notes may be of some help to prepare for the ultimate eventuality.

A surprising number of people fail to make a will, or do not update one when it has become inappropriate because of the passing of the years and the arrival of new circumstances.

Everyone, no matter how large or small their estate, should make a will, properly drawn up by a lawyer; the fee expended on this advice is money well spent if it avoids any complications after death.

Both wife and husband should make wills and everyone moving abroad or retiring to a new country should take advice on the rules which constitute a valid will in the country in which they propose to reside in the future.

In some countries there are laws which protect the family of the deceased and, as a result, the estate has to be divided so as to ensure that the surviving spouse is adequately catered for, also any children, and after this the testator can deal with the remaining estate in accordance with any particular wishes.

So far as the actual arrangements for the burial are concerned, those who wish to be interred in the UK should realise that the cost of sending the body back to the homeland can be substantial, so adequate financial arrangements should be made in advance to cover this by setting up a separate fund, or taking out a special insurance policy.

If you are being buried in the place where you die, the arrangements regarding interment may vary from one country to another. Cremation is not always available in every country, so it may be necessary to purchase a plot in a cemetery.

Spain

On the death of a person in Spain, it is necessary to register the fact immediately at the local Civil Registry. This is generally undertaken by a friend or a relative who will need to have a doctor's certificate stating the cause of death. On receipt of a Spanish death certificate, this should be taken to the nearest British Consul's office who will then register the death and issue a British death certificate.

A lawyer should be instructed immediately to deal with the payment of inheritance taxes, for the assets of anyone dying in Spain cannot be distributed until taxes have been paid.

Burial can be arranged in Spain. Almost all cemeteries are Catholic, but those of any religion may be buried there. Crematoria are scarce, but where available they probably provide the best solution. The ashes can be placed in the urn, which can easily be transported back to the UK.

It is advisable to have a Spanish will, but if this does not exist, the estate can be distributed in such a way that it complies with the deceased's British will. Those who die intestate will have their estate distributed to the next of kin in accordance with Spanish law.

France

In France, a death has to be registered at the local *Mairie* within 24 hours and a doctor's certificate obtained from the doctor who attended the deceased person, or from a medical person who is retained by the local council.

It is not permitted to close a coffin within 24 hours of death; this act can only be undertaken with the authority of the official where the death is registered.

In France, cemeteries belong to the local authorities, who issue licences to undertakers to carry out the actual burial. Despite the fact there are no separate Jewish or Protestant cemeteries, a tradition has grown up whereby parts of many cemeteries are used only by specified religious groups.

For religious reasons, cremation has not been popular in France in the past, but it is now being used more frequently and there are a growing number of crematoria.

Portugal

The tradition in Portugal is for burial to take place very quickly, generally within 24 hours of death. There are undertakers in many towns who have experience of arranging funerals for foreigners, and deaths have to be registered at the local Civil Registry where a doctor's certificate showing the cause of death has to be produced.

It is recommended that the British Consulate be informed of the death, especially if a British death certificate is required.

In places where there is a substantial foreign population, cemeteries permit both Catholic and non-Catholic people to be buried.

There is a British cemetery in Lisbon, but space is very limited and only former parishioners of local Anglican churches can now be buried in this cemetery. Some Portuguese cemeteries permit graves to be occupied for only five years, so it is desirable to ascertain that the choice of final resting place is a permanent one. Cremation is permitted in the recently opened Lisbon crematorium.

One final, essential point is the choice of a storage place for your will. Make sure that your next of kin know where this is located and try at all times to arrange your affairs in a neat and tidy manner so as to make your executor's task as simple as possible.

Often the family solicitor keeps the will and it would be useful if information on bank accounts, insurance policies and so on is also deposited with your legal adviser.

Part 3
A Home Overseas

Chapter 14

Try Before You Buy

As already explained, nobody should consider the purchase of a permanent home abroad without investigating very carefully the facilities, amenities and life-style of the chosen district in considerable detail before entering into any commitment to purchase a property.

Without doubt, the most satisfactory way to do this is to rent a property for a period of several months in the area where you think you would like to reside, if possible in the low season when most of the holiday-makers have gone home and the seasonal attractions are no longer available. This will enable you to experience life with local people and get to know some of the foreigners and your own compatriots who have already settled in the area.

From them it should be possible to obtain information and useful tips about the best places to shop, local medical facilities, clubs for the British or other nationalities, sporting amenities and a whole host of other useful data.

With the advantage of local knowledge and contacts, you will soon become experienced at living in a foreign country and have the opportunity of deciding whether you like the life-style or whether in fact you would do better to remain at home.

During the winter months there is generally a good selection of top-quality apartments and villas available for renting at very reasonable prices and information on these can be obtained from local estate agents or firms in the UK who specialise in self-catering holidays. OSL Travel Plus Club, 4 Broadway, Fiveways, Edgbaston, Birmingham B15 1BB (021-633 3444) publishes an excellent guide to villas and apartments in Spain which are available through them for holidays; both winter and summer editions are issued, prices quoted include return air flights, insurance, transportation from the Spanish airport to your property, and sometimes car hire is included as well.

The *Villa Guide* is a useful publication produced three times a year and available from Private Villas, 52 High Street, Henley in Arden, Solihull, West Midlands B95 5AN. It lists private villas which are available for renting direct from the owners. Here again an inclusive package can include flights from the UK to Spain.

Whichever method you adopt to rent a property, do make sure that you are aware in advance of the terms offered by the owner or the letting company and the points well worth checking are the following:

1. Does the quoted cost include maid service?
2. Do you need to take towels?
3. Are gas and electricity charges included in the rental, or do you have to pay the owner's agent for energy consumed during the time in residence?
4. Location of shops and amenities.
5. How far are the sea and airport from the selected property; are there satisfactory transport arrangements made on your behalf?
6. If your flight is delayed and you arrive later than expected, can you gain access to the property?
7. Does the owner or his agent provide a starter pack of food for use on arrival at the property? (This is specially important if you travel at weekends.)
8. Brochures often describe a property as, say, 'sleeping six'; what extra charges will be levied if only three people travel and use the accommodation?

Some developers arrange to have a limited number of properties available on larger sites for renting to prospective purchasers and the use of this service is well worth while and is generally quite economic.

Having made the momentous decision to purchase a home abroad, do not charge into the transaction blindly, even though it is an exciting proposition which you feel you want to fulfil at the earliest possible moment.

Time will be well spent reflecting on your immediate and future needs and may well ensure that you do not make any hasty decisions that could turn out to be disastrous later on.

Some purchase an apartment in their favourite resort. This may be an excellent choice for annual vacations, but will it be large enough for permanent living and will you really enjoy residing during the summer months in a building where transient occupants provide a constantly changing scene with no opportunity to make permanent friends, and with the recurring problem of late-night parties? Arrivals and departures can disturb the early hours of the morning because of the whims of charter flights to the UK and other parts of Europe.

Security should be adequate in an apartment block with a resident concierge but the winter life could be very lonely if there are only one or two year-round owners in residence.

If you buy an apartment, make sure the block has one or more adequate lifts because as you get older, climbing several flights of stairs may become almost impossible and then you will be dependent on others to fetch your shopping and to undertake errands such as a visit to the bank or post office.

Villa ownership, especially if the property is detached, offers greater privacy, some protection from undue noise and a feeling of true ownership which never seems to come with an apartment.

Many overseas houses have patios or balconies and most have gardens, sometimes large, sometimes small. In retirement you will have more time to potter around your 'estate', but make sure it is planned and laid out so that gardening tasks do not become a burden as you grow older.

The exterior maintenance of a retirement home is an important point to consider in advance. Many units are finished in cement rendering which requires an application of white or coloured emulsion paint every year or two. This is easy to apply on a single storey dwelling, but requires more effort for a two or three storey villa. You may need to employ some professional skill if you find the work too tiring, but the cost should not be too great and it will help to keep costs down if the job can be completed in a few hours.

Even a small villa can easily be made into a permanent home and the purchase price is often not a great deal more than a flat. However, take particular care in your choice of location, for an isolated villa away from shops and facilities could prove particularly inconvenient and lonely, especially if you become less mobile with advancing years and do not possess a car.

How much?

Undoubtedly your very first thought should be how much you can afford to spend on your new home.

Prices in the sunniest countries of southern Europe vary immensely. It is still possible to purchase a modest studio flatlet near the Mediterranean coast of Spain for not much more than £8000 – but it will be very small and not in a prime position or of top-class construction. It could fulfil the holiday needs of a couple who want to escape from the uncertainty of Britain's

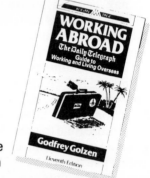

summer climate for two or three weeks annually, but it might well be completely useless as a permanent home or for stays of three months or more.

Opportunities to acquire a large flat or a luxury new detached villa costing £35,000 or more are plentiful in many parts of the sun-belt. If you are very well-off, there should be no difficulty in spending £1 million or more on a modern villa or an old mansion by the sea or in the country in, say, Spain, Portugal or France. Here you can enjoy privacy and live in an elegant style for short or long periods.

After some day-dreaming about your ideal home, a home which you soon discover is beyond your means, re-examine your finances and decide on a sensible sum that will not eat too deeply into your capital or cost you an excessive amount to maintain.

The Abbey National Building Society has established Abbey National (Gibraltar) Ltd at 237 Main Street, Gibraltar to provide a mortgage service to clients purchasing a home in Spain. Loans can be secured on the Spanish property.

Advice on insurance and other matters is also available.

The Alliance & Leicester Building Society is one of the societies prepared to grant mortgages based on the security of a UK property.

Some overseas builders and developers are willing to offer short-term loans, generally for not more than 60 per cent of the purchase price and for periods not exceeding five years. Interest rates tend to be high.

Many older homeowners in the UK have considerable equity locked up in their main residences, with little or no mortgage outstanding. They are in the fortunate position of being able to re-mortgage their property and use the proceeds to buy a home abroad or use the house as security for a loan.

Sheltered housing

Sheltered housing schemes on the Continent for elderly British people are few in number at present, but McCarthy & Stone, the largest UK developer of this category of homes, has acquired a specialist firm in France and will announce details of their proposed output in due course.

Chapter 15

Property Organisations

When purchasing an overseas property there are inevitably greater risks than when buying a home in the UK.

Different laws, contracts in foreign languages, varied financial arrangements, local building methods and firms whose authenticity is difficult to check all add difficulties and hazards to property transactions.

How are members of the public, who are sometimes very gullible and quite ignorant of procedures in the country they have chosen as a place for their holiday or retirement home to be protected?

Currently there are two UK trade associations of agents who specialise in marketing property overseas. In alphabetical order these are ABOPA (Association of British Overseas Property Agents) and FOPDAC (Federation of Overseas Property Developers, Agents and Consultants).

They both require their members to comply with a code of conduct, have entry qualifications, investigate complaints by the public against members and take disciplinary action against member firms who are proved to be treating clients in an unsatisfactory manner.

Many problems arise because members of the public fail to take adequate legal and financial advice before committing themselves to a purchase. The very thought of owning a holiday or retirement home in a favourite resort or country area seems to cause normally sensible business or professional people to throw caution to the wind. As a result, legal documents in a foreign language are often signed without recourse to proper expert advice and substantial sums of money are paid over to relative strangers, either individuals or firms, before any check has been made about their bona fides.

Careful preliminary planning and caution throughout the acquisition period should be adopted by all buyers to minimise the risk of an unsatisfactory transaction.

Association of British Overseas Property Agents (ABOPA)

This association was established in 1980 as a professional body in the field of overseas property. It is a multi-sector organisation of people or firms concerned with selling property overseas and its role is to regulate the professional conduct of its members and to protect the general public. This is done by ensuring that all members satisfy the criteria set by the Association concerning their professional competence and experience.

An arbitrary body will act on a purchaser's behalf in the event of a complaint against a member company which cannot be satisfactorily resolved by direct negotiations with the firm involved.

The conditions of entry for full membership of ABOPA are:

(a) All applicants for membership must be full-time agents actively occupied in the sale of overseas property and based in the United Kingdom or have a separate overseas property division within their organisation. This does not include time-share marketing.

(b) Membership of the Association will be limited to persons or organisations acting as agents in the sale of overseas property, and will exclude developers and builders selling direct to the public. This condition will not affect or exclude an agent who may occasionally sell a property owned personally by him, provided that his principal business is to act as an agent in the sale of property not owned by him.

(c) All applicants for membership must prove their expertise and competence in the sale of overseas property in accordance with the minimum requirements laid down by the founder members.

(d) Applications for membership will be heard at the Annual General Meeting from persons or organisations who satisfy the conditions of membership, or at an Extraordinary Meeting convened by the appointed committee members. All applicants who satisfy these conditions will become members unless a founder member has cause to object to the application. In such cases a full meeting of members will be convened and the applicant will be given the opportunity to state his case. A vote will be taken and in any such vote a simple majority of members present will carry the motion. The candidate shall also sign a form of application for membership giving all particulars required by the Association with an undertaking, if elected, to be bound by the rules and bylaws of the Association. An application form for membership will be supplied outlining the necessary procedure for becoming a member of the Association.

Spanish Property

Eurochoice-Eurosol are the U.K.'s leading Estate Agents, dealing exclusively in Freehold Spanish Property. They have a huge network of High Street shops and agencies throughout Britain and Europe, selling a wide range of luxury properties on the beautiful Cost Blanca and Costa Calida.

There are two ways in which Eurochoice-Eurosol cater specifically for retired people.

Firstly, they cater for people wishing to make a permanent home in Spain. The continually rising costs of living in Britain means many people on fixed incomes are finding it hard to make ends meet. In, Spain the cost of living is much lower and some expenses, such as heating, that are a major consideration

in this country, scarcely exist in Spain where daytime temperatures, even in Winter, rarely fall below 60°F.

The property boom in Britain has meant that many people find that by selling here and buying in Spain they can enjoy a far more comfortable and secure retirment.

Secondly, there are people who wish to buy abroad as an investment and for residence for part of the year. Property prices in Spain have risen 28% over the last year and with the trade prospects for 1992, as well as the 1992 Olympics in Barcelona, this trend is likely to continue for some years. Many people consider the investment potential an important factor in their decision to buy abroad and now is certainly the time to buy while prices are still comparatively low.

To find out more, contact our Head Office in Bournemouth where our staff will be pleased to give you full details of property currently available.

U.K. Head Office
248 Old Christchurch Road,
Bournemouth, Dorset BH1 1PF
☎ (0202) 298386

Affiliated membership

Applications for affiliated membership are considered from persons or companies whose main business activities are management and/or renting of overseas property, flight operators and companies arranging inclusive self-catering holidays. Affiliated members are not subject to the rules observed by full members, but are expected to maintain a high-standard code of business in their activities.

Associate membership

Applications for associate membership are considered from individuals or organisations just starting in the business of selling overseas property and who therefore do not have the necessary experience to be full members.

Applications are also considered from Spanish nationals operating in Spain as licensed agents with the necessary qualification to run an estate agency in Spain. (For an explanation of licensing *see under* 'Buying property' in 'Spain', Chapter 25.) The British agent with whom they are associated must be a full member of ABOPA.

When dealing with resale properties, ABOPA member companies are advised by ABOPA to deal only with licensed agencies in Spain. With regard to new properties in Spain, member companies take out references on the developers with whom they deal, renewable every six months.

Federation of Overseas Property Developers, Agents and Consultants (FOPDAC)

FOPDAC was formed in 1973 with the aim of establishing a code of conduct for its members in their dealings with the public and to try to educate prospective purchasers of overseas residential property on the dos and don'ts of buying villas and apartments outside their native land.

After having made some progress in achieving their objects the organisation went through a period of inactivity between about 1976 and 1980, when the property market was at a low ebb. Following the abandonment of exchange control in 1979 a surge of activity occurred among overseas property agents with many new firms being established and older organisations recommencing business. As a result FOPDAC became active again and now has over 70 members.

Chartered surveyors, architects, planners and developers are now included in the membership as well as tour operators, travel experts, lawyers and, of course, selling agents and builders. Areas covered by the membership include mainland Spain, the Balearic Islands and the Canaries, Andorra, Cyprus, France, Italy, Greece, Malta, Portugal, Switzerland and Austria.

To join FOPDAC, firms or individuals must have well-established businesses and have an integrity that is beyond reasonable question. Principals of companies are required to have sufficient professional expertise and experience to meet the strict requirements of the Federation's code of ethics, a summary of which is given below:

> Members shall make honesty and integrity the standard in all their dealings with their clients and customers. They shall avoid misleading property descriptions, concealment of pertinent information, and exaggerations in advertising. They shall not market property for specific purposes if that property is not accessible and usable for such purposes. Members shall comply with all financial and contractual obligations which comply with all applicable laws, whether of the United Kingdom or not, relating

> to their transactions in overseas property and their clients or customers.
>
> Members shall use their best endeavours to enlist all the professional talents available to them in the fields of ecology, engineering and architecture for the design of a development that strives for the best employment of the land and protection of the environment. They shall use their best endeavours to encourage developments with due consideration for open space and proper environmental controls. Members shall report in writing any violation of these bylaws whether their own or those of others, whether members or not, to the committee.
>
> Where Federation members accept a client's money for payment, whether partial or full for land or property, they must maintain a legally separate client's account which must be properly conducted and disclosure must be given, to the Secretary of the Federation, of the name and address of the bank at which the account is maintained.

Should any member of the general public conducting business through a member of the Federation complain that the member has not acted in accordance with the code of ethics, then the committee will investigate the complaint and arbitrate where necessary. If the committee should decide that a member is in default and he subsequently fails to rectify the matter, then the member would be liable to immediate expulsion from the Federation.

The Federation symbol is displayed on all advertisements and literature distributed by members.

As part of their efforts to help the house-buying public, the Federation publishes several very useful leaflets, including a general guide to 'Buying Property Overseas' plus fact sheets on legal procedures for property purchase in Spain, France, Italy and Portugal. These can be obtained (price £2) from the Secretary, FOPDAC, Imperial House, 15-19 Kingsway, London WC2B 6UU.

Before inspecting any overseas property the Federation suggests that each prospective buyer obtains answers to the following questions:

1. (a) Is the property in which you are interested being offered by its owner, its developer or an agent acting on their behalf?
   (b) Does your British agent have an association with an agent or agents in the locality of your choice who is legally licensed in that country? Does the British agent represent the vendor or the purchaser?
   (c) What are the risks in dealing with an unlicensed local agent?

2. Is the property being offered with clear title? Is it 'free and unencumbered'?
3. (a) Are the costs of connecting water, electricity and drainage included in the selling price of a new home? If not, what are these costs likely to be?

   (b) What are the acquisition and conveyancing costs usually incurred by the purchaser under the traditions and regulations of the locality?
4. (a) What are the formal stages of property purchase in the country in which the property is situated?

   (b) Is the purchase contract binding? Is it in a foreign language?

   (c) What essential points should be covered by the purchase contract to ensure that both parties are adequately protected?
5. (a) Should I seek legal advice on the purchase of an overseas property?

   (b) Must I use a solicitor to draw up the conveyance of my overseas property?

(c) Can I sell my overseas property freely and transfer the proceeds abroad without difficulty?

6. (a) What are the annual costs likely to be incurred by the owner of the property in the country or area chosen?
   (b) If the property is in a development complex are there any charges for communal facilities?
   (c) What is a Community of Owners? Is membership obligatory? What are the benefits? What are the costs? Are the statutes in a foreign language?
7. Can I open a bank account locally? What are the advantages of having a local bank account?
8. Can I insure the property and its contents? What are the rates of premiums to be expected?
9. Can I let the property to friends? Can I make a formal rental agreement with a rental agency? What return can I expect? Will this restrict my own use of the property unduly? Is tax payable on my rental income?
10. Could the view from my property or its amenities be affected by unsightly future development? Is there a zoning plan for the surrounding area?
11. Are there any local regulations which affect the purchase of property by foreign nationals? If so, what are the formalities?
12. (a) If I buy a plot of land on which to build in future, are there any conditions of building permission? Are there time limits for such building? Are there height or size limitations?
    (b) Must I use an architect locally? Must I use an architect who is nominated by the vendor? Must I use a nominated building contractor?
    (c) Are there any other formalities which I should observe if I build a home on a plot I have purchased?
13. (a) Is furniture included in the price of the property, or do I arrange to furnish it myself? What is the approximate cost of furnishings to a basic or a high standard?
    (b) If the property has a garden, is the cost of planting included in the sale price? If not, what is the cost likely to be? Who maintains the garden in my absence? Could a garden be planned and built which requires little or no maintenance?
    (c) How much external maintenance is the property likely to need? Who is responsible for this maintenance? How much is it likely to cost?
    (d) Can a company be appointed locally who will manage the property during my absence and supervise cleaning etc for myself and my guests when we visit?

14. What is the most economical and reliable means of travel to my property? Are there privileges to be obtained for owners and their guests?

The Royal Institution of Chartered Surveyors

Some UK estate agents who operate overseas property departments are members of the Royal Institution of Chartered Surveyors. They are subject to a strict code of conduct and are bonded, so far as their operations in the UK are concerned, but this protection does not cover transactions or work undertaken abroad.

However, a degree of security for buyers does exist as the majority of individuals who are members also have well-established practices in England, Wales, Scotland or Ireland and are unlikely to jeopardise their reputation and professional qualifications by involving themselves in unwise foreign deals.

The Institute of Foreign Property Owners

This organisation was founded in 1983 by Per Svensson, and aims to assist foreigners planning to buy or who have already purchased a home in all the tourist areas of Spain. A monthly magazine is published containing much useful information and data on changes in Spanish law and procedures as they affect property owners. Membership costs about £24 per annum and further information can be obtained from the Institute of Foreign Property Owners, Apartado 35, Calpe, Alicante, Spain, or Sandra Lewin, 2nd Floor South, 72 Tottenham Court Road, London W1.

Chapter 16

Property Inspection Tours

In the late 1960s when there was a considerable boom in overseas property sales, even though the market was still in its infancy, property agents vied with one another to take prospective clients to Spain or Portugal on property inspection tours.

Prices for a long weekend of, say, Friday to Monday, including the flight from London to Malaga or Alicante, for example, plus hotel accommodation, worked out at as little as £40 and even at this figure, some agents subsidised the fares by say £5 or £10 to reduce the cost to around £30.

At these bargain prices, the public soon realised they could enjoy a few days in a sunny Mediterranean country for little more than it cost to go to Scotland. The result was that quite a high proportion of 'prospectives' were in fact joyriders with no intention of buying property.

As the years have passed by, the clients have become more sophisticated in their requirements and much better informed about procedures for house purchase in countries not previously considered as places for holiday or retirement homes.

Consequently, today, most inspection trips are run on quite a small scale with perhaps no more than half a dozen people in one party. The events are well organised to ensure that participants see villas or apartments that closely resemble their previously stated requirements, and efforts are made to ensure that clients are neither tired out with too many visits, nor overloaded with hospitality so that they find it difficult and confusing at the end of the trip to select the property they liked best.

As with all househunting, some flexibility is desirable because there are always a few customers who decide to buy a housing unit that bears no relation to their original stated requirements.

The best advice to the novice prospective purchaser is, do not make an on-the-spot decision the first time you see a property which attracts you, but return for a second or third visit at different times of day to experience the views under different light and weather conditions. Then, if necessary, go home to reflect on

your proposed transaction and, if it is the right one for you, a return visit will settle the matter.

Some developers and their agents still offer subsidised visits for interested clients, but the majority charge a price related to the real expenditure and may then refund part or whole of the charge to those who actually contract to buy.

To avoid wasting a lot of time, do undertake some serious research before flying off for your weekend in the sun. Study books on the area where you propose to purchase your holiday or retirement home, investigate the track record of the builder and his agent by taking up references and, if possible, talking to an existing purchaser. Other important pre-visit jobs include sorting out your financial affairs, especially if you need long- or short-term finance for your purchase, and seeking proper professional advice about any contract you may be required to sign.

Some couples prefer to undertake independent research into the property market during a vacation. This can work satisfactorily, but beware who you deal with, for there are unofficial salesmen who may do you a disservice. In addition you may miss a site that could be ideal for your requirements because of ignorance about all the developments or resale property currently being offered. Although an established agent cannot be expected to have details of every home for sale in a given area, the best firms are very knowledgeable about properties in their area.

Intensive research prior to buying a home abroad is highly recommended and one or more inspection tours are a vital part of this task.

Chapter 17

Timesharing

In a book on living and retiring abroad, this chapter may seem slightly out of place, but timesharing is a method of acquiring experience in living abroad for short periods without the expenditure of large sums of money.

This method of property ownership has been in existence for over 20 years. The first scheme was offered in a French Alpine ski resort in 1967. In the following year timesharing was offered by a co-ownership scheme in Spain promoted by two British businessmen who had built and sold two blocks of apartments in the main street of Javea, on the Costa Blanca, and decided to construct a third block whereby clients could purchase part-ownership of a freehold, two-bedroom flat with names registered on the deeds. The cost of the use in perpetuity of a two-bedroom unit for a fortnight in June was £250, or £500 would purchase the use for all the winter months from November to March. This scheme is still operating successfully. Resales now fetch about £3000 for a week in the summer.

In the UK, a pioneer scheme started 11 years ago in the Highlands of Scotland, at Loch Rannoch. This is now complete and is operating very successfully with nearly 100 units ranging from luxury three-bedroom lodges with huge living areas on the first floor enjoying the fine views across the Loch, down to small apartments. Features on the site include a dry ski slope, hotel and club, boating and fishing opportunities, swimming facilities and various other kinds of sports and pastimes.

It is estimated that more than 40,000 families now own timeshare weeks in about 50 resorts spread throughout the UK from the north of Scotland to Wales, the Midlands, the south coast and the West Country.

The term 'timesharing' originated in America and has also been called 'interval ownership', 'vacation ownership' and 'co-ownership'. There can be up to 50 owners of a single unit of accommodation, each having purchased seven days or more at the time of year when they wish to use their accommodation.

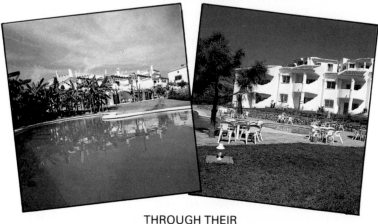

Having paid the purchase price, which can sometimes be spread over two or three years, no further capital payment is required, but there are annual maintenance charges which range from about £40 to £150 per annum at the time of writing and these cover maintenance and management expenses.

In the UK and some other countries it is not possible to transfer legal title to the freehold ownership of a property to more than four people. To overcome this problem many timeshare developers adopt the club trustee system, whereby an independent trustee is appointed to hold the land and buildings on trust for the timeshare owners. Should the promoter get into financial difficulties, timeshare owners' rights are not affected and title cannot be taken away by creditors of the bankrupt company.

An alternative method is to grant a 'right to use' licence. Here the developer who holds the legal title provides the timesharer with a licence which permits use of the accommodation for the period purchased, over an agreed number of years or in perpetuity, the maximum in England and Wales being 80 years.

Normally at least two weeks in the year are not sold by the developers in order to provide a suitable period to cover maintenance and redecoration of properties. The average period of time purchased is between two and three weeks.

To ensure proper management of the scheme, and to spread general outgoings over sufficient owners, a minimum of 16 units is considered to be necessary and, if this is achieved, maintenance fees can be kept to a reasonable level.

Variations to the standard scheme include 'floating weeks' whereby there is no entitlement to a selected week each year and it is necessary to book your period in advance. Those wishing to take a holiday in the peak season may find availability a problem.

Four owners and six owners schemes provide occupation of the selected villa or apartment for three or two months each year. The time segment is usually divided into several periods, so that each owner can enjoy peak weeks, mid-season and low-season periods each year. The periods allocated generally rotate so that each participant has the opportunity to enjoy holidays at differing times each year over, say, a four-year time span.

An objection that some people raise about the purchase of holiday accommodation is that they may tire of going to the same place year after year. This is not a problem experienced with timesharing, for most developments are in membership with one of the two major exchange organisations whereby owners can exchange their accommodation for similar size and quality apartments or villas in upwards of 1000 timeshare developments in most parts of the world.

The best-known organisations are Interval International and Resort Condominiums International. They both have offices in London as well as in the USA, where they were originally founded. They carry out quality checks on all the schemes which apply for membership and have been known to reject a number of sites which do not come up to their strict standards of quality.

To ensure that a development will be a success and will sell readily throughout most of the year, a wide variety of facilities, including sporting activities, shops, restaurants, health clubs and live entertainment, is essential.

Every bit as important as the amenities is the standard of furnishing and the design of the properties themselves. All furniture should be very hardwearing and attractive in appearance; kitchens should be furnished and equipped to luxury standards; bathrooms should be designed and equipped to first-class specification.

In recent years, a number of well-known firms in the building industry, including Wimpey, Barratt and Ideal Homes, have purchased existing or established timesharing schemes in the UK and overseas. The involvement of these firms has helped considerably to build the public's confidence in timesharing and is a good omen for the future.

The timeshare industry has suffered from a certain amount of bad press and a number of schemes have come to grief, mainly because of lack of adequate finance for the initial stages.

Properly organised, developed and managed timesharing schemes will undoubtedly prosper in the future, for they do give families and individuals a safeguard against the escalating cost of vacations. It should be borne in mind that timesharing is not an investment in money terms, simply in future holidays.

Although capital profits have been achieved by many owners who invested at the early stages of the most successful schemes, no capital appreciation should be expected for, say, two or three years, when the developers are still selling the units.

Other specific points to bear in mind, before signing any documents which commit you to purchase, are as follows:

1. Adequate management and maintenance of the development are of vital importance to the future. Ascertain who is going to undertake this work and the proposed charges, including any increase in costs in future years. Will they be based on the cost of living index, or will the figure be fixed annually at the whim of the management organisation?

2. Get details in writing of the facilities that will be offered on the site and, if possible, ensure that these will be available immediately occupation is offered on timeshare units.
3. Details of the furnishings, fixtures and fitments to be included in each unit should be presented to each buyer in inventory form. Check the maximum number of people permitted to use each timeshare unit.
4. If you are paying cash, you may be entitled to a discount if settlement is made by a specified date. If you are financing the purchase on credit, check up on the interest rates to be charged for the period over which repayments are permitted.
5. Investigations into the track record of the project developers are a wise precaution and, with already completed developments, endeavour to speak to one of the existing owners and get their opinion about how well the scheme is organised.
6. Check the terms on which the scheme is being offered, ie either freehold or club trusteeship, and whether segments are sold by the week, or multiple weeks, whether they are for a fixed period every year or for a floating period whereby the weeks vary or rotate each year.

Aggressive methods of marketing are adopted by some timeshare sales organisations who endeavour to interest members of the public on vacation in a resort to visit a local timeshare scheme. Inducements such as a free meal or a gift are often offered by the sales organisation to anyone who is prepared to inspect a show property; these are usually qualified by conditions that require the applicants to be tourists, over the age of 25 and, if married, accompanied by the spouse. These are not perhaps unreasonable qualifications to win a free gift but once inside the show unit, the salesman will try hard to get prospective clients to sign documents committing them to a purchase and will often offer a discount for an immediate decision. No documents should be signed until you have had time to reflect and are absolutely certain that the property is exactly what you want.

Timeshare Developers Association

Until the summer of 1987 there were three trade associations representing various factors of the timeshare industry and endeavouring to give the public reassurance as to the bona fides of their activities. In alphabetical order, these associations were:

British Property Timeshare Association (established 1982)

European Holiday Timeshare Association (established 1985)
Timeshare Developers Group (established 1986).

The existence of three associations representing quite a small industry involved duplicated effort on the part of the associations' administrators, some loss of credibility with government departments and considerable confusion among timeshare owners and those considering the purchase of time-owned property.

It was therefore excellent news to learn in August 1987 that the three associations had decided to amalgamate and to form one body, to be known as the Timeshare Developers Association.

There are two categories of membership, namely developers and exchange organisations.

Developers will be responsible for the behaviour of their marketing agents and the exchange organisations will have data available on each individual scheme in membership with them, following an on-the-spot visit by their inspectors.

A council of 14 members administers the affairs of the association, together with a secretariat comprising a permanent secretary and assistants as necessary.

The council consists of five members each representing the two largest groups of firms, two members from the smaller group and two for the exchange companies, a total of 14 members in all.

A code of conduct to which members are expected to adhere includes the following important clauses:

1. Accurate and clear information must be included in all sales documentation.
2. OPC (Outside Person Contact) employees must be properly dressed and wear a badge indicating the timeshare firm for which they are working. They must *not* solicit business in relaxation areas of resorts and they must comply with local employment laws.
3. Fictitious competitions are not permitted.
4. The name and address of the development firm, together with the location of the development, must be disclosed.
5. Misleading or deceiving information by sales staff is prohibited.
6. Data on resales, contractual obligations, gifts offered, terms of purchase and exchange arrangements should be described in easily understood terms.
7. When a contract to purchase a timeshare unit is signed, a cooling-off period of at least five days must be permitted during which a client can change his mind, cancel the contract and receive a full refund of any deposit paid.

A committee has been appointed by the council to deal with consumer affairs, whose duties will include dealing with complaints and enquiries from the public, investigating complaints against members and arranging arbitration if necessary. The committee also has power to investigate breaches of the code of conduct and to report these to the council.

A second committee deals with public relations and the promotion of the public image of timeshare, also negotiations with governments as appropriate.

Membership application must include a lawyer's report indicating that the developer has proper title to the development(s), also that the use of the land complies with the laws of the country. A paid-up capital of at least £100,000 is required and evidence that sufficient resources exist to complete the development have to be provided. Copies of promotional material have also to be submitted.

Further information on the Timeshare Developers Association is available from 23 Buckingham Gate, London SW1E 6LB.

Holiday property bond

The holiday property bond is not timesharing, but an alternative method of investing a capital sum to provide holiday accommodation each year.

It is marketed in the UK by Villa Owners Club Ltd, H P B House, Newmarket, Suffolk, and comprises a lump sum investment in a life assurance policy with the Isle of Man Assurance Co Ltd, with a minimum premium of £1000. Part of the money is invested in securities, the income from which is used for management and maintenance of holiday properties which are purchased with further funds as available. A points system allows the use of a wide selection of holiday homes in the UK and in many European resorts and in Florida, USA. No rent is charged for use of the property or management fees in the standard scheme.

A new option is available, whereby the payment of a modest user charge gives bondholders 50 per cent more holiday points.

There is a buy-back guarantee after two years and the quality of all accommodation is very high. A property advisory committee, comprising owners with an independent chairman, provides the managers with information about the availability of suitable holiday property and keeps in touch with bondholders to ascertain their preferences regarding new locations for property purchase.

Chapter 18

Title Insurance and Trustees

In the USA, title insurance is an important aspect of house purchase procedure and there are a considerable number of companies which offer this facility at a relatively modest cost. This precaution has not received the same acceptance in the UK. A number of insurance companies have endeavoured to market schemes in England without conspicuous success, although at least one firm has persevered and is gaining ground gradually in respect of properties in the UK and, more especially, on the Continent.

Title insurance is, in effect, an insured statement of the condition of a title to a property which is being transferred to a new owner. It has two advantages, namely: the company issuing the insurance pays for any losses incurred should the title subsequently be found defective and it will also provide an additional cover for the cost of any litigation in defending claims. Purchasers do not have to prove negligence.

For timeshare schemes, both in the UK and abroad, where a divided freehold exists, title insurance provides the purchaser with an independent assurance, backed only after detailed investigation of the title, enforced by a financial guarantee, that the title being passed on by the developers is all that it appears to be.

CECOA, which claims to be Spain's first title company, concerns itself with property searches, rightful title and the investigation of debts or liens on a property. A title company has the right to guarantee its findings via a bank guarantee programme or insurance bond on properties under construction. On finished properties, whether new or a resale, a certificate of documentation and completion is issued. The guarantees are recognised absolutely by the Spanish Courts.

At present the services of CECOA are only exclusively available to clients buying homes on the Costa Blanca and Costa del Sol from Lanes International who are specialist estate agents, based in Brighton, Sussex.

Timeshare Trustees

Claimed to be the largest trust company operating in the European timeshare field, Timeshare Trustees International Ltd provides services to developers in the UK and also in Scandinavia, Germany, Portugal, Spain and Malta. One of the duties of this organisation is to ensure that taxes are paid and buildings insured for all properties held in trust. Computerised records are maintained regarding ownership of weeks and payments for time purchased. The important matter of continuity of management after the developer has completed and sold out the scheme is another vital service which should be provided by the trustee.

TTI is the parent company of a wholly owned subsidiary in the UK, known as Holiday Property Trustees Ltd, which is an authorised custodian trustee under the UK Public Trustee rules. The main purpose of TTI is to make sure that purchasers of timeshare obtain a good legal title to occupation of a completed timeshare property, or if there is a defect the return of money paid to the developer or marketing organisation.

Developers are required to transfer clear legal titles to fully completed properties to TTI, who holds them on behalf of timeshare owners. Before transfer of the title to TTI, all moneys paid by the purchasers are held in a blocked account, and not released to the developer until the title is transferred or until satisfactory completion guarantees have been given.

TTI also helps management companies to collect maintenance charges from owners, and ensures that annual accounts are audited satisfactorily.

Although TTI does provide important services to timeshare resort operators, this organisation is primarily responsible to the owners and cannot be replaced except by the owners themselves.

Further information regarding Timeshare Trustees (International) Ltd can be obtained from the Customer Services Manager, PO Box 10, Tower Street Centre, Ramsey, Isle of Man.

Chapter 19

Flights for Owners

To get maximum benefit from their overseas holiday homes, many owners are keen to obtain the most reasonably priced flights to their chosen destination, not only for themselves, but also for their tenants, when they rent out their property in the summer. There are a number of clubs which provide members with low-cost travel by air and other benefits.

The largest and longest-established organisation is the OSL Travel Plus Club, 4 Broadway, Fiveways, Edgbaston, Birmingham B15 1BB (021-633 3444), which was formed in 1968. The summer service provides regular weekly flights to Spain including the Costa Blanca, Costa del Sol, Balearic and Canary Islands; also to Malta and Corfu and Skiathos in Greece. Competitively priced and mainly daytime departures are available from up to 12 UK airports, with a limited surcharge guarantee. The Club offers a range of additional facilities enabling owners to offer a complete holiday package to friends and the public. These include pre-bookable car hire and overseas coach and taxi transfers, a rental collection service and discounted advertising in *The Sunday Times*. Even free UK airport parking is available at certain times of the year.

Owners Club International of Centurion House, Bircherley Street, Hertford is a more recently established organisation, a subsidiary of the Intasun Leisure Group. A wide choice of flights is available to Spain from Gatwick, Manchester, Bristol and other UK airports at reasonable prices. Free car parking is offered at certain times of the year and there are concessionary rates for car hire and also travel insurance. Rental collection facilities are also available.

Monarch Airlines has a Five Star Owners Club to serve people with overseas holiday homes or timeshare property. They operate flights to many major Mediterranean holiday countries such as Spain and the Canary Islands, Portugal and Greece from eight UK airports, at prices from £88, in winter months, to Malaga.

Their aircraft fleet includes Boeing 757s and 737-300s. A no-surcharge guarantee is offered, bonuses are available for group

travel, and reductions for children under 12 are granted. Further information can be obtained from Monarch Air Travel, Halcyon House, Percival Way, Luton Airport, Luton, Bedfordshire (0582 424211).

The alternative to club membership is to use one of the cut-price flight specialists, many of whom publicise their offers in the national press. However, it is advisable to ascertain if the flight you select is operated under an ATOL number (Air Transport Operators' Licence) and whether the agent making the offer is a member of the Association of British Travel Agents (ABTA). The reputation of certain uncontrolled 'bucket-shops' (as they are known in the trade) has been poor, because of irresponsible behaviour over cancelled flights, late surcharges, unreliable air-craft, and even bankruptcies which have left holiday-makers stranded abroad.

The Air Travel Advisory Bureau, with offices in London and Manchester, offers a data system which discloses details of the operators offering the best-value seats, at the time of application, to numerous destinations. Information can be obtained by telephoning 01-636 5000.

Tour operators also dispose of surplus seats from time to time to selected destinations in southern Europe. Many airlines operating scheduled services are prepared to quote reduced fares to stand-by passengers, but the snag here is that you can rarely be certain you will depart on the flight of your choice until the last minute and you may have to wait patiently for several days at the airport.

Owners Abroad Ltd (051-514 4000) offers low season priced flights throughout the year to Spain, Portugal and Greece, with no surcharge guarantee. The Flight Advice Bureau (0898 900404) provides expert advice on where to buy bargain flights worldwide.

Chapter 20

Security and Safety

Unfortunately, vandalism, violence and burglary are on the increase in most countries, so it is wise to take appropriate countermeasures if you own a property abroad or intend to live overseas.

So far as property is concerned, the precautions you take with an overseas home are much the same as in the British Isles. If you live in a block of apartments with a full-time caretaker your problems are substantially solved, provided the person in charge is reliable and conscientious. Of course, it is wise to have good strong locks on all external doors, plus a spy hole for use when you are in occupation and an unexpected visitor arrives at the front door. Then you can see who is calling and if you have a chain you can open the door a little without allowing direct access.

The concierge or a close friend should have door keys when you are away, so that the property can be aired regularly and checks made to ensure that there is no problem with water, either from a leak in the pipes or a flood from a neighbouring property.

Villas, particularly if they are in a somewhat isolated position, require more detailed planning. In addition to a high standard of door locks, every window that is accessible from the ground should be fitted with security locking devices. In Spain and some other countries metal window grilles are installed as decoration and these also become effective deterrents to house breakers and burglars.

Anyone living alone should have a telephone to call emergency assistance, plus an alarm system with panic button. A loud whistle could also be useful, plus a well-trained house dog who can recognise friend from foe, is obedient to the owner's commands and will bark noisily when disturbed.

One of the first tasks on settling into a new home is to ascertain the best methods of alerting the security authorities. Discover the telephone number of the local police station and find out if it is manned 24 hours a day. Place this information in a prominent position in the dwelling so that it can always be found and add to it instructions for contacting the fire and ambulance services. List the nearest doctor and hospital in case of sudden illness.

On some modern estates where there are perhaps more than 50 dwellings, a private security service is provided permanently and paid for by the owners as part of their community charges.

Chapter 21

Household Insurance

The prudent owner has adequate insurance on his overseas home which provides cover not only for the building but also for the contents.

Under EC regulations household insurance does not have to be underwritten in the country where the property is situated. It is possible, therefore, to take out a policy underwritten by Lloyd's of London, where the premium is payable in sterling and claims are settled quickly in the UK for sterling.

One such policy provides cover for the building against fire, explosion, lightning, earthquakes, subterranean fire, bursting or overflowing of water tanks, apparatus or pipes, bursting or overflowing of fixed oil tanks, apparatus or pipes, aircraft, storm, tempest, flood, impact, riot, strikes and malicious damage, theft or attempted entry. Public and personal liability are also covered.

Full cover is maintained while the property is unoccupied without any additional premium and cover applies to those who live permanently abroad or use the property for short periods and rent it to casual holiday-makers at other times. A typical premium to cover a building for £30,000 at 0.175 per cent and the contents for £4000 at 0.50 per cent would be approximately £72 per annum.

In the insurer's experience one of the most frequent causes of claims is for water damage due to the often erratic water supply abroad and poor standards of plumbing.

If you insure your home with a local company in the country where it is situated you might have to complete a proposal form and cope with a policy in a foreign language which you do not understand. The result may be that you are uncertain about the cover you have obtained or the conditions imposed by the insurance company. In addition you may not be aware of the bona fides of the agent or company with whom you have placed the business.

Spain

Insurance companies in Spain, for instance, have to be registered with the government before they are allowed to operate and are then subject to various regulations concerning the wording of policies (which have to be written in Spanish), taxes and so on.

Sums insured and premiums paid have to be in pesetas and agents must be registered with the College of Agents and have a licence number on an identity card, which indicates they are properly registered.

A new policy created specially for home owners in Spain, France, Italy and Portugal has been arranged by M C Edwards Ltd, 38 Wellingborough Road, Northampton with certain underwriters at Lloyd's.

Much careful thought has been given to the policy terms which cover villas, flats and apartments in respect of damage by earthquakes, tempest and storm, loss of rent and malicious damage.

The policy is worded in English, claims are assessed locally and payable in sterling. Premiums are also paid in sterling in the UK.

Personal accident and baggage insurance is also available through M C Edwards.

Chapter 22

Letting Your Overseas Property

Many families purchase an overseas home with the intention of using it for perhaps only four to six weeks a year, for annual holidays, and perhaps at a later stage, when retirement is in prospect, plan greater use by the parents as they have more leisure time. Grown-up children can possibly have the advantage of using a family-owned property overseas at certain times of the year.

The property will not improve if it is closed up for long periods and if it is not inspected and aired at regular intervals. Damage may occur as a result of freak weather, so some owners decide it is worth going to the trouble of letting their property on a commercial basis.

It should be realised that, generally speaking, this can involve quite a lot of work and the annual return will perhaps not be more than 5 or 6 per cent after all expenses have been paid. To achieve satisfactory results, it is essential to have a good local agent on the spot to see that the property is in a satisfactory condition and ready for occupation as tenants arrive and that it is tidied up after they depart, ready for the next tenant.

Cleaning and maintenance are of great importance and having a local person available at all times to deal with any emergencies such as electricity breakdown or malfunctioning of domestic appliances is highly desirable.

Some new developments have their own management service which they offer to purchasers at a competitive fee, and in the main resort areas there are firms willing to undertake management on behalf of individual owners as a specialist service.

It is unlikely that a property, even in a popular resort, will be let for more than about half of the year. Villas in country or remote locations will probably achieve even less frequent occupation.

The reputation of the management organisation is of paramount importance as it is not unknown for dishonest or careless operators to find a tenant for a week or more and not report the letting to the owner; thus the opportunity is there for them to pocket the rent themselves.

Before deciding finally on letting your property for the weeks or months that you don't require it for yourself, draw up a list of conditions for tenants and have these incorporated in any publicity material that you prepare to assist you in letting the property. For instance, are you prepared to let tenants bring animals on holiday with them, or do you think that your property is not suitable for dogs or cats?

Decide on the maximum number of people you want to occupy the property. Do you expect tenants to pay an additional charge for gas and electricity consumed, or do you include this in the rent? Decide on arrival and departure times for tenants and ensure that there is adequate time between the two to allow for the property to be prepared satisfactorily for the arrival of the new occupants.

If you arrange lettings through a major tour operator there will probably be quite a wide assortment of people using your home and possibly a fairly quick turnover. However, these companies wish to protect their reputation and will ensure a high standard of maintenance and cleanliness. In any case, can you really expect higher standards from people recommended to you than from strangers? Even friends in whom you have complete faith sometimes have lapses and leave places in a horrible mess.

An alternative, although not always a satisfactory one, is to ask a neighbour to manage the property for you in your absence. This means relying on their goodwill to undertake the job properly. Don't forget that they may want a holiday away from their home, just at the peak period when you have several tenants arriving within a short period. Will the job be done to your satisfaction if your 'volunteers' suffer a period of illness, and how much should you pay them as recompense for their trouble? In the long run, professional management is probably more satisfactory.

Chapter 23

Look Before You Leap

As a final reminder, the following checklist should be studied by everyone before they buy a property in a foreign country.

1. Visit the property you plan to buy wherever it is situated. If it is not already completed, ask to see a similar design that is furnished and ready for occupation. Check on the materials and finishes being used and get assurance that any proposed amenities such as swimming pools or tennis courts will be available for use immediately the building programme is complete.
2. Before signing any documents or paying over substantial sums of money, seek advice on the contract, the specification and the terms of business from a qualified legal expert and an accountant. Ask the developer or agent for English translations of all documents which commit you to purchase.
3. Don't be in too much of a hurry to buy a property. The vendor will obviously encourage you to make a quick decision and sign up during your first visit, but it is better to lose the opportunity of purchasing a property which seems to attract you immediately than to make a hasty decision which you may regret later.
4. When purchasing an apartment, obtain written confirmation of maintenance charges and management arrangements.
5. Where estate facilities such as swimming pools, clubs and tennis courts are promised in brochures and publicity, but have not been provided at the time you purchase your property, get confirmation that these will be available within, say, 12 months. In some countries, developers are required to provide the bulk of the amenities and access roads before they launch the sales programme.
6. Ensure that you obtain a proper title to the property you are buying and, where a Land Registry exists, that there are no encumbrances, such as a mortgage, registered. Where a legal expert is employed, these checks will be part of his or her routine work.
7. A completion date in the sales contract is very desirable, but not always easy to obtain.

8. At any early date, compile a list of costs and taxes you will be expected to pay when you purchase the property – then you should not suffer any shocks.
9. When buying a new property still under construction or not yet started, obtain information about stage payments as the work proceeds and check if you are permitted a 5 per cent retention for six months to cover any building faults and if any guarantees are offered for, say, two years to compensate for bad building.
10. Make sure you comply with the fiscal rules of the country of your choice so that you can repatriate your capital on the sale of the property. Also examine the regulations regarding taxation of foreign residents, payment of pensions, medical facilities and so on.

Part 4
Country Surveys

Rates of exchange quoted are those applying on 29 November 1988

Readers are advised to check information about the country they are particularly interested in, as changes occur daily.

Chapter 24

The Islands Around Britain

The Isle of Man and the Channel Islands are the two main groups of offshore islands around the coast of Britain.

They offer interesting financial benefits, but sadly lack a climate which is significantly better than on the mainland.

However, they do attract considerable numbers of tourists and some new residents each year, despite the very strong protective legislation imposed in Jersey.

Isle of Man

The Isle of Man lies in the Irish Sea midway between the Republic of Ireland and Scotland. It has an area of 572 square kilometres (221 square miles) and a population of 64,282 people, a third of whom live in the capital, Douglas, which is on the east coast. Other towns of importance include Ramsey, Peel, Castletown and Port Erin.

The island has never been a part of the United Kingdom and has its own two-tier parliament known as the Tynwald which was founded over 1000 years ago by the Vikings.

Man has a special relationship with the European Community which guarantees free trade in goods with the rest of the Community but there is no involvement with the Community's budget so contributions to the EC are not required, nor is any financial assistance available. Long-term objectives to harmonise tax, social and employment legislation are also not applicable.

As an important part of a programme of economic development, the government is keen to attract new residents and there is a positive welcome to families who would like to live on the island. The aim is to encourage those who will integrate well into Manx society, and will make a contribution to the island's economic well-being.

Why should the Isle of Man government wish to increase the population? The simple answer is that there is ample room for expansion on the island, for the population density is about some six or seven times less than that in the Channel Islands. Also Tynwald prides itself in the quality of its health, education and social services and it is clear that these services could cope readily with an increase in population of 10,000. In fact, many services, particularly electricity supply and other public utilities, benefit greatly from an increase in the number of consumers. Furthermore, the various amenities provided for tourists require a strong domestic market to thrive, and increased consumption by residents will improve the standard of retailing and restaurants available for visitors. In addition, the recreational facilities such as golf, sailing, rambling and fishing, have substantial spare capacity to cater for additional demand.

Businessmen establishing new enterprises in Man are encouraged by the favourable taxation and a loyal, hard-working labour force, plus good communications with the UK and Europe.

Expatriates and retired people enjoy the relaxed way of life and the sophisticated financial facilities, plus the absence of taxes on capital. Domestic labour, as in most developed countries, tends to be scarce, but is available. There is a low crime rate. A sizeable industrial sector provides jobs for skilled engineering craftspeople.

The fact that everyone on the island speaks English and uses a similar currency to the mainland are other advantages.

Residence permits

There is complete freedom of entry and abode to all citizens who have full permanent residency rights in the UK or Irish Republic. Overseas nationals are affected by immigration regulations, details of which can be obtained from a British Embassy or Consulate.

Tax and exchange control

The standard rate of income tax is 15 per cent on the first £6000 of taxable income of resident individuals and 20 per cent on the balance. The rate of income tax is 20 per cent on the whole taxable incomes of non-residents and companies. There are no wealth or capital gains taxes or death duties.

As a tax haven, the island has numerous financial institutions both of local origin and national renown. The island finances all its own services and makes a contribution to the UK for defence and diplomatic services. VAT is charged at 15 per cent on all goods and services, except those which are zero rated.

Currency

The island issues its own £1 notes and pence coinage which are at par with £1 sterling.

Politics

The stability of the Tynwald is enhanced by the absence of party politics and its history of more than 1000 years of independent rule.

Health services

Health, education and social services are of high quality.

Cost of living

The cost of living, excluding housing, is about 5 per cent higher than in the UK. The rate of inflation is similar to that in the UK.

Communications

Air services to London, Manchester, Blackpool, Belfast, Glasgow, Edinburgh, Dublin, Birmingham, Liverpool, Leeds/Bradford, Cardiff and Newcastle. London journey time 60 minutes. Sea ferries to Heysham, Belfast, Dublin, Stranraer, Liverpool and Fleetwood.

Property purchase

There are no restrictions on non-islanders purchasing property in the Isle of Man.

A wide range of homes is available at prices from about £40,000 for an old three-bedroom terrace house to £200,000 plus for a six-bedroom country residence. Considering the size of the island it is pleasing to discover that some of the country properties have extensive grounds up to about 50 acres.

Guernsey

Guernsey (population 55,482) is the second largest Channel Island. It does not attract so many holiday-makers as its neighbour Jersey, but it is a very pleasant place in which to live. Excellent shopping facilities are available in St Peter Port and there are plenty of recreational facilities.

Economy

This is not now so dependent on horticulture although this is still an important employer of labour. The financial sector has expanded, and Guernsey is an offshore tax haven. A large banking sector with over 40 institutions is licensed to undertake deposit business. Many well-known financial institutions have local offices.

Light industry has developed into an important employer and exporter. Tourism and conference trade is fostered. Fishing and 'high-tech' industries are also of importance.

Taxation

Income tax has not changed in the past 23 years – 20p in the pound; no VAT, corporation tax, capital gains tax or inheritance tax. There is a double taxation agreement between the UK and Jersey. A special relationship with the Economic Community exempts Guernsey from most of Common Market law, and there is no need to harmonise taxation and other internal policies with those of the EC.

Medical

There is no health service, but nor are there nursing or maintenance charges in general hospitals. Patients pay fees to their own doctor while in hospital. Private medical insurance is recommended.

Education

Administered by the States Education Council and broadly similar to England. There is a recently built £6 million Grammar School for boys and girls. Well-known private schools include Elizabeth College for boys and Ladies College and Blanchelande College for girls. There are also some small fee-paying schools and a college of further education.

Housing

New residents may occupy 'open market' properties only. These are inscribed on the Housing Control Register and amount to about 10 per cent of total housing stock (16,000), and are effectively properties costing £185,000 upwards. The aim is to protect bona fide locals from speculative purchasers of lower priced properties. A wide variety of properties is available ranging from larger town houses to country residences. Little scope exists for new building due to land shortage.

Conveyance charges amount to approximately 5¼ per cent of purchase price. Rates are very low and in three categories: occupiers' rates levied by the parish, tax on rateable value payable annually to the States, and quarterly water rate. Rateable value has not increased since 1948. Open market houses with a market value of £185,000 pay combined rates including water of about £185 per annum.

The Bristol & West Building Society has an office in Guernsey and many banks and the Guernsey Savings and Loan Corporation offer long-term finance for house purchase.

Purchasing procedures

Verbal contracts are legally binding in Guernsey. The purchaser is represented by an advocate who undertakes the title search and drafts the conveyance. Completion normally takes about four weeks and is effected by appearance before the Royal Court.

Jersey

This is the largest of the Channel Islands and the most southerly of this group of islands.

It is a very popular resort for holiday-makers from the mainland and attractive as a low tax area for wealthy individuals and international businesses. The island has also become a major international banking community with a very wide selection of banks having offices, mainly in St Helier.

Income tax

The standard rate of 20 per cent has remained unchanged since 1940. This rate is charged on residents' gross income less personal allowances and reliefs.

An individual is deemed to be a resident if he is present in the island for six months or more in a fiscal year, or has been present on average for three months per year for four successive years, or if he maintains a place of residence in Jersey available for his use and makes any visits to the island during the year.

No capital taxation is imposed apart from probate duty and stamp duty on authorised share capital of companies (the rate for these two exceptions is 0.5 per cent).

Property purchase and residency

In order to protect local people, and maintain a balance between economic development and the preservation of the environment, it has been necessary to impose restrictions on the movement of people into the island.

This is achieved by local licensing laws which prevent individuals who do not have birth or marriage qualifications from buying or leasing freehold or leasehold residential accommodation unless approved by the Jersey Housing Committee.

One way of obtaining this approval is to be essentially employed in one of what are considered to be the most important professions such as medicine, accountancy and banking. The applicant needs to be employed by a well-established company in the island and able to prove this. The Committee will need to be satisfied that the individual applying offers the island sufficient potential benefit through the essential employment he is to undertake.

Having obtained the Committee's permission, the employing company can then purchase or rent a property for the employee to live in. The individual cannot buy a property in his own name unless resident in the island for 20 years or more.

Wealthy immigrants

The only other way of obtaining a residence permit is as a wealthy immigrant. Each application is considered on its merit and requirements do vary. As a general guide, an annual income of more than £50,000 per annum is required and total wealth in the region of £2 million upwards. Very few people of this status are accepted each year.

Having satisfied the authorities that their financial qualifications fulfil the requirements, wealthy immigrants are then permitted to purchase a home, probably costing in excess of £200,000.

Because there is a shortage of homes for local residents, any property purchased on 'economic grounds', ie where the wealthy immigrant is making a substantial tax contribution to Jersey, must not be in a category which might deprive a native Jersey family of accommodation which was affordable to them and might otherwise be available to them.

Under Jersey law the legal title to property does not depend on deeds. Title only passes when the Royal Court of Jersey decrees. The Court will only do this when the parties have indicated their mutual agreement to the terms and have also previously satisfied the Housing Committee that the proposed new occupant has the necessary residential qualifications. Thus the housing purchase regulations are enforced without undue difficulties.

Chapter 25

Europe and the Mediterranean

Andorra

General information

Status. Co-principality
Capital. Andorra la Vella
Area. 465 sq. km (180 sq miles)
Population. 40,000 (approx)

Location

Longitude 43°N; latitude 0°E. Landlocked territory in the Eastern Pyrenees, surrounded by France and Spain, roughly the same size as the Isle of Wight and having very mountainous terrain.

Political stability

Excellent. It has a unique record of diplomatic non-intervention in European affairs over a period of 700 years. Despite the fact that Andorra enjoys the protection of the French President and the Spanish Bishop of Urgel (as princes), the status of an independent republic is maintained. The government comprises 28 citizens elected to the General Council and a six-person cabinet. There are no political parties and no defence expenditure.

Economy

Currency. Andorra does not have its own currency but uses the Spanish peseta and the French franc.

Cost of living. The economy is very sound. As import duties are so low, luxury items such as alcohol, electrical goods and jewellery are especially cheap. The cost of food and other living expenses are well below the charges in Britain and roughly on a par with Spain. Fuel costs are substantially lower than in most European countries (electricity is generated by hydro-electric power) and telephones, property insurance and normal household expenses are not high.

Taxation. As a tax haven, Andorra is virtually unrivalled. There is no income tax, capital gains tax, inheritance tax or VAT. The country's revenues come from a tiny duty on imported goods.

Exchange rate. As for Spanish pesetas and French francs.

Exchange control. None.

Language

Catalan, Spanish and French are the main spoken languages, but English is spoken and understood in some areas, especially tourist parts.

Expatriate community

Only about 25 per cent of the population are native Andorrans, the rest being about 18,000 Spanish residents, 8000 from France and the rest a mixture of other nationalities including about 1000 Britons.

Because of the large immigrant community, Andorrans are obviously welcoming in their attitude.

Security

Andorrans are generally law-abiding citizens with few 'black sheep', who are mostly visitors and foreign workers. The crime rate is very low and the country itself has no army.

Residence permits

For retired people of independent means, there are no problems, the only financial requirement being the production of evidence showing at least £5000 in a bank account.

Andorra does not have to be the main base or home, but the authorities do want new residents to spend a few months each year in Andorra, not just a couple of weeks' holiday. However, this requirement is not recorded in writing.

Work permits

People wishing to seek employment face great problems in gaining a work permit.

Personal effects

No duties are payable.

Housing

There is a good selection of villas and apartments available, both in residential towns and villages, as well as the skiing districts.

Buying property

The procedure is simple and uncomplicated. Legal formalities must be completed by a local lawyer. Generally, property is freehold, with the buyer and the seller appearing before one of the two notaries involved to complete the transaction.

Where to live

Avoid the main highway, which is noisy because the heavy goods vehicles use this route between France and Spain.

Inspection flights

Inspection visits are available most weekends at a cost of about £190 inclusive of travel, food and accommodation.

Communications

Air. Daily services from Heathrow and Gatwick to Barcelona. A good taxi service from Barcelona takes about 3 hours.

Rail. By rail from London via Paris, Toulouse and Hospitalet, close to the Andorran border, then by connecting bus service. Overnight sleeper from London arrives at 7 am the following morning.

Road. The trans-Pyrenean highway linking Toulouse with Barcelona passes within 40 km of Andorra's capital.

Driving. Driving is on the right.

Recreation

Andorra's growing reputation for a quiet and relaxed life-style does not detract in any way from the abundance of recreational facilities available. Skiing is a major sport and facilities are constantly being improved. Facilities are also available for swimming, squash, tennis, riding, fishing, shooting and walking. Less energetic pursuits include the cinema, theatre and art galleries. The capital, Andorra la Vella, is an interesting and busy place, and throughout the country, fiestas with Catalan dancing and music frequently occur.

Health services

Two modern hospitals provide a high standard of health care. There is also a comprehensive social security plan.

Climate

Spring (April-May). Maximum temperature 22°C, minimum 4°C. Generally warm but with variable rain or snow showers.

Summer (June-September). Maximum temperature 26°C, minimum 10°C. Mostly dry hot days, with cooler nights. No humidity.

Autumn (October-November). Maximum temperature 18°C, minimum 2°C. Clear skies, fresh mornings and evenings. No fog.

Winter (December-March). Maximum temperature 15°C, minimum 7°C. Snow on most higher altitudes, mostly sunny days and not damp.

Austria

General information

Status. Republic
Capital. Vienna
Area. 83,855 sq km (32,367 sq miles)
Population. 7,555,338

Location

Longitude 48°N; latitude 10°E to 16°E. Austria is situated in southern central Europe covering part of the eastern Alps and the Danube region. Though landlocked, the country has a wide variety of landscape, vegetation and climate, ranging from Alpine highlands, through the foothills to lowland plains.

Political stability

Despite a history of political and territorial instability, post-war Austria has gained a reputation for comparative continuity and stability. It is a federal republic, which effectively gives considerable autonomy to the regions. Party politics, although well developed, have created some problems and there is now a coalition government.

Austria's position of neutrality helps to enhance the policy of cordial relations with all nations, whether NATO or Warsaw Pact. In economic matters, Austria is also non-aligned as she is not a member of the European Community.

Economy

Cost of living. The Austrian economy is undoubtedly very stable. Prudent policies and efficient industry have combined to produce a high level of employment and, generally, a high standard of living for most of the inhabitants. Prices are high when compared with the UK but this is compensated for by high wages.

Taxation. A double taxation agreement between Britain and Austria does exist. VAT varies, depending on the type of goods, from 8-10 per cent to 32 per cent (luxury goods). Income tax varies from a minimum of 10 per cent to a maximum of 50 per cent.

Exchange rate. Austrian schillings 22.38 = £1.

Exchange control. There are no limits to the amount of foreign currency which can be imported or exported. The Austrian schilling is one of the most stable currencies in the world.

Language

98 per cent of the population are German speaking, so a knowledge of the language would be useful. However, English is fairly widespread in Austria, especially among the well educated.

Expatriate community

There are very few expatriate Britons in Austria.

Security

Austria is a secure nation and faces no specific problems.

Residence permits

A residence permit may only be granted on specific authorisation from the Ministry of the Interior. Material independence is usually required. Where family reunion is concerned, the name, nationality and address of the relatives are required too. A temporary visa for six months can be acquired but all applications must be made in the mother country.

Work permits

A work permit can only be applied for prior to departure from the UK. They are issued in line with existing conditions in Austria, and so, because of the unemployment situation, they are currently very hard to get. A sound knowledge of German is required.

Personal effects

Household goods may be imported duty free, so long as they are accompanied by the household goods inventory (*see* Chapter 8).

Housing

In order to protect local inhabitants from growing shortages and escalating prices of residential property, a quota system has been imposed on the purchase by foreigners of homes in certain regions. As a result, it is virtually impossible to purchase property in some regions of the country if you are not Austrian. In other communities the restrictions are not severe. In the centre of the country the Steiermark district offers good opportunities for property purchase. Ski lodges and apartments appeal most to the British. Small studios can be acquired for around £20,000, while chalets can cost from £85,000 to around £400,000.

Buying property

The property agreement is written in German, with an English translation, and this can be signed in either Austria or the UK. A copy is given to the purchaser. The lawyer acts for both parties and can have a power of attorney to act on behalf of the purchaser. He can also prepare a mortgage agreement if a loan is required.

Deposits are not normally necessary. The documents are signed before an official of the Austrian Embassy and then returned to the lawyer with a draft or cheque for the purchase price. The money is then placed in a trustee account in Germany or Austria where it remains until completion takes place. Meanwhile the new title to the property is registered at the land registry and this may take four weeks or more. When registration is complete the taxes and fees are paid and the purchase price released to the vendor.

The land registry fee amounts to 1 per cent of the purchase price. Trustee management of the purchase price by an attorney or a notary costs about 3 per cent and the purchase tax 8 per cent. Where land is bought prior to building, the tax is on the land value only.

Where to live

See 'Housing' above.

Inspection flights

Regular personal inspection visits.

Communications

Austria has excellent communications both internally and externally, including six commercial airports, well over 1000 km of motorways, 5800 km of railways, plus large stretches of navigable waterways, not to mention thousands of cable-based mountain lifts. Public transport in Austria is well developed.

Austria has a dense network of postal communications and news media, including fully automatic telephone, telegraph and telex as well as radio and television.

Recreation

Leisure facilities in Austria are excellent. The environment is one of stunning beauty, which encourages outdoor pursuits such as walking, camping and climbing, not to mention the ideal alpine skiing conditions which make skiing Austria's national sport. Other popular physical pursuits include football, swimming, judo and motor racing. There is also a very strong tradition of horse riding. In general, sports facilities are excellent.

Culture and the arts also provide a rich source of interest for residents. Literature, opera, choirs and festivals combine with the fine architecture to promote Austria's cultural image. The main cities such as Vienna and Salzburg are especially fascinating.

Driving

Driving in Austria is on the right and really much the same as elsewhere in mainland Europe.

Health services

The Austrian health service is very well equipped, with an average of one doctor for every 370 patients. There are 322 hospitals in all. Each province has its own health administration and health office. In principle, anybody is entitled to make use of the facilities in the health service as the costs are borne by the social insurance and social welfare scheme.

The recent influence of the Socialists in Austria has led to the development of a carefully worked-out welfare programme. An agreement does exist between the UK and Austria and details are given in DSS pamphlet SA25.

Climate

Austria belongs to the central European climatic zone, with the influence of the Atlantic felt in the west and the continental influence more strongly in the east. In general, the climatic seasonal changes are far less pronounced in the west than in the east. For the purposes of describing climate, Austria can be divided into three areas:

East – continental Pannonian climate: mean temperature for July above 19°C, annual rainfall less than 800 mm.

Central Alpine region: high precipitation with long winters and short summers.

European climatic zone: wet and temperate, July temperature 14-19°C, annual precipitation 700-2000 mm.

Cyprus

General information

Status. Independent Republic
Capital. Nicosia
Area. 9251 sq km (3570 sq miles)
Population. 650,000

Location

Longitude 30°N; latitude 32°E. The island of Cyprus, at the east-

ern end of the Mediterranean, is a land of contrast. In the south where the majority of Greek Cypriots live, there is little unemployment and considerable prosperity and vast sums have been invested in recent years in the construction of new roads, hotels and residential accommodation. A new airport has been opened at Paphos and the facilities at Larnaca are considerably improved.

The main business centre is Nicosia, the capital, which is partitioned by an armoured line. The towns of Larnaca, Limassol and Paphos, all on the southern coast and controlled by Greek Cypriots, have a multitude of sandy beaches which are much enjoyed by the tourist; they also benefit from considerable business activity.

In the middle of the island is Trudos, a mountain range where it is possible to ski in the winter and then descend to sea level to enjoy a swim in the Mediterranean, all on the same day.

The northern parts of the island, including the once popular resorts of Kyrenia and Famagusta, are under the jurisdiction of Turkish Cypriots who are supported by a considerable contingent of the Turkish army. By comparison, tourism is at a low ebb compared with the rest of the island.

Political stability

Although the island is partitioned, stability seems to have been achieved but there is no apparent intercommunication.

The Greek Cypriot part of the area has one of the lowest crime rates in the world with offences such as muggings practically non-existent. The safety of individuals and property is no great problem and the risks are minimal.

Economy

Cost of living. In general, prices are lower than the UK, especially local produce. Imports are expensive. Heavy clothes are not required and heating costs are negligible (solar power is cheap and popular).

Taxation. A taxation agreement between the UK and Cyprus has existed since 1973, so tax paid in the UK can be offset against tax due in Cyprus. Investment income and pensions remitted to Cyprus are exempt from tax on the first C£2000. Any amount in excess of this figure is taxed at 5 per cent. An individual who is not resident in Cyprus for more than six months in any one year is not liable for income tax on any income arising outside Cyprus, even if it is received in the island. The actual levels of tax are very low.

No capital gains tax on the sale of property is charged and the proceeds may be remitted abroad. There is no VAT.

Exchange rate. Cyprus pound (C£) 0.83 = £1.

Exchange control. In operation.

Language

English is spoken by practically everybody. About 70 per cent of local TV programmes are in English and there are two English language papers. In addition, the local British Forces radio broadcast round the clock every day.

Expatriate community

Links between the UK and Cyprus have always been strong, and are illustrated in many ways, such as the similarity of property registration procedure, driving laws and the existence of a substantial Cypriot community in Britain. Links are compounded by the presence of a British military base on the island so it is not surprising that about 3000 Britons are resident in Cyprus and many more own holiday property there.

Security

The Cypriots themselves are generally open and honest and so personal property is not especially at risk. Cyprus is, however, strategically vital to the west for monitoring the Middle East, and also there is an undercurrent of uncertainty because of the partition of the island. However, any fears should be allayed by the comforting presence of the UN peace-keeping force.

Residence permits

A permanent residence permit can be easily obtained on proof that you are self-supporting and no burden to the state.

Work permits

Aliens wishing to work in Cyprus require a permit from the government under the Aliens Immigration Law.

Personal effects

Personal baggage can be imported free of duty.

Housing

A wide range of recently built and new villas and apartments is available at prices from about £20,000. Also available are village houses for modernisation.

Buying property

The Cyprus legal system is based on its English counterpart. The authorities do not consider that foreigners need a solicitor to handle property transactions as the system of transfer and registration is simple, but in the author's opinion, it is better to be safe than sorry.

First, the vendor and purchaser sign a private contract in the form of general and sale agreements. These documents are in a standard form to protect both parties.

Purchasers of property in Cyprus are required to pay stamp duty on signing a contract, amounting to 15 cents per C£100 up to C£10,000 rising to 20 cents per C£100 on purchase monies exceeding C£100,000.

When the land is registered at the land registry, transfer fees are payable at 5 per cent on prices up to C£10,000 rising by 0.5 per cent increments to 8 per cent where the price exceeds C£75,000.

The annual property tax is low. For properties valued at C£35,000, for example, the tax is C£52.50 per annum.

Aliens must produce evidence that foreign currency has been imported to pay for any property purchased. A permit has to be obtained from the Council of Ministers when acquiring immovable property in Cyprus. This is normally a routine task.

Where to live

Property is available mostly in the southern (Greek) sector.

Renting property

In order to protect the tourist industry, a regulation prevents foreigners from letting their property in Cyprus to holiday-makers. However, this rule does not seem to be imposed very vigorously.

Inspection flights

Scheduled flights only, unless a package tour is booked.

Communications

British Airways and Cyprus Airways between them run daily services to Larnaca (flying time about 3½ hours). On leaving, an airport tax of about £1.50 is levied. There are also scheduled flights to Paphos (4 hours).

Telecommunications are excellent, with automatic direct dialling available on a 24-hour basis to over 60 countries.

Health and welfare

Cyprus has one of the healthiest climates in the world. Medical treatment costs in government hospitals are low. Also there are plenty of specialist doctors and surgeons, and private practices for consultation.

A social security agreement exists between the UK and Cyprus covering National Insurance and various benefits including pensions. Details are given in DSS pamphlet SA12.

Climate

	Average daily temperature (°C)	*Rainfall Average days*	*Sea temperature* (°C)	*Sunshine hours*
January	9-18	12	18	169
February	9-19	8	18	197
March	10-20	7	18	255
April	11-21	4	18	285
May	15-27	4	20	355
June	18-30	1	21	379
July	21-35	0.3	26	399
August	21-35	0.4	27	358
September	18-32	1	29	321
October	17-27	3	25	277
November	11-24	6	21	231
December	8-17	11	17	175

France

General information

Status. Republic
Capital. Paris
Area. 551,000 sq km (220,400 sq miles)
Population. 55 million (approx)

Location

Longitude 42°N to 51°N; latitude 5°W to 5°E. France is surrounded by mountains and water and its natural boundaries are the Pyrenees and the Alps, the river Rhine, the Channel, the Atlantic and the Mediterranean.

Political stability

The France of today no longer suffers from its earlier weaknesses and uncertainty, and strong and responsible governments have become the rule. France is a leading light in European affairs. Although there were worries about the resurgence of the extreme right, in the 1988 elections only one National Front member was elected (compared with 34 in 1986). This member has since resigned, leaving the National Front with no representation in the National Assembly.

Economy

Cost of living. The economy is fairly strong, instilling financial stability. In general, prices are a little higher than in the UK, although this is offset locally by higher wages. This is especially the case in Paris. Local products, especially food and wine, are good value. The French are, however, self-sufficient in outlook and so foreign goods are not so easy to acquire cheaply.

Taxation. There is a double taxation agreement between the UK and France. Non-residents do not normally pay income tax if they are using a property as a holiday home. There is a 33.33 per cent tax on capital gains when selling property but generous allowances always reduce the actual assessment quite substantially. Owner-occupiers are now allowed a tax credit for major repairs if they have owned the house for 15 years, providing it is their principal residence. Local rates based on the annual rental value of the property vary from one area to another. In line with European Community regulations, VAT is also levied at various rates.

Exchange rate. French francs 10.87 = £1.

Exchange control. On a sale of a property in France, foreigners are permitted to repatriate the proceeds provided the original funds emanated from outside the country and proof of this is recorded in the purchase deeds.

Language

French is a comparatively easy language to learn and the effort is well worth while if you live in France for any length of time.

Expatriate community

A considerable number of retired people live in the south, particularly along the Côte d'Azur and in the Languedoc-Roussillon region. Many business executives reside in Paris and other major cities. The attitude of the French to foreigners is generally restrained.

Residence permits

People intending to take up permanent residence require a *visa de longue durée* which will ultimately lead to the issue of a *carte de séjour*. Application has to be made to a nominated French Consulate-General in your own country.

Work permits

Work permits are not required but entry into some professions is restricted.

Personal effects

Permission is granted to import free of duty and VAT all furniture and furnishings to equip your holiday or retirement home provided they have been in your ownership for more than six months. It is necessary to sign a declaration in triplicate to the effect that the goods are your own and will continue to be used by you in your new residence. You are thus bound not to sell or even give away any of the goods admitted.

Housing

Some property is available to rent in the Paris area, also in certain holiday resorts. Property prices are somewhat similar to UK ones in urban and coastal areas and conurbations, but in depopulated rural villages they are often lower. Properties available vary from châteaux in the countryside and villas on the coast, to lodges in the Alps.

Buying property

The system of property transfer is quite simple and fair. Briefly, France has no 'subject to contract' convention and so once the initial agreement to buy is made, a preliminary contract *(compromis de vente)* is signed and a 10 per cent deposit is paid to the *notaire* (lawyer). If the deal falls through, the deposit or an equivalent amount from the vendor is forfeited. Completion of the deal takes two or three months, during which time the *acte* (conveyance) is drafted. Once signed, the *acte* goes to the land registry for the final verification.

Roughly 10 per cent of the cost of the property goes on buying

costs incurred (unless the property is new). The *notaire* receives about 2½ per cent, and added to this is the registration tax, but this tax is not levied on properties less than five years old.

Where to live

See page 200.

Inspection flights

None.

Communications

Air. Excellent. Internal flights from airports such as Paris, Nice, Lyon and Bordeaux link up with a wide range of external flights to other parts of Europe and the world.

Rail. A very efficient network of railways connects the various areas of France, with the express services especially good.

Sea. As France is effectively Britain's neighbour, communication links across the Channel are very good. The ferry services are regular and fairly cheap. The Channel will, of course, be even less of an obstacle once the fixed link Channel tunnel is completed.

Recreation

France's favourite national pastime is without doubt imbibing good wine and food. Restaurants exist in abundance serving exemplary meals at quite reasonable prices (when compared with top quality British equivalents). Good food guides are available to show the novice the ropes, but exploring French cuisine should in any event be a delight.

The scope and standard of entertainment is wide, especially in Paris, although theatres and cinemas are quite expensive. Art is also taken very seriously and some of the world's finest paintings are to be found in French galleries.

Sport is probably not so popular in France as elsewhere in Europe, although facilities such as tennis courts and swimming pools are to be found in most areas. The most popular sports in France are football, rugby, cycling, motor racing and skiing. The beautiful French countryside is also a great source of pleasure, either for merely driving and touring, or for serious walking and camping.

Driving

Traffic rules are almost the same as in the UK except that you drive on the right instead of the left. In built-up areas, you must always give way to traffic coming out of a side turning on the right, but at roundabouts with special signs you give way to cars already on the roundabout.

The following points should always be remembered: the minimum age to drive is 18 and driving on a provisional licence is not permitted. Seat belts must be worn by the driver and the front seat passenger, and children under the age of 10 must not travel in the front seat. Stop signs really mean stop and creeping forward slowly is not permitted. A red warning triangle should be carried in case of a breakdown. Everyone must carry a complete spare bulb kit. Headlights must emit a yellow beam and lights must also dip to the right. Headlights must be used at night everywhere except in built-up areas. The maximum speed limits vary depending on the type of road, from 60 kmh in towns to 130 kmh on toll motorways. When roads are wet, speed limits are slightly reduced. For the first year after passing the driving test, new drivers may not go faster than 90 kmh.

You may drive on a British registration and with British number plates for six months after entry, after which you must re-register your car with the French authorities. If you sell your car within two years of entry, you will have to pay import duties.

One important thing to note is that lead-free petrol, which is unsuitable for cars that have not been modified, is available from pumps marked *'Essence sans plomb'*.

Health services

A reciprocal agreement between the UK and France does exist but private treatment is expensive, so adequate health insurance is advisable. There is no need to enrol with any one doctor once there so you may consult with as many as you wish. Fees are paid directly to the doctor but you will receive 70 per cent of the medical costs back, so long as the doctor abides by the recommended charges. With health insurance, this will cut the bill to about 10 per cent of the original cost. The same applies to hospital and prescription costs. Full reimbursement is given for a long illness and for injuries sustained at work. Dental costs are also covered.

Details of social security, health care and pension rights are given in DSS pamphlet SA29.

Climate

France is more than twice the size of Britain and has coastlines on

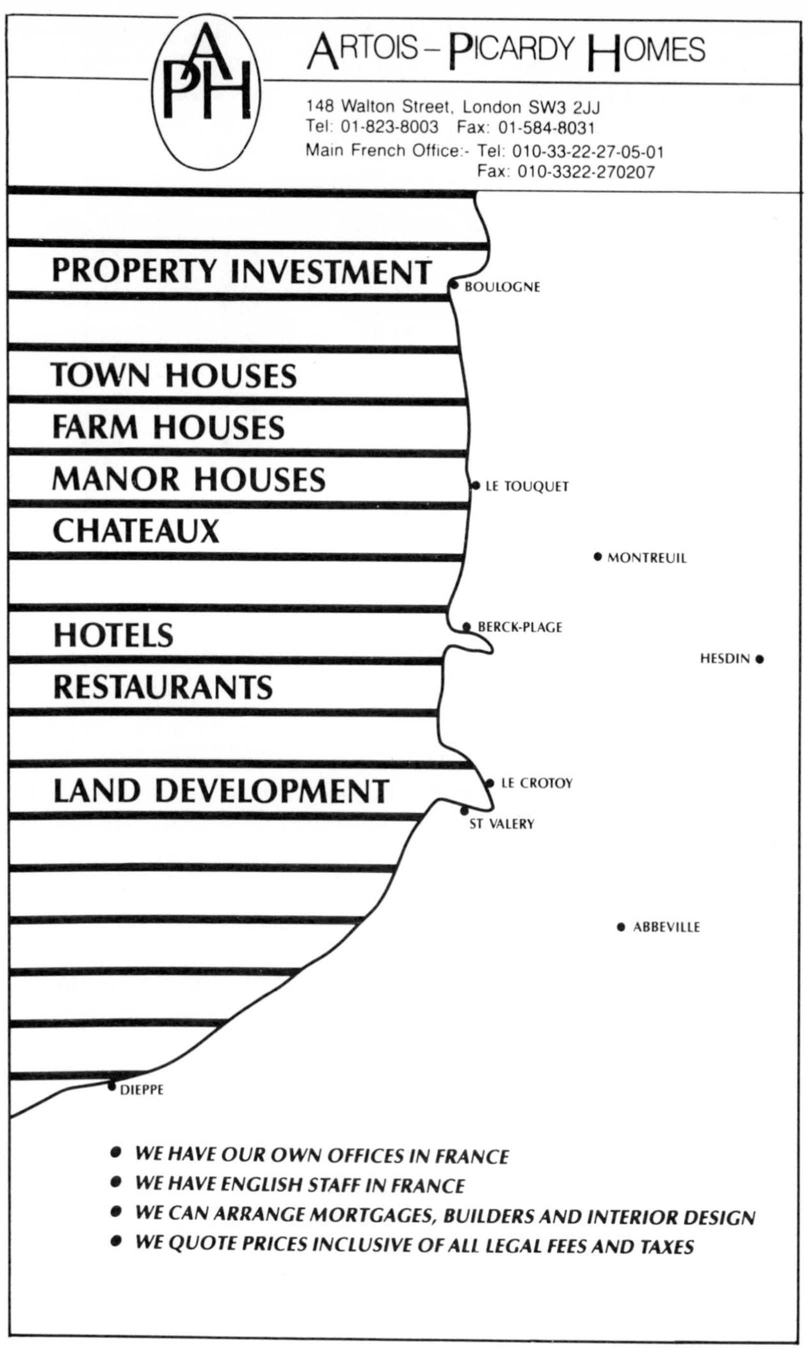
APH
ARTOIS – PICARDY HOMES
148 Walton Street, London SW3 2JJ
Tel: 01-823-8003 Fax: 01-584-8031
Main French Office:- Tel: 010-33-22-27-05-01
Fax: 010-3322-270207
PROPERTY INVESTMENT
TOWN HOUSES
FARM HOUSES
MANOR HOUSES
CHATEAUX
HOTELS
RESTAURANTS
LAND DEVELOPMENT
BOULOGNE
LE TOUQUET
MONTREUIL
BERCK-PLAGE
HESDIN
LE CROTOY
ST VALERY
ABBEVILLE
DIEPPE
• WE HAVE OUR OWN OFFICES IN FRANCE
• WE HAVE ENGLISH STAFF IN FRANCE
• WE CAN ARRANGE MORTGAGES, BUILDERS AND INTERIOR DESIGN
• WE QUOTE PRICES INCLUSIVE OF ALL LEGAL FEES AND TAXES

the Channel, Bay of Biscay and Mediterranean, so the climate varies from one region to another. In the south it is temperate, with warm summers and generally mild winters, but in the north there is not much difference from London.

Average daily temperatures (°C)

	Britanny	*Normandy*	*Provence*	*Côte d'Azur*
January	9.3	7.6	12.1	12.2
February	8.6	6.4	11.9	11.9
March	11.1	8.4	14.3	14.3
April	17.1	13.0	18.5	18.5
May	16.0	14.0	20.8	20.8
June	22.7	20.0	26.6	26.6
July	25.1	21.6	28.1	28.1
August	24.1	22.0	28.4	28.4
September	21.1	18.2	25.2	25.2
October	16.5	14.5	22.2	22.2
November	12.1	10.8	16.8	16.8
December	9.3	7.9	14.1	14.1

Where to live

Aquitaine

The Aquitaine region includes the Dordogne, a district long favoured by British families searching for an old farmhouse or cottage for modernisation. Sadly the selection of properties of this type is now limited but there are always resale properties on the market for those prepared to forgo the fun and the worry of creating a home with modern standards out of a near wreck.

South-west France is well known for the local culinary delights and fine wines. Much of the countryside is dramatic in appearance with its panoramic views, rivers, fine old fortified churches and châteaux plus hillside villages. Bastides (small towns which were built during the Hundred Years' War, surrounded by ramparts), which had a good system of roads for quick reinforcement of areas under attack and an arcaded central square, can also be seen.

The river Dordogne is one of the dominant features of the department with the same name, and the capital is Perigueux on the banks of the river Isle. The large white Byzantine cathedral on a hill, with its five domes, dominates the view and contrasts with the red-brown roofs of the ancient part of the town.

From a commercial point of view the town is the centre of the *foie gras* and truffle industry. Metal and railway engineering pro-

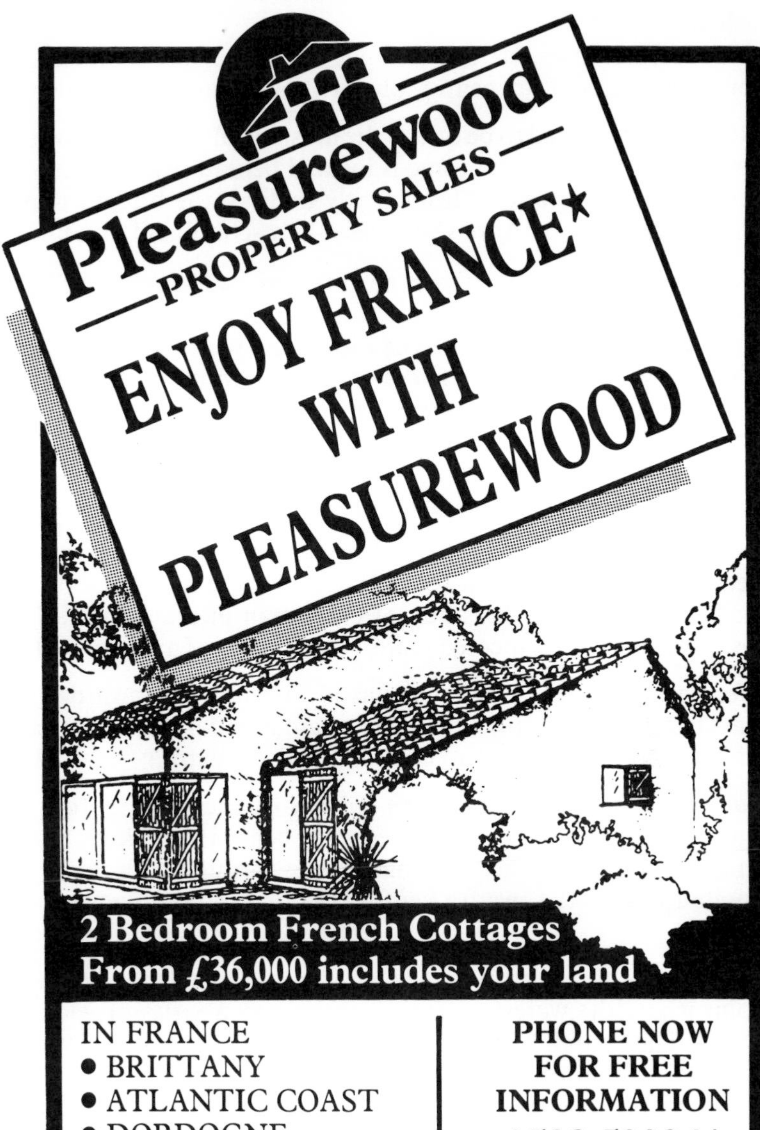
Pleasurewood
PROPERTY SALES
ENJOY FRANCE*
WITH
PLEASUREWOOD
2 Bedroom French Cottages
From £36,000 includes your land

vide employment and a stamp printing works has been established.

The largest town on the Dordogne river is Bergerac, which is an important agriculture centre, also with wine and light industry.

Brantôme. Claimed to be one of the most beautiful small towns in south-west France, Brantôme is located behind two branches of the river Dronne which flows gently under stone bridges past a former Benedictine Abbey now used as a school and museum.

Domme. Originally a hilltop bastide, this well-preserved little town still has one original gateway. The narrow streets climb steeply up past old houses to the top square where there is a variety of ochre stone houses and a church. Beyond the church is a stone balustrade built at the edge of a dramatic descent to the river below. The views from this point are extensive and very impressive. The old Halle in the centre of the square gives access to a series of caves with stalactites.

Les Eyzies-de-Tayac. Described as the 'capital of prehistory' because a century ago in the valley of Vézère discoveries were made which turned the study of early man into a science. The resulting museum is located in the rebuilt ruins of a feudal castle.

Monpazier. A well-preserved bastide begun by Edward I of England in 1284. It still retains the original grid pattern of streets with a fortified church and central arcaded square.

La Roque-Gaseac. Situated on a bend of the river Dordogne with a huge cliff rearing up immediately behind the village. Steep lanes wind upwards between old houses through archways and on an upper level a twelfth-century church looks out across the river.

Trémolat. Another attractive village on the Dordogne river, at a point where the waterway traverses through a series of wide S-bends. The church has four domes and was built in the eleventh and twelfth centuries with military features including arrow-slits and a defensive belfry. Nearby a large loop in the river has created an expanse of calm water where rowing and sailing can be enjoyed and regattas are held in the summer.

Gironde. Most of the rivers of Aquitaine terminate eventually in the Gironde estuary. These include the Garonne which rises high in the Pyrenees, and the Dordogne which joins the Garonne north of Bordeaux. The Aveyron and the Tarn flow through rug-

ged gorges and join together near Montauban to flow into the Garonne near Moissac.

Bordeaux. One of the most important cities of France, Bordeaux is situated on the river Garonne at a point where it is about 400 metres wide. It is the centre for the wine trade and a long-established commercial port.

In the heart of the city a fine open square has a fountain with wide boulevards nearby which are lined with classical terraced houses with balconies overlooking the plane trees along the thoroughfares. Well worth a visit are the neighbouring luxury shops, the pavement cafés and the many excellent restaurants. On the opposite side of the river is the huge industrial zone.

A new suspension bridge has been built high above the river on the northern outskirts of the city to link up with the Paris autoroute, also with the local airport and the Toulouse autoroute. This has improved the accessibility of Bordeaux.

Arcachon. Sixty miles west of Bordeaux this popular Atlantic coast resort has sandy beaches, a marina for 1000 yachts and tamarisk-lined boulevards. The Arcachon basin is one of the most important locations for oyster production in France.

The town has a variety of expensive hotels, apartment blocks where many families from Bordeaux spend weekends, tourist shops, restaurants and oyster bars.

At the western end of the town between sand dunes smart villas have been built amid pine woods.

Within easy reach is Cap Ferrat, another seaside resort which is at the end of a peninsula forming the western side of the Arcachon basin.

Entre-Deux-Mers. A renowned wine producing district in beautiful countryside. The ‘two seas’ are in fact the rivers Dordogne and Garonne. The area is noteworthy for woodland, streams and private châteaux amid gently undulating hills. On sloping fields vines are grown in strips alongside other crops.

Libourne. Another important wine trading town, situated at the confluence of the Isle and Dordogne rivers. It was probably named after Englishman Roger de Leyburn who built the town as a bastide about 1270 on the orders of Edward I. Until the beginning of this century the riverside quays were busy with wine barrels being loaded on to foreign ships. This was superseded by the development of road haulage.

La Kéole. This old stronghold on high ground above the banks of the Garonne has one of the oldest town halls in France (twelfth to fourteenth century). It is an active little agricultural market town with narrow streets of old houses and enjoys good views towards Bayas.

Les Landes. South-west of Bordeaux lies a large triangular area of sand dunes, pine forest and lakes. The dunes, believed to be the highest in Europe, have formed over the centuries as the result of the action of the Atlantic rollers and gales from the west which have driven sand inshore. These formed ever-expanding treeless deserts which began to threaten the wine districts of Bordeaux.

To stabilise the dunes, gorse, broom and pine seedlings were planted early in the nineteenth century. These have prospered and as a result the Landes is one of the richest areas of timber in France occupying nearly all the area between the rivers Adour and Garonne. Part of this area has been designated as a regional park and special trains take tourists for four hours through the forest to an open air museum at Marquèze.

Mont-de-Marsan. Located on the perimeter of the pine forest, Mont-de-Marsan is the capital of the Landes and a centre for local products. These include *foie gras*, jam, poultry, resin distilleries and saw mills.

The rivers Midou and Douze meet in the old quarter of the town and become the river Midouze. The area houses a local form of bullfighting in summer and there is a well-known racecourse.

Lot et Garonne

Agen. Capital of the department, on the right-hand bank of the Garonne in a valley between Toulouse and Bordeaux. It is an important rail and road junction close to an autoroute which leads south to Narbonne on the Mediterranean coast, also north to Poitiers and beyond. A 23-arched aqueduct carries the lateral canal over the river in the north-west of the town.

This is a busy market town with a fertile plateau to the north where a mild climate helps the production of orchard fruit including plums and prunes for which the district is well known.

Nérac. 30 km west of Agen is this interesting little town. The older part has a number of narrow streets on the bank of the river Baise, which is reached by an old Gothic hump-back bridge. At the west end of the 'new' bridge is a Renaissance château formerly the court of Marguerite of Navarre.

Villeneuve-sur-Lot. Located on the N21 road between Agen and Bergerac. About 30 km north of Agen, this municipality straddles the river Lot and operates a thriving market for dried fruit and plums.

Pyrénées-Atlantiques

The Basque country lies to the south of the Landes in an area bounded by the Pyrenees, the river Adour and the Gulf of Gascony. Over 80 per cent of the Basque people live in Spain and the remainder in this corner of France. They exist mainly by mountain farming, also fishing, and are a fiercely independent people keen to preserve their way of life, customs, language and unity.

Bayonne. Bayonne, 6 km from the sea, is the capital of the Basque country. It has a long history from the days of the Romans but in modern times it has become a thriving port following the construction of a breakwater which prevents the channel sanding up, so large ships can navigate the entrance to the port.

Exploration of natural gas and by-products in the foothills of the Pyrenees has ensured improved prosperity to the area which is now also a major exporter of sulphur.

Biarritz. A small fishing port near Bayonne which grew into a fashionable resort in the nineteenth century, frequently patronised by European royalty. There is still evidence of the period in the elegant hotels and restaurants which remain.

Today it is a popular seaside resort patronised particularly by the French, also Spaniards from the Basque country across the border. Facilities include four golf courses, tennis courts, heated indoor swimming pools and excellent beaches, with rocky coves stretching north along the Côte d'Argent and south on the Côte Basque.

Hendaye. The last town on the Basque coast is Hendaye which is a popular seaside resort with sandy beaches and opportunities for various sports. Some streets are named after flowers which grow prolifically among the hotels, villas and camping sites, eg Avenue de Mimosas. A little way inland the Pyrenees begin to rise steeply from the lowland.

Nearby is St Jean de Luz, a thriving fishing port which is also a yachting centre with a casino, hotels and a popular beach.

Pau. Capital of the Pyrénées-Atlantiques department, Pau is an administrative centre well located for visitors to the Pyrenees mountains. Pau was popular with the British during part of the nineteenth century and at one time they formed about 15 per cent of the resident population.

The inland town of Eaux-Bonnes, 40 km south of Pau, is a ski resort and spa in mountain surroundings. The temperate climate and the local waters attract sufferers from rheumatic and respiratory problems.

Another well-known town south-east of Pau is Lourdes, which is visited by 3 million pilgrims every year.

Languedoc-Roussillon

Languedoc-Roussillon is the name for a region of France with a Mediterranean coastline and a border with Spain. It comprises the departments of Aude, Gard, Hérault, Lozère and Pyrénées-Orientales.

The land along the coast between Montpellier and Perpignan is of special interest to foreigners desirous of acquiring a holiday or retirement home in the south-west, because the French government supervised a comprehensive development scheme which created half a dozen new resorts built in modern style with many high-rise buildings adjacent to beaches and plenty of facilities to encourage tourism.

The four important towns of Perpignan, Narbonne, Montpellier and Nimes are all inland and have histories dating back over many centuries. They have large populations (Montpellier has 200,000 inhabitants) and excellent residential amenities.

From Perpignan the new towns comprise:

St Cyprien. Golfers enjoy St Cyprien which is a few kilometres south-east of Perpignan. Two courses totalling 27 holes are available and have views of the Pyrenees. Other sports are also available.

Port Bacarès. The yacht harbour provides berths for 200 yachts. The Centre Méditerrané du Nautisme has a skin diving and sailing school and marina club and there are opportunities for water-skiing. Nightclubs and restaurants are in abundance; tennis and riding establishments are also available.

Port Leucate. Situated on a piece of land about 1 km wide between Perpignan and Narbonne which separates a lagoon from the sea, the harbour has about 500 quayside berths for yachts and a sailing club and watersports school are available.

Sète and Cap d'Agde. Sète is the second largest port in France on the Mediterranean coast and is located on the seaward part of the biggest lagoon in the Languedoc-Roussillon. It is the premier fishing harbour in this region and also handles the importation of much Algerian wine.

At the base of a former volcano and Mont St Martin, a marine resort was commenced in 1969, known as Cap d'Agde. Pedestrianised streets and squares are a feature and on the outskirts is a naturist holiday village.

La Grande Motte. Situated about 20 km from Montpellier, La Grande Motte is a resort where the architecture is ultra modern. Multi-storey blocks of flats in pyramid form dominate the landscape to the regret of many and the joy of some. Plenty of holiday villages, hotels and camping sites provide accommodation for around 15,000 vacationists and the marina can berth about 1000 craft. A casino, many shops and restaurants plus beaches 3 km long are among other popular facilities. Port Camargue is another pleasure port and resort.

Provence

Provence is the most easterly department of France with a long coastline on the Mediterranean, a border with Italy and a mountainous region to the north.

For over two centuries intrepid British and other foreign travellers found their way to the exotic coast which we call the French Riviera and settled in the vicinity of Nice and Cannes. They built palace-like villas in the old days but today's settlers are much more likely to live in a tall modern block of flats.

Some of the towns most popular with the British are:

Nice. Recognised as the capital of the Riviera, Nice is the fifth largest town in France. It is very accessible to all parts of Europe via the international airport on the perimeter of the town. The

shingle beach disappoints some visitors but other attributes more than make up for this hardship.

The spectacular Promenade des Anglais, which stretches along a vast part of the sea front, indicates the popularity of the resort with the British. Shopping opportunities are prolific and annual events which attract large crowds include the two-week carnival before Lent, the battle of the flowers in the summer, and festivals for ballet, dogs and books. Colourful public gardens are abundant.

The port accommodates fishing boats, yachts and commercial shipping.

Antibes. The old town has narrow streets full of interest, but the new resort with many beaches and a large port with yachting facilities has an air of spaciousness and calm. A varied range of homes in both price and location is generally available.

Cannes. Claimed to be the most fashionable resort on the Riviera, modern Cannes has a coastline of more than 6 km where there are several large yacht harbours and marinas. Also blocks of apartments and hotels along the Boulevard de la Croisette, two casinos and sandy beaches which are crowded with sunseekers during the peak season, between June and September. Golf, yachting and tennis were introduced to the town by the British.

Property prices are high in the centre of Cannes where an overabundance of apartment blocks, often of nondescript design, has been built. Better value can be found in some of the nearby smaller resorts.

St Raphaël. St Raphaël, south-west of Cannes, has an Anglican church and a golf course, which was the result of British enterprise, dating back to the early part of this century. As a sedate watering place it still retains some interest with older generations of the British.

St Tropez. The neighbouring town of St Tropez was probably put on the map by de Maupassant and a group of post-impressionist painters, including Matisse, at the end of the nineteenth century.

Although quiet in winter, St Tropez is now a town full of action in the summer with plenty of visitors using the two large yacht harbours, enjoying the beaches, shops, restaurants and getting involved in fêtes, musical events and folklore festivals. This is another district where homes are expensive.

Monaco. Although an independent principality, Monaco is very much part of the Riviera. It covers less than 2 sq km in area yet has a population of around 25,000 people including foreign residents.

The Monégasques do not pay any taxes and are not liable for military service. Large numbers of visitors flock to Monte Carlo to enjoy the varied events, sightsee and visit the Casino, which is probably the best in the world. The annual Monte Carlo Rally brings considerable publicity to the commune. In addition the opera, music festival, Musée Océanographique, Botanical Garden and Zoo all provide items of interest to visitors.

Property prices on average are higher than in almost any part of France including Paris.

Inland from the Côte d'Azur. Interesting developments are now frequently available a few miles inland from the most popular resorts and prices tend to be lower, with the exception of the area around Grasse, centre of the perfume industry, where high prices can be paid for living accommodation of good quality.

Federal Republic of Germany

General information

Status. Federal Republic
Capital. Bonn
Area. 248,574 sq km (95,975 sq miles)
Population. 62 million (approx)

Location

Longitude 47°N to 54°N; latitude 6°E to 13°E. The Federal Republic of Germany is, in terms of population, size, geography and influence, the dominant country of central northern Europe. Although the climate is generally the same throughout most of the country (Continental influenced by the Atlantic), there are many contrasting environments ranging from the Alpine south, the flat plains of the north and the river basins of the west. The vegetation also varies considerably, ranging from the Alpine mosses and the thick forests to the agricultural lands. The country is highly urbanised, especially in the Rhineland and the Baltic coast. One of the stranger aspects of West Germany's geography is the peculiar position of West Berlin, totally surrounded by another country (the German Democratic Republic).

Political stability

Conflict and instability have, until the post-war era, been constantly present in German history. Germany, of course, featured prominently in both world wars and has consequently earned a certain notoriety. Indeed, the running sore of German nationalism could easily have initiated further instability following the Second World War, but for partition.

Therefore, it is indeed remarkable that the Federal Republic has enjoyed a stable, moderate and successful government, leading the way in European unity (through the European Community) and, more than most, wanting peaceful diplomatic co-existence with the Communist bloc.

Economy

Cost of living. Generally speaking, the German economy is an example to the capitalist west. Living standards, wages and consumption are at very high levels when compared with elsewhere (including the UK). Inflation is nominal and unemployment is comparatively low. Goods and services are readily available and of high quality, and although prices are far higher than in the UK, this is compensated for by local wage levels.

Taxation. Direct income tax levels are lower in West Germany than in Britain. A single person's tax-free allowance is currently DM5616 per annum and a married couple's allowance is DM11,232 (provided only one has an income). Earnings above these thresholds are taxed at 19 per cent up to DM18,000 (single), or DM36,000 (married), rising progressively to the highest rate of 53 per cent. National insurance schemes covering pensions, unemployment and health are also payable by both the employer and the employee. A church tax is paid by members of the Roman Catholic and Lutheran Protestant churches of 7-9 per cent of their income tax. No capital gains tax for non-speculative transactions is payable and a property tax amounts to just 0.5 per cent.

Exchange rate. Deutschmark (DM) 3.18 = £1.

Exchange control. There are no exchange controls in operation.

Language

German. Knowledge of English is widespread.

Expatriate community

Few people move to Germany to retire. Many more, however, move as a result of the thriving economy or because they were stationed there as part of the army presence.

Residence permits

For those people residing in Germany for more than three months it is necessary to acquire a residence permit. This is obtained by British citizens from the Aliens Office of the local council. Non-EC nationals need a visa before entering Germany.

Work permits

No work permit is required by British citizens.

Personal effects

They may be imported free of duty so long as the owner has been in possession of large items for more than six months.

Housing

The cost of housing in West Germany is often so high that renting is common. These high prices are a huge disincentive for people to move there, but if one can afford to, the best buys are often older houses in need of a little attention. These may prove especially attractive if they are situated in an aesthetically pleasant area. Furnished accommodation is in very short supply and is the most costly. A deposit of two months' rent is usually charged to cover the cost of dilapidations at the end of the lease. Rarely is low-priced public housing available to foreigners. Nevertheless houses are, of course, an excellent investment.

Buying property

Foreign nationals can purchase real estate without any restrictions. All contracts to purchase must be certified by the notary public. The title only passes to the purchaser on registration in the land register, which is maintained by the district court. Fees of 1-1.5 per cent are paid for conveyance and certification of the land sale. A tax of 7 per cent on conveyance may be added. Generally, estate agents are paid a fee of 3 per cent of the purchase price plus VAT by both parties to the transaction.

Where to live

For people who wish to retire to Germany, the most quiet and tranquil region is the south, as a healthy and restful life-style may be achieved in both the Alps and the Black Forest.

Inspection flights

Foreign nationals acquire property on the free German market and so no flights for inspection are available.

Communications

As you would expect, Europe's most successful industrial power is very well served by its infrastructure. Communications are excellent whether by road, rail, water, air, telephone or telex.

Recreation

Such a large and interesting country as Germany is obviously full of opportunities for leisure activities.

The Germans are especially keen on sport, particularly football, athletics and motor racing. Facilities like swimming pools and tennis courts are excellent.

Hiking is a very popular pastime and this complements the fine German countryside and the passion for camping. There are currently over 2000 camp sites. Sailing is also growing in popularity on the North and Baltic Seas.

Eating out is enjoyed by many Germans, especially as every region specialises in a different type of food, wine or beer.

Driving

There is no requirement to take a German driving test so long as you have been in possession of a full British licence for more than one year. It is also possible to drive a British registered car for one year before it has to be registered with the German authorities.

Third party insurance is obligatory and more expensive than the UK. Vehicle tax will be levied, the level depending on the size of the car's engine.

It is important to note that lead-free petrol, which is unsuited to British engines that have not been modified, is readily available where it says *'Bleifrei'*.

Speed limits are marginally higher in Germany, and on the autobahns the upper limit of 130 kmh is only 'advised'.

Health services

All foreign nationals employed in Germany are subject to the same health insurance scheme as German nationals. Contribution rates on taxable income are 10-14 per cent for health, 18 per cent for pensions and 3 per cent for unemployment benefit. Details of European Community rights are given in DSS pamphlet SA29.

Climate

Germany lies on the western edge of the European-Asiatic continent. The climate is mainly maritime in nature, but occasionally

Continental climatic conditions impose intense hot or cold periods. Mostly, the climate is comparable with that of the UK.

Average monthly temperatures (°C)

	Berlin	*Frankfurt*	*Hamburg*	*Munich*
January	– 1.3	0.7	0.3	–0.6
February	0.1	2.2	1.0	0.2
March	3.4	5.3	3.5	3.8
April	7.9	9.3	7.5	7.8
May	13.2	14.3	12.3	12.9
June	16.2	17.3	15.4	15.9
July	18.0	18.7	17.1	17.8
August	16.7	17.7	16.3	17.0
September	13.5	14.4	13.6	13.5
October	8.4	9.4	8.8	8.3
November	3.5	4.7	4.3	3.1
December	0.7	1.9	1.6	0.0

Gibraltar

General information

Status. British Crown Colony
Capital. Gibraltar
Area. 5.5 sq km (2 sq miles)
Population. 29,000 (approx)

Location

Longitude 36°N; latitude 5°W. The British colony of Gibraltar lies on the southern tip of Spain where the Mediterranean Sea and the Atlantic Ocean meet. It is dominated by a 430 m-high block of limestone and is itself an isthmus.

The population density is the second largest in Europe.

Political stability

After enduring 15 years of isolation when the border with Spain was closed, Gibraltar remains steadfast in its British connections and desires to remain part of the Commonwealth.

Economy

Currency. Gibraltar pound, but UK coinage is legal tender.

Cost of living. The rocky terrain is not suitable for food production and there is little scope for primary production, so the inhabitants rely heavily on the port for their prosperity. Resourceful

local entrepreneurs trade in the world markets and import goods from the most competitive sources, so prices are quite reasonable. Now that the border with Spain is open again, cheap agricultural goods can be imported, again keeping down living costs. Cigarettes (at £5.30 for 200 at time of writing) and drink (£4.50 for a bottle of whisky) are also cheap.

Taxation. There are no death duties, surtax, capital gains tax or VAT in Gibraltar. Exempt companies can be registered for a fee of £225 and do not have to pay local taxes, regardless of profit, for a guaranteed 25-year period.

Exchange rate. G£1 = £1.

Exchange control. There are no exchange controls.

Language

English is the official language; Spanish is widely spoken.

Expatriate community

There is a modest expatriate community, many of whom are devoted to yachting, naval and marine pastimes.

Security

The 4 km-long isthmus which has only one point of exit apart from the sea, means that Gibraltar is safe from many undesirables.

Residence permits

European Community nationals can remain on Gibraltar with a provisional permit for six months to find work or establish a business. On achieving this, they are granted a residential permit.

Work permits

These are not necessary as you enter on a provisional permit on condition that you get work within six months.

Personal effects

No duty is payable on personal effects.

Housing

Over the past three years more than £12 million have been invested in speculative real estate developments and this should produce about 200 housing units, 20,000 sq ft of shopping and 50,000 sq ft of office space.

Cornwall's Parade off Main Street is one of the most ambitious schemes with commercial and retail premises grouped around a central piazza, plus top-class apartments with car parking.

About 90 per cent of residential property is purchased by Gibraltarians so there is not much choice available for other nationalities.

Buying property

Gibraltar law closely follows its British counterpart and so therefore does the procedure for acquiring property.

Where to live

As property on the market is very scarce, and the Rock is so small, it is difficult to give guidance on where to live.

Inspection flights

Very rare.

Communications

GB Airways is the flag carrier; also Air Europe and British Airways between them have daily scheduled flights from Gatwick and Heathrow (2½ hours). Charter flights are offered by various operators including Britannia and GB. The journey time is about 2 hours and the cheapest scheduled return fare £149.

A regular flight by GB Airways to the city of Tangier just across the Straits provides a popular excursion in just 20 minutes. The same destination can be reached by the Bland ferry in about 2½ hours, and in 1 hour by jet catamaran.

International direct dialling and telex make worldwide communications simple.

Recreation

Existing amenities include three beaches, two cinemas, a casino, crazy golf and scenic tours. Sights include the caves, the apes on Upper Rock, Moorish Castle, Trafalgar Cemetery and Europa Point lighthouse.

For other hobbies, a trip over the border into Spain is necessary where extensive golfing, tennis and hiking opportunities exist as well as numerous social activities.

Gibraltar Broadcasting Station operates its own radio and TV services which can also be heard or viewed along some parts of the Spanish Costa del Sol. Reception of BBC World Service is good.

Health services

A reciprocal health service agreement between the UK and Gibraltar covers emergency medical treatment required in Gibraltar. EC nationals can receive free medical treatment on production of form 111.

Climate

	Monthly rainfall (mm)	*Average daily temperature (°C)*	*Average daily sunshine hours*
January	15.4	13.6	6.05
February	64.9	13.7	6.69
March	108.7	13.8	5.35
April	12.6	16.9	5.89
May	79.8	17.1	8.98
June	6.7	20.1	9.78
July	—	24.1	10.46
August	1.7	24.3	9.25
September	0.2	23.5	9.16
October	14.7	18.9	7.12
November	15.2	16.4	4.45
December	14.4	14.5	3.94

Greece

General information

Status. Republic
Capital. Athens
Area. 131,990 sq km (51,245 sq miles)
Population. 9.7 million (approx)

Location

Longitude 31°N to 41°N; latitude 36°W to 39°W. Greece occupies the southern part of the Balkan peninsula and also has many attractive islands both large and small. The principal one is Crete, while Rhodes is also very well known. Four-fifths of the mainland is mountainous and there are at least 20 mountains over 2000 m with a permanent snow line. Another striking characteristic is the huge areas of woodland in Greece, with the 89 million hectares covering almost two-thirds of the country. Also, no part of Greece is more than 100 km away from the coast. Athens has many historic associations and is visited by millions of international tourists every year.

Political stability

As with a number of Mediterranean countries, steady democracy

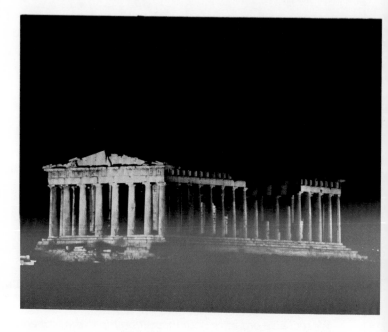

has only recently triumphed over its oppressors. In Greece's case, the military junta that was running the country in an excessively brutal fashion collapsed in 1974 in a bloodless coup and was replaced by a democratic government led by Karamanlis. The current Socialist government is under pressure as a result of financial scandals. Greece is a full member of the European Community.

Economy

Cost of living. At the moment, the Greek government is trying to deal with the uncomfortably high level of inflation (about 16 per cent) and rising unemployment. Greece faces a major problem in that she is becoming increasingly reliant on the tourist trade for her prosperity, while other sectors of the economy are in dire straits. It is noticeable that living standards in Greece are appreciably lower than in most other EC nations. This being the case, it is less than surprising that essentials such as food, especially from the markets, are very good value for money. This, however, is not the case with luxury items.

Taxation. Personal taxation is calculated on the worldwide income of residents. A personal allowance and a wife's allowance is granted to retirees and income tax rises from 12 to 50 per cent. When tax payers submit returns showing their income, they must also submit their expenditure for the previous year, and if the authorities believe the life-style is too high for a person on that level of declared income, the tax demand will be set at a more suitable level, unless the person can prove that the expenditure emanated from funds already taxed. VAT is levied at 16 per cent with a reduced rate of 6 per cent.

Exchange rate. Drachmas 265.43 = £1.

Exchange control. In operation.

Language

A basic understanding of the fundamentals of Greek is advisable as knowledge of English is not especially widespread.

Expatriate community

Greece has become steadily more popular during the last few years. Many people have chosen to retire there and also over 3000 people are in employment.

Security

Activities involving Middle East terrorists at Athens international airport emphasise Greece's proximity to one of the world's troubled areas, and security is very tight. Internally, it is prudent to take standard precautions against theft and burglary by installing security equipment.

Residence permits

British subjects can stay in Greece for up to three months without any formalities, thereafter a temporary residence permit is granted for one year, which is generally renewable annually, provided the applicant can produce evidence of having a permanent address in Greece and an adequate income emanating from outside the country.

Work permits

Under the European Community, work permits are no longer required.

Personal effects

No duties are payable as long as a certificate has been acquired from the Greek Embassy. Arrangements are also possible for temporary stays in Greece, when exportation of effects is certified by production of a passport with clearance to do so.

Housing

Although there has been quite a lot of interest in the purchase of homes in Greece during the past two decades, there has been a dearth of specialist agencies able to offer a service to prospective purchasers. This situation has improved recently and there are at least three well-established firms with departments handling homes on the mainland and the islands.

A mistaken impression that foreigners were not allowed to own property in Greece became established, following the Greek government's restrictions for security reasons on the purchase of residential property in designated border areas and islands (including Crete and Corfu) close to the borders with Turkey. However, it should be made clear that in most parts of the country non-Greeks may buy and sell freehold property.

New methods of protecting foreign clients' interests are now available to those who purchase homes through the Cassimatis Organisation of Athens (UK agents Whiteway Properties of

Knaresborough, Yorkshire). This long-established firm, with substantial experience in shipping and tourism, has made arrangements with a large Swiss-based company who are represented in 140 countries, including Greece, to undertake legal examination and certification of property titles and report on the state of a new property on completion. This should overcome many of the title problems which arose in the past.

Buying property

The purchaser and the vendor sign a contract of sale before a Greek notary public to transfer the titles of ownership of land and property in Greece. The sale contract can be drafted through the Consulate General of Greece in London.

Foreigners have the same civil rights as Greeks and may, in principle, buy or sell real estate on a freehold basis provided the property is not located in border areas or on certain of the islands. Border areas are designated as follows: Florina, Kilkis, Drama,

Rodopi, Evros, Thesprotia, Xanthi, Kastoria, Ionnina, Preveza, Pella, Serrae, Samos, Chios, Lesvos, Thessaloniki, Kozani, Kavala, the Dodecanese, Imathia, Pieria and Grevena. The islands popular with foreigners are: Crete, Cephalonia, Anafi, Lemnos, Corfu, Skyros and Ios (and the surrounding small islands).

For further information about procedures for property purchase in Greece, the National Tourist Organisation of Greece suggests that interested parties should contact a Greek solicitor.

Inspection flights

No flights especially for inspecting property exist.

Communications

British Airways and Olympic Airways have scheduled flights from Gatwick, Heathrow and provincial airports to Athens and other destinations in Greece. The normal return fare is around £560 but reduced Superpex fares are available at £196 on weekdays and £206 at weekends. Charter flights are also available to many destinations, particularly in summer.

Despite the fact that Greece is perhaps a little isolated from western Europe, road and rail links via Yugoslavia are surprisingly good.

Recreation

The legacy of the past 5000 years of Greek civilisation is probably one of the greatest attractions in Greece today. Unique examples of architecture and sculpture exist in abundance, with perhaps the most impressive relic being the Parthenon which stands, together with other masterpieces, on the rock of the Acropolis in Athens, and receives about 1.5 million visitors per year. Greek culture extends into theatre, dancing and festivals.

Greek cuisine is generally very good but limited, and eating out is both popular and cheap.

Modern leisure facilities such as swimming pools and tennis courts are quite plentiful, especially in the popular resorts. Also, because of the number of islands and the large amount of coastline, water-based pursuits such as sailing, waterskiing and windsurfing are popular.

Many of Greece's recreational facilities are very much orientated to the tourists, but because of the pleasant climate all year round, the tourist trade is not as seasonal as in some countries and so the facilities are maintained at the highest level throughout the year.

Health services

With over 550 hospitals and more than 29,000 doctors, the state-run Greek health service is adequate. However, as there are often long waiting lists for treatment, private medical insurance is advisable.

Climate

The term generally associated with the Greek weather is that of an 'olive climate'. The fundamental characteristic of it is the smooth transition from one season to the next. A short spring with moderate temperatures, followed by a long, hot summer, and then by a pleasant autumn with average temperatures above those in spring, lead finally to a mild and sunny winter. There are about 3000 hours of sunshine each year, rain in summer is an unknown phenomenon and the cooling north-west winds blow. Rainfall varies throughout the country, from about 1500 mm to less than a third of that in the south.

Republic of Ireland

General information

Status. Republic
Capital. Dublin
Area. 70,282 sq km (27,165 sq miles)
Population. 3,480,000

Location

Longitude 52°N to 55°N; latitude 5°W to 10°W. On the extreme west of the European sub-continent, jutting out into the north Atlantic lies an island of comparatively little urbanisation or modern agricultural land. Instead, large areas are still in their most natural state, whether it be bleak moor or rocky coastline. In some areas, only the traditional crofters make use of the unspoilt land. The Irish Republic is dominated on the eastern side by the capital city, Dublin, which is about the closest point to mainland Britain and hence one of the main trade and communication arteries. The west, however, is far more the property of nature, that is, either the influence of the Atlantic Ocean or the river Shannon.

Political stability

Ireland has for many years been a source of great instability, not only on the Irish mainland but in Britain too. The issue of sovereignty of Northern Ireland is still unresolved, and the extreme elements on both sides of the sectarian divide still pose major problems. However, the violence is largely confined to the North, and the Republic is free of most of the direct effects of the 'troubles'. Politically, recent governments have been weak and often without a working majority, and it is this that has provided the greatest internal instability for the Republic. External links with the UK have improved considerably and this can only benefit internal stability.

Economy

Cost of living. The Irish economy has never been very strong and has been hit by economic recession. Backward methods and a general lack of resources are inherent problems for the government. With VAT at 23 per cent and petrol at £2.60 per gallon, the cost of living is high.

Taxation. There is a double taxation agreement between the UK and the Republic of Ireland. Income tax is charged currently at 0 per cent on the first £3050, 37 per cent on the next £5700, 48 per cent on the next £2900 and 58 per cent on the rest.

Exchange rate. Punts (£IR) 1.19 = £1.

Exchange controls. There are no restrictions on importing money into Ireland, but care should be taken to record transactions involving imported funds with the Central Bank of Ireland in Dublin, so that permission to export the proceeds of any sale may be granted.

Language

Everybody speaks the Irish version of English with Gaelic as a second tongue for many. Knowledge of Gaelic is essential for all top government employees, and is a qualification for many posts.

Expatriate community

Partly because of traditional links with the UK and partly because of geographical proximity, there are a large number of Britons in Ireland.

Security

Ireland does have a problem with house-breakers and petty thieves, so it is worth while installing burglar alarms (preferably those linked to the Garda (police station) or a security company). Away from border areas, the 'troubles' have few practical repercussions.

Residence permits

There are no restrictions for those who are citizens of European Community countries over entering Ireland. Similarly, any person who can prove that at least one parent or grandparent was born in Ireland can enter without restriction.

Work permits

EC citizens do not require a work permit to take up employment in Ireland. Citizens of other countries require a permit from the Irish Ministry of Labour.

Personal effects

These can be imported duty free by persons wanting to set up permanent residence if the items have been owned for over six months. Normally, importation should be within six months of arrival.

Housing

The property market in Ireland has been depressed and so a wide variety of properties is available, ranging from tiny farm cottages in need of renovation to large mansions and castles. Prices vary according to location and quality. Rural cottages in County Kerry can be bought for around £IR13,000, new two-bedroom detached bungalows in County Cork for about £IR21,500, while a five-bedroom mansion with 250 acres of good land has been offered at £IR650,000. A substantial number of estate agents and surveyors exist, including the Irish Auctioneers and Valuers Association. Also, the magazine *Property Ireland* produces a list of interesting property.

Buying property

The procedure for buying property in Ireland is no different from that in Britain. Stamp duty starts at 3 per cent for properties costing between £IR10,000 and £IR20,000 and reaches double this for sales over £IR50,000. Some houses are exempt from stamp duty subject to obtaining a Certificate of Reasonable Value from the developer. Deposits of 10 per cent are normally demanded by the vendors or their estate agents. Solicitors charge about 1 per cent plus £IR100 plus VAT at 23 per cent on the total fees. Other outlays include registration charges at between £IR25 and £IR200 and also search fees of about £IR25. For a principal private residence where sale price reflects the current use value, exemption is granted from capital gains tax. The tax, where these conditions do not apply, is on the excess of the sale price over prime cost plus expenditure on certain improvements, the cost of selling and inflation adjustments in certain cases.

Where to live

The most appealing areas are probably the quiet rural areas in the west of Ireland in County Kerry, County Cork and County Clare. They offer a quiet and tranquil life-style.

Communications

Air. Aer Lingus, British Airways and charter companies provide frequent flights to Dublin and Shannon throughout the year, with a journey time to Dublin of about 65 minutes.

Sea. Services from Britain are available on luxury car ferries from Liverpool, Holyhead, Swansea, Pembroke and Fishguard.

Recreation

The greatest facet of the Irish Republic is undoubtedly the countryside and this therefore provides the richest source of pleasure through recreational pursuits such as walking, climbing, camping and orienteering. The river Shannon also provides water-based activities such as boating and canoeing. Other sports facilities are available in the main centres like Dublin and Cork such as swimming pools and tennis courts. Golf courses are also fairly abundant. The most popular sports in Ireland are rugby, Gaelic football and hurling.

The Gaelic culture and many of the old traditional crafts, songs and dances provide a great source of pleasure.

Health services

Medical standards in Ireland are high and, subject to income limits, free medical care can be obtained in general wards of public hospitals and from certain general practitioners. Interfund agreements exist between Irish medical insurance companies and

BUPA, PPP and WPA in the UK. British retirement pensions can also be paid in Ireland. Details can be obtained from the DSS.

Climate

Changeable weather is a major feature of the climate; rain falls almost every month, with the western part of the country being the wettest. Also, humidity is quite high. The months of May and June have the most sunshine, while July and August are the warmest periods. January and February are the coldest months with an average temperature of between 4° and 7°C.

Israel

General information

Status. Republic
Capital. Jerusalem
Area. 27,817 sq km (10,840 sq miles)
Population. 4,455,000

Location

Longitude 30°N to 33°N; latitude 35°E. Israel, the land of the Bible and historic homeland of the Jewish people, is situated in the Middle East, along the eastern coastline of the Mediterranean. The geographical diversity of Israel is quite remarkable for such a small country, as it has mountains and plains, fertile fields and barren deserts, sea coast and rocky uplands. In Galilee in the north, forested highlands merge with green valleys. Sand dunes and citrus groves mark the coastal plain bordering the Mediterranean. Deserts stretching southwards through Negev and Arava meet the tropical waters of the Gulf of Eilat on the Red Sea.

Political stability

Israel's short history has certainly been a stormy one. The Jewish homeland, created after the Second World War, has been the subject of conflict in the Middle East. The main current problem is the Palestinian crisis. The Palestinian people, aggrieved at losing their own country to accommodate the Jewish state, have turned to terrorism, and this, combined with the long-standing feud with the Arabs, has created a potentially explosive situation.

This explains the Israeli government's 'vigorous' foreign policy, huge defence expenditure and attempted assimilation of the Palestinian people still within Israel.

The coalition government cannot rely on majority support, due mainly to the consequences of a proportional representation system that allows undue weight and influence to political extremists and religious zealots. This being the case, it means governments progress slowly and carefully, sometimes having to fudge important yet unpopular policies.

Economy

Cost of living. Israel lacks the natural resources necessary to back up its rapid economic growth. Infrastructural growth, welfare services and massive defence expenditure have put a huge strain on the economy. Since 1987 inflation has been approximately 16 per cent, mainly as a result of the Economic Recovery Plan introduced in 1984. Economic stability is much improved and there has been an improvement in Israel's foreign reserves. Immigrants can expect to have a high standard of living, mainly because of the strength of their home currencies. Israeli produce is of the highest standard and is reasonably priced. Petrol costs much the same as in the UK.

Taxation. Special compensations for new immigrants do exist in terms of tax regulations. All savings are tax free for the first 20 years of residence. VAT is charged on all goods and services (except in duty-free Eilat).

Exchange rate. Shekels 2.91 = £1.

Exchange control. It is possible to bring into Israel an unlimited amount of foreign currency, travellers' cheques and Israeli shekels. There are restrictions on what can be taken out, and a tax is payable on departure.

Language

The official languages are Hebrew and Arabic. English is widely spoken.

Expatriate community

Since the creation of Israel in 1948, immigration (especially by Jews) has been extensive. Eastern European, North American, Asian and African migrants have all flocked to the country.

There has also been considerable migration from Britain with almost 20,000 British Jews having made the journey. Clearly then, Israel's society is very cosmopolitan.

Security

Fears for Israel's future, prompted by her encirclement by potentially unfriendly nations, and Palestinian terrorism, have made security a primary issue for the government. The result is that the country has one of the best equipped and most rigorously trained armies in the world. Potential adversaries realise that Israel is willing to meet force with more force.

Residence permits

All applications must be made to the Ministry of the Interior. An initial tourist visa of three months may be extended by the Ministry, on consideration of the application.

Work permits

It is necessary for the potential employer to make an application for a work permit on your behalf to the Ministry of the Interior.

Personal effects

No duties are payable on household goods.

Housing

Housing in Israel varies from the Arab-style villas of simple design and the red-tile-roofed houses of the early settlers, to ultra-modern seaside cottages built to exacting architectural specifications. Most Israelis, however, live in apartment blocks, ranging from one-room studios to ones with four bedrooms. Many of these flats are in fact rented, as this is cheap compared with buying property. A three-bedroom apartment for rent costs about $200 per month.

Where to live

This is very much a personal choice. Some choose big cities, others the quieter country villages. Some move to the coast whereas others prefer it inland. Some choose to live a sophisticated modern life, while others want to live on a kibbutz.

Inspection flights

None.

Communications

Air. Eighteen international airlines operate flights to Israel's Ben-Gurion international airport, which is 18 km from Tel Aviv and 50 km from Jerusalem. International charter flights also operate, as well as many internal services.

Sea. Shipping lines offer regular sailings from Europe and arrive at Haifa port.

Road. Over 1500 km of new roads have been built during the past decade and previously existing roads have also been improved.

Telecommunications. Israel is fully integrated into international communications systems by means of underwater cables and communications satellites.

Recreation

Being a warm Mediterranean nation, all kinds of outdoor activities are popular. Facilities provided by the municipalities such as swimming pools and tennis courts are generally good, as are the ones in the tourist coastal regions. Spectator sports such as football and especially basketball are popular too.

Israeli cuisine is regarded as very good, although non-kosher food is a little harder to get. Therefore, those with a taste for pork, shellfish or dairy produce with meat meals will have to search for a private restaurant to cater for them (not hotels or large restaurants which sell only kosher food).

Israel is, of course, the Holy Land, and so is scattered with monuments and architecture celebrating that fact. Museums, theatre and cinema are also popular.

Driving

It is possible to drive in Israel on a valid UK licence. International traffic signs are used and also the sign posts are in English.

Insurance is quite expensive, with compulsory third party cover costing about £100 and fully comprehensive over £500. The maximum no claims bonus is only 30 per cent, which possibly reflects the quality of Israeli driving.

Seat belts are compulsory in the front seats.

Health services

The Ministry of Health is responsible for all health services in Israel. It prepares health legislation and oversees its implementation, controls medical standards and supervises the planning and construction of hospitals. In total, there are some 145 hospitals in Israel. The cost of medical treatment is quite high though, so health insurance is available.

A social security agreement does exist between the UK and Israel. Details are given in DSS pamphlet SA14.

Climate

Israel's climate is characterised by hot, dry summers from April through to October and wet winters from November to March. The rainfall, in general, is higher in the north and west of the country than in the south and east.

Average monthly temperatures (°C)

	Tel Aviv	*Haifa*	*Eilat*
January	9.4-18.3	7.6-17.4	9.6-21.3
February	8.7-18.8	8.5-17.8	10.8-22.8
March	10.1-20.3	8.3-21.3	13.4-26.3
April	12.4-22.3	12.6-25.5	17.1-30.7
May	17.3-25.0	14.5-24.6	20.6-34.8
June	19.3-28.3	17.7-27.6	24.1-37.1
July	21.0-30.2	20.0-29.9	25.3-39.9
August	22.1-30.1	21.2-30.0	26.0-39.9
September	20.3-31.4	19.7-29.6	23.7-36.4
October	15.0-28.8	15.0-28.8	20.4-33.3
November	12.2-24.5	12.2-24.5	16.0-28.3
December	8.8-19.0	8.8-19.0	10.6-23.3

Italy

General information

Status. Republic
Capital. Rome
Area. 301,247 sq km (116,303 sq miles)
Population. 56,336,000

Location

Longitude 36°N to 47°N; latitude 6°E to 18°E. Geographically, Italy lies in the temperate and hot temperate zone. The climate is influenced by both the Mediterranean Sea that virtually surrounds it and to a lesser extent the continent to the north. Another feature of Italy is the startling length of its coastline, and there can be little doubt that this, more than anything else, has had the most profound influence on Italy's development. The vegetation varies greatly, depending on the climatic and geological factors. On the one hand, in the north there are considerable areas of woodland and productive land, whereas in the south, scrubland tends to predominate. The main population centres are mostly in the central northern region. A number of islands form part of the country including Sardinia, Elba and the most well known, Sicily.

Political stability

The Italian people are probably not renowned for their stability and inner calmness and, to some extent, this has been mirrored by their political system. The Republic, having fully recovered from the traumas of Fascist dictatorship, now has all the trappings of a parliamentary democracy, with the President as head of state. The one-time grip of the army, church and judiciary has been loosened, leaving sovereignty where it belongs. But for all this,

Italy has been beset by political problems in recent years, caused by the inability of governments to achieve a workable majority. The party and electoral system encourages coalition governments, and their recent failings have helped to initiate a growth in popularity of more extreme elements. Nevertheless, Italy's image today is no longer one of political chaos, and her growing standing in world affairs, due in no small way to membership of the European Community and NATO, is encouraging.

Economy

Cost of living. Italy's post-war industrial development has been quite considerable and has brought prosperity to many people. However, the economy is weakened by the high level of inflation (around 16 per cent) and unemployment at around 12 per cent. Also, Italy is very much a divided nation in terms of wealth and living standards, as the south is far less affluent and successful. Prices in Italy are about the same as in the UK although some goods, especially market produce and local wine, are very cheap. Top-quality goods, such as clothes, china and glassware and fine furniture, are very expensive.

Taxation. The current Italian tax system comprises a series of taxes of a varying nature. Personal income tax (IRPEF) and corporation tax (IRPEG) are levelled directly. Indirect taxes including VAT (IVA) exist on much the same lines as in Britain. The other indirect taxes are stamp duty and registration tax. An international agreement between Italy and the UK has been in existence since 1962 to prevent additional burdens on expatriate residents.

Exchange rate. Lira 2359 = £1.

Exchange control. A maximum of 400,000 lira per person (including children) may be brought into and taken out of Italy. Foreign currency can be imported without limitations, and may be taken out of the country to a value of up to 1 million lira. To export any more, a special declaration from the customs police is needed.

Language

Knowledge of Italian is very useful as English is only spoken in the more popular tourist regions.

Expatriate community

A modest number of British people take up residence in Italy every year but not on the same scale as in Spain or Portugal. Expatriate diplomatic communities exist in Rome and Naples. British business executives are especially active in the northern cities.

Security

Wealthy people have been subjected to kidnapping particularly in some of the larger cities. Also, petty crime and muggings do occur in popular resorts but this is no more a problem in Italy than elsewhere. However, one place where it is perhaps a little harder to guarantee security is Sicily, because of the Mafia.

Residence permits

British citizens, like all other EC nationals, have free entry into Italy. They must obtain a residence permit within three days of arrival, which is valid for five years and automatically renewable. For full-time permanent residence, a certificate of residence is needed, to make the applicant subject to Italian laws and taxes.

Work permits

These are not necessary.

Personal effects

They may be imported free of duty by holders of a certificate of residence.

Housing

Unlike many other Mediterranean countries, there are few developments aimed at attracting foreign nationals, and so it may be necessary to seek a place on the open market. In general, land is not cheap, but bargains are available for houses of varying size, age and quality.

When seeking a house, it is wise to show no undue interest should a property appear that meets your requirements, as keenness is often met by a price increase. It is best to leave it to the selling agent to settle matters later on. It is always advisable to deal with reputable firms. Personal contacts, say in a bar, are less desirable, because if a deal is ever finalised, under Italian law the contact is entitled to a commission as a result of his introduction.

Buying a property

Prior to signing any document for the purchase of a property, it is advisable to make enquiries at the local land registry and municipality to ensure that: the vendor has a registered title to the property and that chain of title is unbroken; there are no mortgages or charges against the property and that planning consents have been obtained and building regulations complied with; municipal taxes are paid up and if the property includes agricultural land, there are no pre-emptive rights of adjoining landowners.

Sometimes, the first legal step is to sign a document of intent which sets out the details of the transaction and generally involves the payment of a holding deposit of around 2 per cent which is refundable if the transaction does not proceed.

Next, a preliminary contract *(compromesso)* is drawn up by a *notorio* (public lawyer). His job is to ensure that the transfer takes place according to law. The *compromesso* is a legally binding commitment to purchase on the terms stated and a deposit of 10 to 30 per cent is payable. This is forfeited if the purchaser does not conclude the deal and if the vendor reneges he has to compensate the prospective purchaser with a sum of twice the deposit paid.

The final act of formal conveyance transfers ownership of the property from the vendor to the purchaser and necessitates the payment of the balance of the purchase price. The document is generally drawn up and witnessed by a *notorio* who then registers it at the land registry after registering it at the stamp duty office for tax assessment.

A certified copy of the conveyance document is evidence of title and contains the names of the two parties in the transaction, description of the property with map references, boundaries, price, method of payment or receipt of payment, details of rights of way and warranties, that the vendor is legal owner, that the property is sold with vacant possession and it is not subject to any charges.

To advise you personally and to guide you through the transaction it is worth while employing your own *avvocato* (lawyer). Remember, all documents you sign will be in Italian, so make sure you know your commitments.

There are a number of costs to be borne during and after the transaction. Stamp duty at 8 per cent of the declared value is payable where a property is purchased from an individual owner and this is reduced to 6 per cent where a resale occurs within five years. Under-declaration of the purchase price is common to reduce the vendor's capital gains tax and the purchaser's transfer costs, but the registration office can revise declared prices and charge additional fees. When a property is purchased from a limited company whose main business is buying and selling property, VAT at 2 per cent is payable. Otherwise, the rate is 15 per cent. Land registry fees are usually around 2 per cent. In addition, there will be payments to your own *avvocato* and interpreter/translation services if required.

Where to live

Tuscany, Umbria, Lazio and Marche in the centre of Italy between Florence and Rome are the most popular locations for British property buyers as prices are still reasonable. The areas near the northern lakes are more expensive because of their proximity to other European countries.

Inspection flights

Some charter flights are available.

Communications

Air. Italy has very good internal and external air services. There are some 26 airports, 15 of which are international and have services from Britain, with the main ones being Rome, Milan, Bologna, Venice, Pisa and Naples. Flying time from London and Manchester is between 2 and 3 hours.

Rail. The Italian State Railway has a network of over 16,000 km of track and every day carries over 1 million people. The railways form an integral part of the commuter services.

Sea. Italy's islands are linked to the mainland by comprehensive ferry services.

Road. An autostrada network, totalling 5910 km, is the country's main artery, but tolls are charged. In general, Italian roads are good and often very spectacular.

Recreation

Italy has a great deal to offer new settlers, with a vivid history and unrivalled classical traditions and superb monuments, yet an up-to-date outlook. Italy was, of course, the birthplace of the Renaissance and it is consequently impossible even to try to list the marvellous examples of art and architecture to be found in many of the great Italian cities such as Florence, Rome and Venice. Suffice to say that anyone who appreciates fine art and beauty will appreciate Italy.

More modern arts are also very much alive and well in the form of cinema and theatre. Equally popular is opera, which is not centralised in the main centres but performed throughout the nation in many small towns.

Sports facilities such as gymnasiums, swimming pools, golf courses and tennis courts exist in abundance. Skiing in the northern Alpine region is popular too. The most favoured spectator sport is undoubtedly football and Italian clubs such as Juventus, Roma and Inter Milan are recognised as having some of the world's best players.

Italians enjoy eating out and plenty of good restaurants are to be found. Every region has its own speciality dish. Several different styles of eating house exist, including a *ristorante* (conventional restaurant), a *trattoria* (family-owned cheaper restaurant), a *rosticceria* (hot food) and *pizzeria* (pizzas).

Driving

It is not necessary to retake your driving test in Italy as a British licence may be converted into an Italian one, which lasts for ten years. It is also possible to drive on British number plates for the first six months, after which the car must be re-registered in Italy. In Italy, road tax is assessed depending on the car's engine size. The general rules of the road are much the same as elsewhere in mainland Europe. The traffic police have a reputation for applying the law to the letter and are inclined to impose on-the-spot fines. Maintenance costs are roughly the same as in Britain.

Health services

Health benefits are not nationally administered in Italy but are directed by a number of semi-public bodies which are state subsidised, but mainly financed by contributory schemes. Generally speaking, all medicines and treatment are free, but there are often long waiting lists.

Full details of social security rights can be obtained from the DSS.

Climate

The geographical aspects, such as the influence of the Alps in the north and the Mediterranean in the south, make for an interesting climatic pattern.

	Rome		*The Alps*		*The Lakes*		*Adriatic Coast*	
	average		*average*		*average*		*average*	
	temp (°C)	*ppt (mm)*	*temp (°C)*	*ppt (mm)*	*temp (°C)*	*ppt (mm)*	*temp (°C)*	*ppt (mm)*
January	7.4	74	– 2.3	51	6.0	74	6.7	11
February	8.0	87	– 1.3	447	7.0	218	9.1	43
March	11.5	79	1.8	82	9.2	91	10.3	35
April	14.4	62	5.2	138	13.3	47	13.5	42
May	18.4	57	9.1	132	16.5	105	17.7	62
June	22.9	39	13.5	128	19.7	88	21.8	66
July	25.7	6	15.8	148	23.7	12	24.3	95
August	25.5	23	15.4	117	24.3	117	23.4	69
September	22.4	66	12.7	115	18.5	35	20.0	43
October	17.7	123	7.6	119	9.8	20	10.5	132
November	13.4	121	2.8	116	8.4	79	9.8	54
December	8.9	93	– 1.6	59	7.3	70	5.7	12

temp = temperature
ppt = precipitation

Malta

General information

Status. Republic
Capital. Valletta
Area. 320 sq km (122 sq miles)
Population. 360,000

Location

Longitude 35°N; latitude 14°E. Malta, and its two sister islands,

Gozo and Comino, is about half the size of the Isle of Wight. It is situated in the middle of the Mediterranean, about 36 km from Sicily and 290 km from the North African coast.

Political stability

A new, more realistic attitude has become apparent under the nationalist premier, Dr Eddie Fenech Adami, who is planning to encourage new residents.

Economy

Cost of living. In general, prices compare favourably with the UK, especially in food and essential services. Inflation is negligible.

Taxation. A flat rate of 15 per cent is levied on all income (less personal allowances) received in or remitted to Malta, whether from foreign or Maltese sources, subject to a minimum amount of LM1000 per annum. A double taxation agreement exists between Britain and Malta. Death duties are charged on estate in Malta only.

Exchange rate. Maltese lira (LM) 0.59 = £1. Sterling sums mentioned below are based on this exchange rate.

Exchange control. Some restrictions.

Language

The national language is Maltese, but English is spoken almost universally.

Expatriate community

Evidence of the century and a half of British rule in Malta is still to be found in many shapes and forms, from red letterboxes to a statue of Queen Victoria. The substantial British community of more than 1000, combined with a further 3000 who own property there, maintain the link with the past.

The links between the UK and Malta are still apparent and this, combined with the friendly and hospitable attitude of the Maltese, makes for a pleasant atmosphere.

Security

Standard precautions against theft and burglary are advisable.

Residence qualifications

For those with higher incomes, there is an optional residency

LIVING IN A DREAM WORLD

In association with the ALCYMAR Co., we are able to offer you building projects for 2 or 3 bedroom villas on plots of land of 500 and 600m². Furthermore, when you purchase a plot in this outstanding community we also offer you the expert guidance and advice of our architects and interior decorator, who will be pleased to discuss the plans, design and furnishings of your future villa.

Our 2 and 3 bedroom villas, of 135m² and 160m² respectively, are built to the highest possible standards. We lay the finest quality tiles on the floors, and we finish our bathroom washbasins in elegant marble. In addition to a refrigerator and stove we install a washing machine, a dishwasher and an extra refrigerator for drinks only. As a finishing touch, we not only landscape the villas' gardens with a few exotic shrubs and some flowering plants, but we will also add a splendid lawn. At last you can enjoy a relaxing evening on your covered terrace, overlooking your own swimming pool in mosaic design and with an underwater lighting system.

OWNERS FLIGHT PROGRAMME
Inspection flights and accommodation arranged.

Esta-Sol
ESTATES IN THE SUN

On the West Coast of the island of Ibiza lies a 100 acre luxury estate; a tranquil and sophisticated haven of splendid sunsets, panoramic views, extensive gardens and a unique architecture — the kind of world that everybody dreams about. But this is no dream. Thanks to the imagination and enterprising spirit of Calo d'en Real, this unique experience in prestigious living could be yours.

Our fully qualified maintenance team is taking great care to conserve the general condition, as well as the beauty, of the estate. And for easy living we provide our property owners with a wide range of amenities: housekeeping services, technical assistance, garden maintenance, and a babysitting service for parents who want to be at ease while enjoying the long Ibiza nights.

Without leaving the estate, villa owners can enjoy refreshing drinks and exquisite dining in our bar-restaurant "Mezcal" and in the pool side restaurant "Estrella" Or enjoy the many amenities of the "village hotel" — the restaurant, sauna, whirlpool, massage, gymnasium and swimming pool to name but a few. We will also look after your garden and villa during your absence, if you wish. And should you not be able to come during the summer months, then we could be helpful in renting your property. So why live in a dream world when you could just as easily be living in a Calo D'en Real-World?

We are leading agents for all Mediterranean islands, including Malta, Majorca and Menorca.

TRAVELCADE

4 QUEENS AVENUE, HASTINGS, EAST SUSSEX TN34 1PA.
TEL: (0424) 443444. TELEX: 957265 SENLAC G

scheme which allows them to pay income tax in Malta at the special flat rate of 15 per cent, less personal allowances. To qualify, an individual is required to have an annual income of about £17,300 anywhere in the world plus £1730 per dependant. Of this, at least £12,110 must be remitted to Malta per couple.

Alternatively, an individual is required to have access to proven capital of £259,500 worldwide. This does not have to be brought into Malta and can be part of the value of the applicant's property in the island.

Holders of permanent residence permits are allowed to repatriate any unspent income above the minimum requirements; also the proceeds of the sale of their property or any other investments in Malta.

Property purchased must cost in excess of approximately £34,500 for a flat or £52,000 for a house or villa.

Expatriates are not allowed to be employed or to engage in business without the authority of the Maltese government. Tourists and non-residents with entry visas do not require permits and may visit the island at any time, provided each sojourn does not exceed three months. Any property purchased for vacation purposes must cost over £14,000.

Those spending less than six months in Malta, in any one year, do not pay tax on sums brought into the island.

Temporary residents staying for periods in excess of three months can apply to the immigration authorities to renew the entry visa once a year. This is a simple formality and many British people live in Malta on this basis.

They are not entitled to the taxation advantages for permanent residents, but are normally subject to local tax conditions if their stay exceeds six months in one continuous period and then only on income remitted to Malta. Proof needs to be provided, however, that they have sufficient income to live in the island without becoming a financial burden to the government and any property purchased must exceed about £14,000 in value.

Property can only be used as a permanent or holiday residence by the purchaser or his immediate family, but guests can be accommodated when the owner or a member of his family is staying in the property. Funds for property purchase must originate from outside Malta.

Personal effects

Once a residence permit is acquired, no duties are payable on personal effects. Exemption from customs duty is granted on house-

MALTA with its stable economic and political climate is creating an environment for people seeking a permanent home or a second home in the Mediterranean and an ideal opportunity for the investor.

To meet this demand

KB K.B. REAL ESTATE LTD has pleasure to announce the availability of 'Quality Homes in the Sun' in best locations for permanent and holiday home buyers and 'Commercial and Investment' propositions with immense potential for the investor.

KB
K.B. REAL ESTATE LTD.

Dingli Street, Sliema. Malta.
Tel: 313020, 334971.

A reputation built on sound foundation.

hold and personal effects and also a car imported within six months of arrival in Malta.

Housing

A wide range of modern and well-established villas and apartments is available for sale all over the island. Expatriates are limited in that they can own only one property, which must be of a value exceeding £14,000 (if renovating an old property, this can be the total amount including building costs), in order to prevent speculation on the property market at the expense of the local residents. In general, Malta may be described as a buyer's market, with plenty of property available at a reasonable price. Prices are, however, rising because of an increase in demand from foreigners.

Buying property

The procedure for buying property can take some time, as all foreigners must apply to the government for a licence to purchase. Having satisfied the government of their eligibility, buyers may proceed to the next stage.

While searching for property, people may visit the island as often as they like, providing the stay does not exceed three months. Once a property has been found, the usual procedure is for the buyer to pay a 10 per cent deposit (forfeited on failure to proceed). At this stage, the buyer should engage a notary public to establish the title of the property, and submit the necessary applications to the government.

Purchasing costs break down as follows: 3.5 per cent for stamp duty; 1 per cent for the notary; a Ministry of Finance fee of £170; and finally a recognition fee paid to the original owner of the land.

Where to live

On this small island, there is not a great deal of difference between locations. The Valletta area is more built up.

Inspection flights

At present these cost around £165 for a four-day inclusive visit, during the winter months. Details from Association of Estate Agents in Malta.

Communications

There are regular flights to Malta operated by Air Malta and British Airways.

Recreation

Facilities exist for football, water sports, horse racing, hockey, cycling, athletics, fishing and netball. Indoors there are opportunities for billiards, snooker, ten-pin bowling and table tennis. Non-sporting pursuits include the cinema and the theatre; 700 years of historical development provide a fine heritage of remarkable architecture.

Driving

At times, standards are a little erratic. Cars drive on the left, officially.

Health services

The climate is good, and the hygienic conditions help the Maltese to enjoy a high standard of health. A free health and hospital service is available to local residents.

There is a social services agreement between the UK and Malta aiming to protect your entitlement to benefit and to give equality of treatment. The UK benefits covered by the agreement are unemployment, sickness, invalidity and industrial injuries benefits, retirement pensions, widows' benefit and guardians' allowance. Details of the agreement are given in DSS pamphlet SA11.

Climate

	Average daily temperatures (°C)	*Monthly rainfall (mm)*	*Sea temperature (°C)*	*Sunshine hours*
January	9.5-15.0	88.2	14.5	5.3
February	9.4-15.4	61.4	14.5	6.3
March	10.2-16.7	44.0	14.5	7.3
April	11.8-18.7	27.5	16.1	8.3
May	14.9-23.0	9.7	18.4	10.0
June	18.6-27.4	3.4	21.1	11.2
July	21.0-32.2	0.9	24.5	12.1
August	21.8-30.6	9.3	25.6	11.3
September	20.2-27.0	44.4	25.0	8.9
October	17.1-23.7	117.9	22.2	7.3
November	13.8-19.9	75.5	19.5	6.3
December	11.1-16.7	96.0	16.7	5.2

Portugal and Madeira

General information

Status. Republic
Capital. Lisbon
Area. 92,000 sq km (32,225 sq miles)
Population. 9.8 million

Location

Longitude 37°N; latitude 6°W. Situated on the south-western tip of the European mainland, Portugal has very obvious attractions. The environment is today still pretty unspoilt and so the perfect beaches provide the same incentive to move that her Iberian neighbour had 20 years before. Being on the Atlantic coast means that greenery flourishes, whereas elsewhere on equal latitudes, scrub and thorn prevail. Therefore, Portugal is subjected to the warmth befitting its proximity to the equator and the cooling influence of the Atlantic, which together combine to provide ideal conditions.

Political stability

Despite many changes in government and a bloodless revolution in 1974, which overthrew nearly 50 years of virtual dictatorship, the present regime appears to have adequate control. Portugal's stability has been enhanced by entry into the European Community.

Economy

Cost of living. The country suffers from a fairly high rate of inflation and the after-effects of the return of many expatriates from Africa. Indeed, residents of the Algarve have been known to travel across the frontier into Spain in order to stock up on cheap household goods. However, local produce such as fruit and vegetables is cheap and of good quality. Other food products cost about the same as equivalents in the UK, except for those which have been specially imported. In general, prices are a little lower than in the UK. Inflation is about 10 per cent per year.

Taxation. There is a double taxation agreement with the UK. Income tax ranges from 16-45 per cent. The normal rate of VAT is 17 per cent, but for Madeira and the Azores the rate is 12 per cent.

Exchange rate. Escudos (written $): $263 = £1.

Exchange controls. Non-residents can bring into the country unlimited foreign currency, including travellers cheques, but no more than 50,000 escudos in notes or coins. When leaving the country foreigners can take out the same amount of escudos. In order to ensure repatriation of funds when selling a property in Portugal, it is vital to obtain consent from the Bank of Portugal to import the money at the time of the original purchase. It will be necessary to produce the import licence when the conveyance is prepared.

Language

Portuguese is spoken and some knowledge of it would be useful. However, English is fairly common in tourist areas, especially where there is a substantial expatriate community.

Expatriate community

The southern coastline (Algarve) attracts a variety of European citizens, particularly from the UK, Germany and Scandinavia. The business community is settled around Lisbon and Oporto.

Security

It is a good idea to install a security system to protect your property from undesirables.

Residence permits

Applications should be made to the Portuguese Consulate for a residence permit before arrival in Portugal.

Work permits

A work permit is required by all residents (expatriate) who wish to take a job. The prospective employer is responsible for contacting the Ministry of Labour for one.

Personal effects

These may be imported free of duty so long as they have been in the owner's possession for more than 12 months. Household goods need a *residencia* or *escritura* if they are to be imported duty free.

Housing

Many villa and apartment estates have been built on the Algarve in recent years and in resorts close to Lisbon. Old properties for modernisation come on the market quite frequently.

Buying property

Having selected a suitable property the prospective purchaser is expected to sign a promissory contract of sale and pay a deposit amounting to 10 per cent of the purchase price. The contract records the agreed price, details of the property being purchased and promises to buy or sell from the purchaser and vendor respectively. It is legally binding and if the vendor fails to proceed, he must pay the purchaser a sum equivalent to 20 per cent of the proposed purchase price. Likewise, when a purchaser does not complete the contract, the vendor is entitled to retain the 10 per cent deposit as contractual damages. This arrangement does help to reduce the number of abortive deals and offers some protection against irresponsible behaviour by either party. British buyers must remember there is no subject to contract arrangement.

Transfer documents *(escritura)* are generally prepared by the municipality's notary where the property is registered and signed by both parties to the contract. The full purchase price is then paid. The *escritura* remains in the possession of the notary but an official copy is sent to the owner and this acts as the deeds.

Before any final commitment is made, the buyer's legal adviser should check at the municipal offices for any outstanding mortgages or charges against the property, that planning permission has been granted and building regulations been complied with and that there are no municipal taxes outstanding and unpaid.

After the *escritura* has been signed and entered in the notary's official book, the new owner is responsible for registering the property at the land registry and also with the Inland Revenue Office so that the authorities can calculate the annual property tax. This tax is about 18 per cent of the rateable value, but a 10-year exemption is granted if the property is the permanent habitation of the owner.

SISA (Portuguese property purchase tax) is charged at the rate of 10 per cent of the property (not including fixtures and fittings) where it is an urban building or land for building, valued at more than $10 million. Rural property and land are taxed at a reduced rate of 8 per cent. Newly built or established properties for permanent occupation valued at under $10 million are generally exempt from SISA, but professional advice is worth while.

Capital gains tax is not payable when individual properties are resold.

Value Added Tax is levied on the supply of services, including building contracts, at the rate of 17 per cent.

Inspection flights

Cheap flights to inspect property are available via charter services throughout the year.

Communications

There are daily flights from the UK to Lisbon and Faro by British Airways and Portuguese Airlines (TAP), less often to Madeira. Internal flights (including Madeira and the Azores) are run by TAP.

Train services are available via Paris (journey time approximately 24 hours Paris-Lisbon).

Recreation

Spectator sports are a very popular form of leisure in Portugal, especially football and also the traditional bullfight (more merciful in character than the Spanish version). Golf is a popular pastime with a number of good courses within reach of Lisbon

and a half dozen along the Algarve. Horse riding, water sports and camping are among other enjoyable pursuits.

Eating out is common, with restaurants plentiful and open until late. The food is possibly as good as anywhere in Europe.

So far as the arts are concerned, Portugal has its own theatre tradition, abundant museums and galleries, fine orchestras and beautiful and arresting architecture. The cinema is popular and films are often dubbed into English.

There are also many clubs and societies for expatriates' use. The Algarve region has a Lions Club and also a Lioness Club, an archaeological association, and meetings of the Rotarians and the British Legion. Bridge tournaments are held in some hotels and bingo has now been legalised. Other clubs and associations elsewhere include the Royal British Club, the Charity Bridge Association and the Royal Society of St George (or David or Andrew). The British Council in Lisbon also helps organise exhibitions, lectures, films and concerts.

Driving

Foreign registered cars may enter Portugal for a period of up to six months on production of the registration document. A Green

Card (from your insurance company) is not required by law but is recommended.

It is advisable to carry a spare parts kit and obtain GB stickers while the car is still registered in Britain. British driving licences are valid. Carrying petrol in cars is forbidden.

Portugal uses the international road sign system. The rule of the road is to keep to the right. Traffic approaching from the right must be given priority, except when entering a public road from a private driveway or a side road with a stop sign. The speed limits are roughly the same as elsewhere on the mainland of Europe, ranging from 50 to 120 kph.

Health services

There are many English-speaking doctors in Portugal and a British Hospital in Lisbon. Free emergency out-patient treatment is available to any Briton who produces a British passport. For permanent residents, private health insurance is advisable.

There is a social security agreement between the UK and Portugal. For further details, contact the DSS and ask for pamphlet SA31.

Climate

Portugal is regarded by many as having one of the most pleasant climates in Europe. Throughout the year, the temperature is warm without ever being sweltering. The proximity of the country to the Atlantic means that the air is freshened by the sea breezes that bring with them the moisture that allows vegetation other than scrub to flourish. The average temperatures in the two most popular areas for migration are as follows:

Average temperatures (°C)

	Algarve	*Lisbon/Estoril*
January	12	12
February	13	12
March	14	14
April	16	16
May	18	17
June	21	20
July	24	21
August	24	22
September	22	21
October	19	18
November	16	15
December	13	12

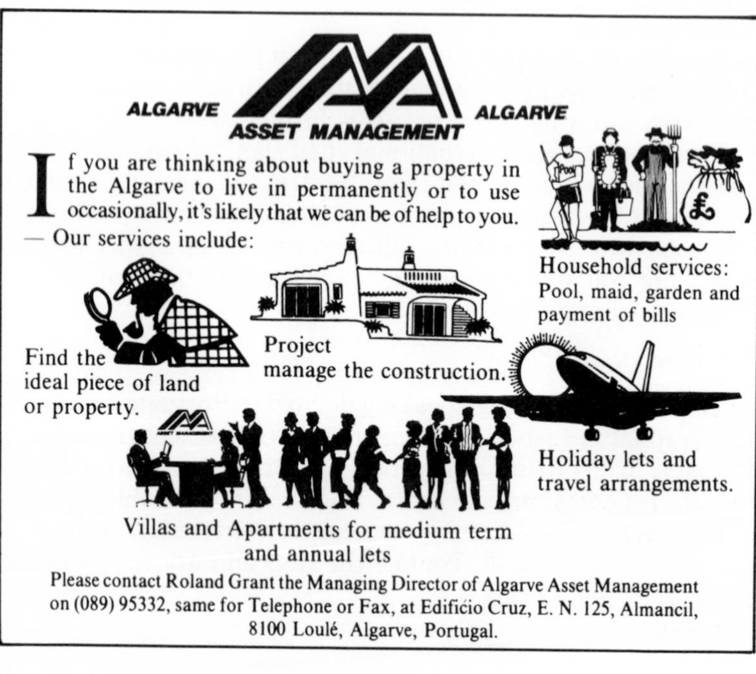

Where to live

The two regions most preferred by expatriates for permanent residence or a holiday home are the Algarve coast in the deep south of the country, or the towns close to Lisbon such as Cascais and Estoril.

The Algarve

The Algarve is favoured with a wide range of sandy beaches stretching from the border with Spain as far west as Cape St Vincent.

Twenty years ago, this region was almost unknown in the international tourist world, but following the expansion of facilities on the southern Spanish coast, the Algarve began to develop, slowly at first and with a good deal more caution than its neighbouring state. Some lessons were learned from the over-development of parts of the Costa del Sol and although there are some multi-storey horrors of both hotels and apartments on the Algarve, they are not so blatantly objectionable as in Spain.

The capital of the region is Faro, and the conversion of the local airstrip into an international airport speeded up the development of the whole coast as it became accessible to most northern European countries in about 2½ hours' flying time. Faro has a population of about 50,000 and is a good shopping centre. It has a small harbour and some pleasant municipal gardens, several museums and interesting churches.

To the east of the regional capital are a few places of interest including Olhao, a fishing port, Tavira which is surrounded by a prosperous agricultural area and some fine beaches which spread as far as Monte Gordo, a pleasant resort with an immense sandy beach, only a short distance from the border with Spain.

West of Faro the coastline becomes more indented with rocky coves, islets and sandy beaches which are very reminiscent of the Cornish coastline. The nearest town of note to Faro is Almansil, a regional shopping centre, and on the coast are three major resort towns namely Quinta do Lago, Vale do Lobo and Quarteira. Facilities include golf courses, tennis clubs, hotels and a wide range of villas and apartments used either for summer holidays or permanent living.

Further west along the coast is the well-known resort of Albufeira, originally a fishermen's town, with a large open-air market. The beaches are popular, with unusual rock formations; above on the clifftop the winding street layouts have a variety of well-established and recently built properties. An abundant supply of retail establishments, restaurants and bars serve the local population and also the considerable number of holiday-makers who visit the town every summer. From nearly every vantage point, there are views of the sea.

The next major town on the inland road is Lagoa (not to be confused with the port of Lagos, further to the west). As the wine capital of the province, Lagoa is considered important as an agricultural market town.

Portimao is a large fishing port at the mouth of the river Arade, but its popular residential suburb is Praia da Rocha which has a large sandy beach, interesting cliffs and attractive rock formations. This is a family resort with a wide choice of new properties and hotels.

The last large town going westwards along the coast is Lagos which has a variety of entertainment and shopping opportunities. At one time, Lagos was the capital of the Algarve. Small resorts of interest from the residential point of view near Lagos include Praia da Luz, a true family resort, also Burgau and Salema. This part of the coastline is memorable for the many rugged tiny coves where the sand is regularly washed clean by the Atlantic waves.

The Lisbon area

Lisbon is a fine city located near the mouth of the river Tejo with many grand buildings, and the huge variety of commercial establishments makes it an ideal centre for sightseeing. This is not perhaps a place where many British people decide to spend their retirement years.

Of greater interest in this respect is Estoril, about 24 km west of Lisbon, known for most of this century as a cosmopolitan town, because it provided shelter for many former administrators and even kings from bygone European states. The town has a good beach on the Atlantic and is well known for entertainment activities which include a large casino, night clubs, restaurants, exhibition halls and theatres. Modern apartment blocks vie with Victorian villas to attract those who want to live near the facilities.

Nearby Cascais is a fishing port and also the home of many well-to-do people from various nations.

A few miles inland is the ancient hill town of Sintra where Portuguese kings made their summer home from the fourteenth century. There are many fascinating buildings to be visited and sites to be seen.

Costa Verde

This is the northern sea coast of Portugal (the green coast) and lies between the frontier with Spain in the north and the mouth of the river Douro in the south.

It is not an area where many foreigners have settled for retirement, but it does attract tourists looking for somewhere different.

Oporto is the main centre of habitation and this town can be reached by domestic flights from Lisbon in a flying time of about 40 minutes. There are also rail and coach services from the capital.

As the second largest city in Portugal, it is also well known for having given its name to the famous wine – port – and British expatriates there tend to be connected with the trade.

Located at the mouth of the river Douro, this mainly working city does not necessarily impress at first sight but with time and effort many attractions can be discovered. Three famous bridges are among the best-known buildings. The oldest, Maria Pia, was opened in 1877 and was the work of a famous engineer Gerard Eiffel. In 1886 a two-tiered road bridge was opened which also bears the influence of Eiffel's design and in 1963 the Arrábida bridge was built and its 270 m span of reinforced concrete is believed to be the largest concrete arch in the world. Other important buildings are the cathedral, the Archbishop's Palace, also the nineteenth-century Palácio da Bolsa which is the home of the Stock Exchange. There are numerous museums and a good selection of hotels, plus leisure amenities.

Among coastal resorts is Espinho, south of Oporto, which has a long sandy beach.

To the north of Oporto lies a large fishing port known as Póvoa da Varzim, an excellent seaside resort with good facilities for tourists, and to the north again lies Ofir which has a long stretch of white sand backed by pinewoods, while a few kilometres inland is Barcelos which is well known for the large open-air market held on Thursday each week.

Another seaside resort is Viana do Castelo, 71 km from Oporto. Located near the mouth of the river Lima, the town has various hotels and good shopping. The folk costumes of the local people are among the most colourful in the land. Hand-embroidered clothes, ceramics, filigree work and rugs are among other items offered locally.

The Anglo-Portuguese Society, Canning House, 2 Belgrave Square, London SW1X 8PJ (tel. 01-245 9738) publishes a quarterly newsletter for members and arranges events in Great Britain to inform people about Portugal. Meetings are also held for members at the headquarters.

Madeira

This Atlantic island which belongs to Portugal lies about 1000 km south-west of Lisbon, but much closer to the African coast. It is 56 km long by 21 km wide and the terrain is very mountainous because of its volcanic origins. The coastline is largely steep cliffs so there are few beaches, but inland greenery and colourful flowers are to be seen everywhere.

About one-third of the island's population of 300,000 inhabitants lives in Funchal, the capital, and the rest are scattered in towns, villages and hamlets in the countryside.

Funchal is built on a hillside overlooking the bay and harbour. The main hotels are located in or on the perimeter of the town and the central zone is packed with buildings ancient and modern containing the major shopping premises and administrative headquarters.

The choice of homes for sale to foreigners is limited and few

UK firms of estate agents specialise in selling Madeira real estate, but there are a number of local firms willing to assist foreigners.

The holiday island of Porto Santo has some fine sandy beaches. It lies 40 km north-east of Madeira and has a population of 3000. There are plenty of natural pastimes, but man-made events are scarce. A local airport has regular flights to Madeira and also to Lisbon.

All procedures and taxes in the mainland of Portugal apply to Madeira.

Average temperatures range from 16°C in January to March to 22°C in August and September.

Spain

General information

Status. Kingdom
Capital. Madrid
Area. 510,000 sq km (197,000 sq miles)
Population. 37,973,000

Location

Longitude 36°N to 43°N; latitude 8°W to 6°E. The popular image of Spain is that of Benidorm or Torremolinos, one of high-rise hotels, crowded streets and an endless nightlife. Yet there is far more to Spain than the commercialism of the popular holiday resorts. Blessed by an idyllic climate and at times breathtaking countryside, there is a different Spain which has been popular for many years among those looking for their place in the sun. Sun, of course, is one of the main attractions of the Iberian peninsula, but Spain's appeal is not limited to its climate.

Residence permits

UK citizens can visit Spain as tourists for up to 90 days, without requiring a visa, provided they have a valid passport. Thereafter the tourist should apply for a *permancia* which extends the period allowed to remain in Spain by a further 90 days. This is obtained by having the passport stamped at a police station with a foreigners department. If you intend to remain in Spain for a lengthy period, an application should be made during the currency of the *permancia* for a *residencia*. This is normally valid for five years and can be renewed for a further five years.

To obtain a *residencia* you will need a current visa in your passport issued by a Spanish Consul in the UK, confirmation that you are registered with the local British Consul, evidence from your Spanish bank indicating that you have sufficient means (ie capital and income) to support yourself and your dependants so that you will not become a burden on the state and evidence that you have accommodation available in Spain, ie either the *escritura* of the property you have bought or a long-term lease of an apartment or flat. You may also be asked for proof that you are covered by a private health insurance scheme valid in Spain or that you are covered by Spanish national health insurance.

Work permits

Work permits are not now required in Spain by EC nationals who wish to work for themselves, nor do they require an entry visa. They must, however, acquire a card authorising them to start work. This can be obtained from the nearest police station with a foreigners department in the place where they wish to start a business or trade.

A tax identification card (*licencia fiscal*) must be obtained and the Spanish Social Security Service has to be joined and the monthly contribution made until retirement age.

It is well worth while paying a *gestoria* (an administrator who specialises in certain legal problems and the paperwork involved) to handle these matters for you. The fees for the work are not high.

Professional people such as doctors, dentists, lawyers, accountants, etc, are now allowed to practise in Spain on their own account, but are required to have their qualifications confirmed and may be required to pass a written examination.

If you want to work for others in Spain, an official work permit is needed but no entry permit. Preference is given to EC citizens. Prospective employees normally obtain these permits, but support documents generally required include a current British passport, a medical certificate issued by the health authority in Spain, a certificate from the British consulate in Spain confirming that you are registered with them, four recent colour photographs and two copies of the work contract.

EC nationals receive an initial permit for one year which is renewable for five-year periods thereafter.

Personal effects

No import duties are imposed on goods that have not been bought within the previous six months.

SABLO ....

NO IT'S NOT TOO GOOD TO BE TRUE!

"I like to think that any of us from SABLO can get in our car", says Charles Chaundy Brain, one of the partners in the U.K. estate agency and Spanish building company, "and drive anywhere we like, and be made welcome by our former clients".

Equally impressive is what SABLO of Javea has to say in it about itself. "We pay all *your* Solicitors' fees and give you full legal protection". Even after you've bought, there's a first-class, unlimited after-sales service including assistance in obtaining such things as *residencias* and Spanish driving licences. To sum all this up, the SABLO brochure categorically states, "We handle the total documentation *free of charge,* making this a service unrivalled in Spain. It is our caring attitude towards our customers that guarantees your security".

"The result of all this", he continued, "is that most of our business has been by personal recommendation. And, if you want to go round and ask our clients, I'm sure you'll find they sing our praises pretty highly".

A truer word was never spoken!

"They're so kind and helpful, it's unbelievable", was Betty's opinion, a few days later in *Costa Nova Ambolo II.* "You hear such awful things, it makes you happy you've chosen the right ones".

Elly and Norman—those are their real names as is Betty's—were equally fulsome in their praise. "You hear all those stories about how you have to be on your guard, so we came over to Spain with a bit of trepidation. I thought what SABLO told us was too good to be true, but we decided there and then and said okay". That was Norman speaking, but their instant decision was due to the instincts of his wife, Elly. "If my wife takes to somebody, she's seldom wrong, and she took to Charles. She said, 'Look, I trust that man', and that was good enough for me".

Their trust was such that they didn't come out again until their villa was completed. While it was being built, however, SABLO sent them photographs of every stage of the operations, and, if he had any queries, he telephoned them. "It became a joke in our family", Norman recalled, "if Charles says it's all right, that'll do us!"

But the greatest praise of all came from someone who *wasn't* a client. When Sarah and her husband, another Norman, bought in Spain, they found themselves in a "nightmare" over the final payment. They gave a cheque to the agent in Britain, but he paid the builder with one that bounced. They first met Charles in the notary's office, and told him of their predicament. "A week later, he called in on us", Sarah said, "and he's just helped us from there on. He's been a good friend and that's what we needed. He's under no obligation to us, but he's a good man, an excellent man".

So there you are, some honest opinions from some honest people speaking as they've found. In their experience, buying with SABLO had been a very wise move on their part, not least for the friendly way in which they were still cared for long after they'd bought.

Perhaps you're thinking of buying property in Spain, and would like to see what SABLO can offer? Let Charles Brain explain. "There's no pressure put on any client. Even if they're anxious to buy, before they make a final decision or we let them sign a contract, we encourage them to go away with what they have from us and see somebody else". Then he continues with absolute confidence. "We know that nobody else is going to do for them what we do!"

PUERTO SOTOGRANDE

A unique holiday home and an outstanding investment.

...nd an average 320 days of sunshine each year!)
...agine, if you will, sitting on your terrace, ...king up the warm sun and sipping a cool ...nk. Behind you, a luxury, air conditioned, ...hitect designed apartment of the highest ...ality. In front of you, the new marina, ...bably the most sophisticated and well ...uipped in Europe – boats of all sizes lying ...amily at anchor, owners and visitors alike ...axing around the restaurants and cafes and, ... you, gazing out over the harbour towards ... Puerto Sotogrande Beach Club, miles of ...crowded beach, which seem to stretch ...broken to Gibraltar, just 10 miles distant. ...his is the life . . ."

...e New Harbour Village at Puerto ...togrande has been described as "the most ...iting development in the South of Spain". ...he stunning Italian Style architecture has ...eady won an award for its fascinating ...our scheme). Whether you are looking for ... perfect holiday home for yourself and your ...nily, a marina berth for your yacht or just a ...t class investment, you will not find better.

...artments currently available from ...25,000 (2 bed, 2 bath), £160,000 (3 bed, 3 ...h) and £140,000 (penthouse).
...arina berths may be purchased from around ...9,000 (12 metre).
...e are also pleased to announce the ...ning of our "Club Maritimo", a new yacht club/hotel which is situated in The Harbour Village with direct frontage to the marina. Fully furnished rooms and suites are available for purchase on a long leasehold basis from around £60,000.

FINANCE AVAILABLE UP TO 70% BASED ON THE SPANISH PROPERTY FOR UP TO 20 YEARS (SUBJECT TO STATUS).

If you are considering a purchase in this exceptional development, why not take a weekend visit to see it all for yourself? Flights are available from Gatwick to Gibraltar, which is only 20 mins drive from Puerto Sotogrande. Transport from Gibraltar and accommodation can be arranged through our London office.

BOOK YOUR VISIT NOW OR COME TO OUR PERMANENT EXHIBITION AT OUR LONDON OFFICE. PLEASE TELEPHONE OR RETURN THE COUPON BELOW FOR DETAILS.

PUERTO SOTOGRANDE,
3 Shepherd Market,
London W1Y 7HS
Tel: 01-495 3630 (24 hrs).

PLEASE SEND DETAILS TO:

NAME ____________________

ADDRESS ____________________

HOME TELEPHONE NUMBER ____________________

OFFICE TELEPHONE NUMBER ____________________

DATE ____________________

T1

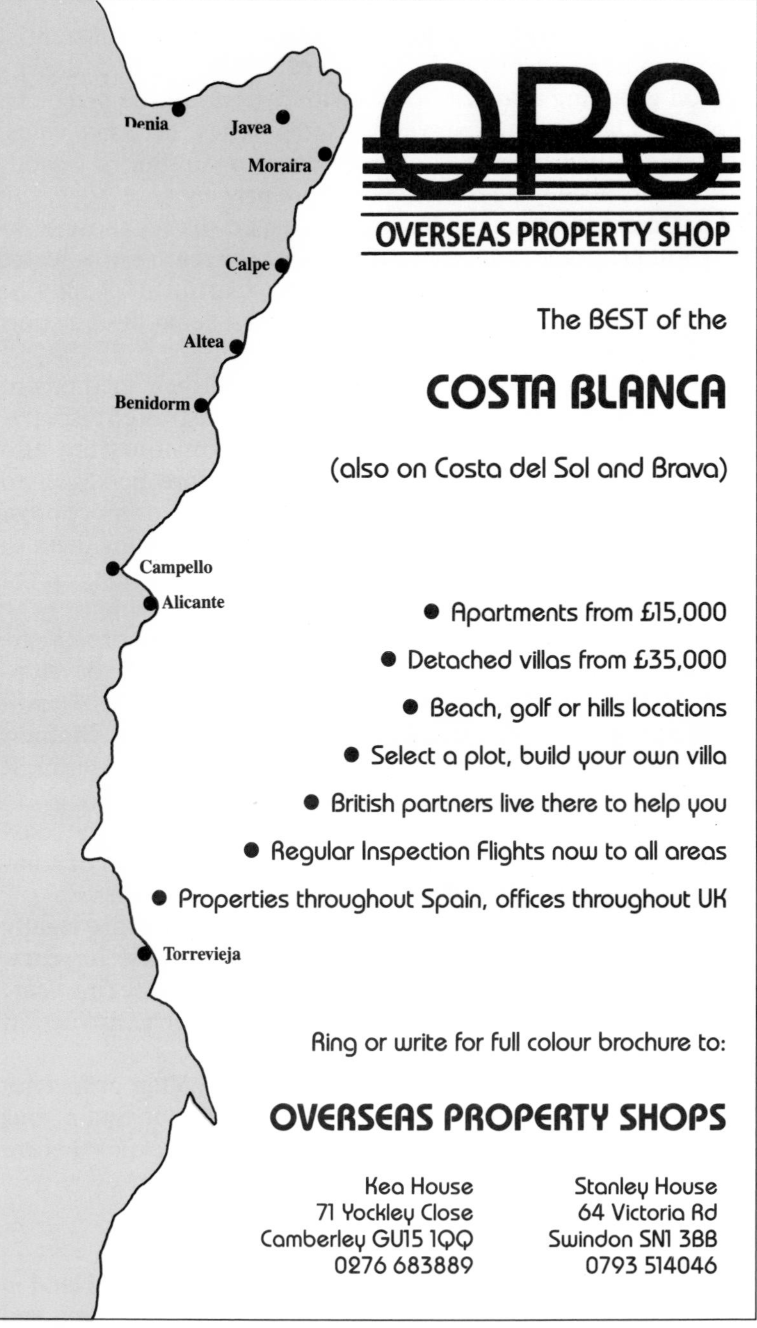
Denia
Javea
Moraira
Calpe
Altea
Benidorm
Campello
Alicante
Torrevieja
OPS
OVERSEAS PROPERTY SHOP
The BEST of the
COSTA BLANCA
(also on Costa del Sol and Brava)
• Apartments from £15,000
• Detached villas from £35,000
• Beach, golf or hills locations
• Select a plot, build your own villa
• British partners live there to help you
• Regular Inspection Flights now to all areas
• Properties throughout Spain, offices throughout UK
Ring or write for full colour brochure to:
OVERSEAS PROPERTY SHOPS
Kea House
71 Yockley Close
Camberley GU15 1QQ
0276 683889
Stanley House
64 Victoria Rd
Swindon SN1 3BB
0793 514046

Housing

Spanish pueblo-style developments have been of substantial interest to overseas buyers in recent years. This is a high density method grouping terraced houses with pedestrianised precincts. Those with larger sums to invest tend to purchase detached villas, especially if they are going to live in them for substantial periods of the year, as they do offer much more privacy.

Apartments continue to be popular, especially for those seeking a holiday home, but types overlooking the sea are now scarce and expensive, so for reasonably priced apartments it may be necessary to examine the possibility of units being built a short distance inland.

Both developers and agents have improved their methods of presentation and marketing by using more sophisticated displays, models and specialised exhibitions. Inspection tours are also offered, but generally these are now of a more personalised nature and the previous practice of taking a dozen or more prospective buyers on a weekend visit to Spain, and keeping them so busy that they only have time to see the properties being offered by the agent or developer, have now gone out of fashion.

A confidence-building trend apparent over the past few years has been the entry of leading UK housebuilders into the development of residential property in southern Spain. Well-known names now active in this sector include Barratt, Costain, McInerney, Norwest Holst, Kenning, Wimpey, Bovis, Lovell, Heron, R K Francis Group, Langdale Group and DMI plc.

Very few mobile homes seem to be available on any of the coastal sites due, in part at any rate, to the high import costs of complete units such as can be found in the UK and elsewhere.

On new property the developer and the architect are legally responsible for any structural defects during the first 10 years. Internal defects are covered by the developer during the first year. Developers who sell their properties while under construction must have insurance cover against bankruptcy.

There is still a wide selection of old farm and other properties suitable for conversion, particularly in the hills of Spain, but sound local advice and experience are highly necessary before becoming involved in such projects.

Investment in agriculture

Several firms specialise in offering farms and agricultural land in Spain to the UK market, particularly the farming fraternity, and

the properties include orange and lemon groves, cork forests, vineyards, avocado cultivation, olives and animal husbandry.

The future

It is likely that low-priced seaside apartments and secondary sites in the larger towns will decline in importance in the near future.

A greater demand exists for individually built villas in rural areas in southern Spain which offer convenient access to the important towns and a high degree of luxury which can be enjoyed in retirement.

The trend all over Europe for longer holidays is likely to increase the demand for apartments and villas suitable for vacations because the number of people able to afford to stay five or six weeks a year in a hotel is not likely to increase, whereas those with a capital sum can invest in a home and cater for themselves.

Areas likely to have sites available for expansion include the Costa de la Luz, between Cadiz and Huelva, on the Atlantic coast.

The terrain is very varied with attractive beaches on the north and south coast, immense mountainous regions inland and fertile plains behind the Mediterranean coastline, close to the border of southern Portugal and in Catalonia.

Two groups of islands also come within the jurisdiction of the mainland government, namely the Balearics in the Mediterranean and the Canaries, which lie in the Atlantic off the coast of Morocco and Western Sahara.

Political stability

The twentieth century has been a period of internal confusion and instability which resulted in a bloody revolution followed by General Franco's conservative and repressive regime. In the 1980s, however, the signs are that Spain is recovering well from the traumas of the Franco years and, although there have been a few scares, the stability of the administration seems to be satisfactory and the bulk of the inhabitants appear to be behind the government. The king has played an effective role by maintaining the calm. Also, Spain's entry into the European Community and her continuing membership of NATO means that she is no longer of peripheral importance in European affairs.

Economy

Cost of living. The Spanish economy is not without its problems, notably inflation (around 8 per cent) and unemployment. This is

GOLF

CANYAMEL - MALLORCA

Imagine a perfect village, built to appeal to the most discerning golfer. An area of comfortable, elegant apartments overlooked by golf course and sea. Picture this set against a backdrop of gently rolling hills, lying next to the only 19 hole golf course in Europe. Then think that this idyll is only a 10 minute stroll from quiet, unspoilt beaches. Beaches with silver sand and silky water. Beaches which incredibly remain uncrowded even in high summer.

The place you're imagining is a new development called Golf Apartments Canyamel.
Golf Apartments Canyamel set a new standard in developments of this kind offering privacy, comfort, superbly designed accommodation and consequently an excellent investment opportunity.
Set in spacious, lush surroundings, each apartment enjoys views of the sea, the golf course—or both—and has the use of any one of five private swimming pools which are part of the development.
'Golf Apartments Canyamel have been designed to meet all needs and requirements. To this end, there are three types of apartment of varying sizes, all having the advantage of spacious, pleasant terraces and delightful views.

The course was designed by the celebrated Spanish golf architect Jose (Pepe) Gancedo, a man responsible for some of the finest courses in southern Europe. Like Torrequebrada on the Costa del Sol, Golf de Sur in Tenerife, Parque da Foresta in the Algarve and Pollensa Majorca.
This unique course, with its optional 19th hole, is expected to play host to the 1990 Majorcan Open Golf Championship.

**Your purchase price includes membership and starts from as low as £46,000. Security is also guaranteed. All money is held by the bank in a trust account until the titles and deeds are exchanged.
We know of no other development that offers this security. We know of no other development that offers mortgages at the rate we can.**

FOR MORE INFORMATION DIAL 100 & ASK FOR FREEFONE CANYAMEL

When it comes to that very special home in ıe sun – one British builder ıines out above all thers.

The name is Lovell and ıe difference is a quality, reativity and craftsmanship robably unequalled in the hole of southern Spain.

Visit Puebla Aida or White earl Beach on Spain's Costa el Sol and you'll discover the ifference.

Puebla Aida is arguably ne of the classic visions of outhern Spain – a unique ndalucian hillside village estling on the edge of the ıxuriant Mijas Golf.

Here Lovell has created a ide selection of individually esigned homes with an nagination and style that's reathtaking.

By contrast, White Pearl each offers the delightful etting of one of Marbella's nest beaches – next to the

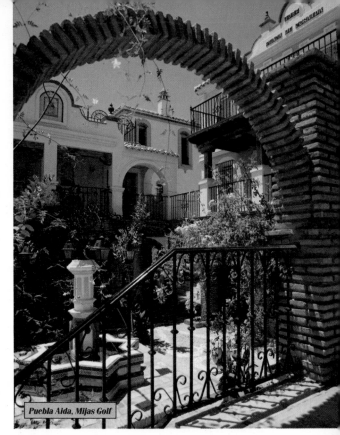

Puebla Aida, Mijas Golf

THE DEGREE OF DIFFERENCE IS MORE THAN JUST THE CLIMATE

White Pearl Beach, Marbella

famous Don Carlos Hotel.

Here 100 luxury garden apartments garland themselves around an exquisite sub-tropical landscape to form what will probably be the area's most exclusive circle of homeowners. Both locations offer a home and investment opportunity of rare quality, so call us now for further details and video of Lovell homes in Spain.

Lovell España

FOR FURTHER DETAILS CONTACT: OVERSEAS RESIDENTIAL PROPERTIES LTD., OVERSEAS HOUSE, 5 BROADWAY COURT, CHESHAM, BUCKS HP5 1DB. TEL: (0494) 791779 why, despite recent devaluations, the cost of living in Spain is now only slightly less than in the UK. Thus a move to Spain is not so economically advantageous as it once was. But, having said that, items such as fish, fruit, wine and vegetables are very cheap, and while energy prices are high (especially electricity), petrol costs about the same as in Britain.

Taxation. Income tax is levied on anybody who stays in Spain for more than 182 days every year, whether resident or tourist. However, there is a double tax agreement between Britain and Spain. A wealth tax is payable by all non-residents on their assets in Spain, as well as by all resident foreigners who have more than 4 million pesetas, wherever deposited. It is, at present, at a very low level, amounting to about 0.2 per cent after deductions of certain allowances. No demand is submitted by the tax authorities, as everybody must make a wealth declaration prior to 10 June each year. Local taxes are low but there is a surcharge for late payment.

Recent legislation announced by the Spanish government tax department requires that all foreigners who have any dealings with the tax authorities must have a foreigner's tax identification number. This is obtained by visiting a police station with a foreigners department with the applicant's passport. Forms are then issued for forwarding to the appropriate tax office. One of the reasons, it is stated, for this requirement is the government's need to obtain trustworthy statistics regarding the number of foreigners who live and work in Spain and who own property locally. This information appears to be sadly lacking at present.

There are three rates of VAT: 6 per cent (reduced rate), 12 per cent (standard rate, which applies to most items) and 33 per cent (increased rate).

VAT at a reduced rate of 6 per cent is charged on new building, including land from a developer, or on a purchase from a developer on land already owned by you. On the purchase of land or property from a private owner, a property transfer tax of 5.5 per cent is charged. VAT is not payable in the Canary Islands.

Another tax is *plus valia* which is a penalty on the increase of the value of the land on which property is built. It is often payable by the purchaser, but should morally be paid by the vendor who made the capital gain. A table of values is prepared by the municipality indicating the current values in various parts of an area together with past values. The increase in value is expressed as a percentage of the lower value and this figure is divided by the number of years since the title last changed hands. The coefficient pro-

duced by this calculation is the basis of the tax to be charged; where the figure is less than 5, 15 per cent of the increase is levied, rising progressively to 40 per cent where the coefficient is over 50.

A new local finance law is proposed and should apply in 1989-90. Under law all municipal taxes (except car registration tax) will be deductible for income tax purposes by resident individuals. Current urban real estate tax will be redesignated immovable property tax and will be treated as a deductible expense with respect to owner-occupied homes and taxpayers will be able to credit against their income tax liability the local capital gains tax for sales of developed land.

Exchange rate. Pesetas 208 = £1.

Exchange control. When you import foreign currency into Spain to purchase property, you must obtain a certificate from the bank which is attached to the *escritura* (deeds). This will enable you to repatriate the money on eventual sale. In due course, these regulations may be eased due to EC membership.

Language

A knowledge of Spanish would be very useful although many Spaniards do speak English, especially in the tourist regions.

Expatriate community

There are more British people living in the country than any other expatriate nationality, but there are also substantial numbers of residents from Germany, Holland, Belgium and Scandinavia.

Security

It is wise to be wary and to take precautions against theft by installing adequate security systems. Also, street crime and muggings in the holiday resorts are a problem. It is also a good idea to be aware of Spain's terrorist problem involving Basque separatists, who have struck in the popular areas.

Now that Gibraltar is open, this area is much more accessible by air from other European countries than in the past and this must encourage expansion along the attractive coastline where there are sandy beaches and few high-rise schemes.

Costa del Azahar and Costa Dorada have scope for future expansion, so do the Canary Islands of La Palma and Fuerteventura.

An All Round Experience in Southern Tenerife

THE AMARILLA GOLF & COUNTRY CLUB, SITUATED IN THE MOST PICTURESQUE PART OF TENERIFE, OFFERS THE ULTIMATE IN LEISURE ACTIVITIES AND PROPERTY INVESTMENT IN THE CANARIES.

IN THE ALL YEAR ROUND SUB-TROPICAL SUNSHINE, YOU CAN RELAX WITH A ROUND OF GOLF ON OUR 18-HOLE CHAMPIONSHIP COURSES, OR SIMPLY SPEND THE DAY AT THE CLUBHOUSE WHERE YOU CAN SWIM, OR HAVE LUNCH IN OUR RESTAURANT AND MAYBE ROUND THE DAY OFF WITH A GAME OF TENNIS. IF YOU'VE NOT EXPERIENCED THE JOYS OF HORSERIDING, THEN AMARILLA'S EQUESTRIAN CENTRE IS THE PLACE TO START. THERE'S EVEN A 300 BERTH MARINA NEAR COMPLETION – A SAFE HAVEN TO SATISFY THE MOST DEMANDING YACHTSMAN.

WHY NOT SPEND YOUR NEXT HOLIDAY AT AMARILLA – YOU'LL ENJOY IT SO MUCH THAT YOU'LL BE TEMPTED TO BUY YOUR OWN APARTMENT OR VILLA OVERLOOKING EITHER THE SEA OR FAIRWAYS FROM AS LITTLE AS £37,000.

EAMON DARCY CAPTAIN OF THE IRISH TEAM, WINNERS OF THE DUNHILL CUP SAYS:
"I believe this course, in its idyllic setting, will develop to a true championship standard and I have no hesitation in recommending it".

WRITE OR DIAL 100 AND ASK FOR FREEFONE AMARILLA FOR A FREE BROCHURE AND DISCOVER THE ALL ROUND EXPERIENCE OF THE AMARILLA GOLF & COUNTRY CLUB.

Amarilla Golf & Country Club

Cornwall Buildings, 45 Newhall Street, Birmingham B3 3QR. Tel. 021-233 1117

Buying property

It is advisable, when buying property in Spain, to take all the professional help and advice available because of the presence of less reputable property dealers, the long-winded process and the smattering of sub-standard, mostly older property.

When working through an estate agent, it is sensible to ascertain their reputation and experience. According to Spanish law, the title 'estate agent' can only be used by individuals of Spanish nationality who are qualified by examination and registered. But some licensed estate agents are little more than sleeping partners in foreign (British) firms having few qualms about the firm's reputation. Consequently, some lapses in professional standards do occur. Although builders and developers are not required to comply with such standards, again it is advisable to check their respectability and financial soundness.

Having found a property and negotiated a price, it is usual to pay a deposit of some 40-50 per cent, with the balance to be paid in six months. The sizeable deposit is forfeited if the transaction is halted by the buyer.

The legal process is simple, but often drawn out. It is very desirable to employ an *abogado*, the Spanish equivalent of a solicitor in Britain, to act on behalf of the purchaser. He checks the title to make sure there are no encumbrances and to ensure that building permits and planning permissions are in order. He also arranges for a *notario* to prepare the *escritura* (title deed).

The *notario* is a public official who ensures that the requirements of the law are carried out in connection with the preparation and signing of the *escritura*. He is not there to advise either party to the transaction.

By tradition the *notario*'s fees should be paid by the vendor, but nowadays contracts often provide for the purchaser to pay them. It is advisable to allow 10 per cent of the purchase price to cover the various fees and expenses.

The local land registry *(registro de la propriedad)* is where the names of all owners of the land in the district are registered and until the purchaser's name appears in the register he/she is not the full owner. Only the true owner, as recorded, is capable of legally transferring full ownership.

A *finca urbana* is a plot which is zoned for construction and building licence is usually easily obtainable from the local town hall, but there may be restrictions due to an alteration in the town planning because the residential services for the area are insuffi-

CLUB MARITIM, LANZAROTE

Lanzarote, the most easterly of the Canary Islands, is possibly one of the most curious and beautiful places in world.

Location: This small and select complex is located in the heart of the Teguise Coast Urbanisation opposite a extensive green belt and sports area with views of the sea and only a short distance from two excellent beaches the pleasure craft harbour.

IN THE MARITIME RESIDENTIAL CLUB
We have set out to create and intimate and high quality complex. This has been realised through spacious living areas and their superb environmental features which in turn are enriched by the select luxury furnishings and decoration. Spacious terraces, garden areas, swimming pools and an adjoining car park complete this high return investment property.

Island of Lanzarote

Apartment Type I
(Ground Floor)
Entrance Hall, 2 Double Beds, Large Reception, raised Dining Area, fully fitted Kitchen, Bathroom, Large Terrace, Private Garden.
£61,000 (Exchange rates correct on press date)

Apartment Type II
(1st and 2nd Floor)
Duplex apartment with master Bedroom suite with own Terrace and en suite Bathroom, Large Reception, Kitchen, Double Bedroom, Utility Room, Large Terrace.
£71,000 (Exchange rates correct on press date)

Islands' location

Sterling Mortgages can be arranged subject to status

FOR COLOUR BROCHURE AND FURTHER DETAILS CONTACT
Castlefields, 450-452 Edgware Road, London W2 1EG. Tel: 01-402 2196

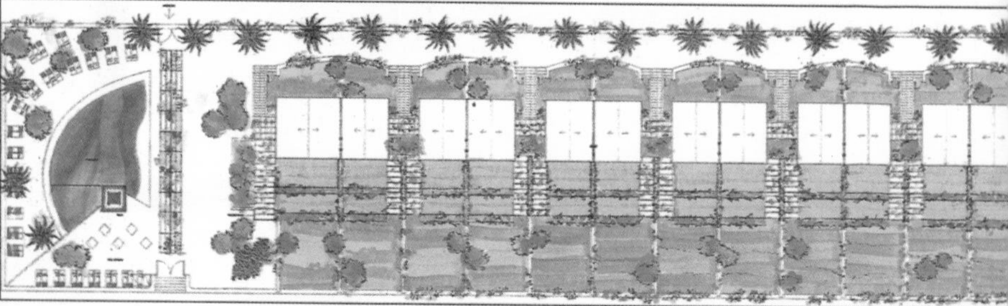

cient. A *finca rustica* is agricultural land where normally it is only possible to build for agricultural purposes. Building permits are sometimes given by municipalities on land in this category, but they may impose density restrictions, and also dictate the distance property may be built from the road, its height and distance from neighbour's property and so on.

Community of owners

In Spain, the Law of Horizontal Ownership requires that in property with communal facilities such as shared gardens, swimming pools, tennis courts or public entrance halls and passages, and in blocks of apartments or pueblo-style villa schemes and others it is the owners who decide how their development is to be maintained and managed day by day. Thus the Community is run according to the decisions approved by the majority of owners, yet the rights of minorities have to be protected.

Each Community of Owners must have its own regulations which are known in Spain as the *estatutos* (statutes) and these should describe in detail the parts which are jointly owned by all the members and those that belong entirely to individual owners.

The proportionate share of the common property belonging to each owner should also be stated and so should many other matters of importance to the general well-being of all the parties concerned.

Before making any purchase in this type of scheme it is vital that every prospective owner should be fully aware of the obligations involved, so reading the appropriate documents is essential.

Every owner is required to pay his or her appropriate share of the Community expenses and, under article 9 of the Law of Horizontal Ownership, owners are required to:

1. Maintain the property, fittings and installations in satisfactory repair so that no damage or danger will occur to the other owners.
2. Care for all installations in the individual's property which are for the benefit of other owners. This includes water pipes, mains drainage and electrical wiring.
3. Allow work to be carried out in the property as is necessary to provide new services for other owners.
4. Obey Community rules and regulations contained in the statutes or imposed as the result of resolutions passed at general meetings of members.

In accordance with the law, a chairman of the Community must

be elected every year. He is known as the *Presidente* and represents all the owners. He is also responsible for ensuring that the Community's affairs are conducted in accordance with the law and in the interests of everyone.

If an administrator is not appointed to handle day-to-day affairs then the *Presidente* undertakes the tasks of an administrator. The latter need not be an owner, but the *Presidente* must own a property in the development.

An administrator's duties include ensuring the affairs of the Community are run satisfactorily and that services are adequately maintained. He also deals with the maintenance and repairs of the buildings and other joint property belonging to the Community, prepares an annual budget for approval by the owners and, if no treasurer has been appointed, the administrator collects owners' annual contributions and also keeps adequate records of meetings.

An Annual General Meeting of the Community must be held at least once a year and notice in writing has to be sent to every owner, not less than six days before the appointed day.

A general meeting can be called by the chairman at any time of the year, or by a group of owners representing at least 25 per cent of the total of owners.

Matters to be dealt with at the AGM include election or re-election of the officers, approval of the Community's accounts for the previous year and of a quotation of expected expenses for the next year, also to fix owners' contributions towards these expenses.

Voting at meetings is undertaken on a majority basis by the members or their proxy. Voting is based on the size of the property owned by the voting member, but the total of those attending a meeting must hold at least 50 per cent of community property to pass a valid resolution.

Minorities are protected by the rule that states that a group of owners who between them own at least 25 per cent can apply within one month to a judge for a decision where they consider their rights have been prejudiced by a resolution.

A resolution can be declared invalid by a judge on the application of just one owner, where it is contrary to the laws of Spain or if it is against the Community's own regulations.

Where to live

The choice of where to live in retirement or for holiday periods is extensive. The weather is perhaps one of the most important

COSTA BLANCA
COSTA DEL SOL

Low-Rise Apartments · Pueblo Houses
Semi & Detached Villas

Freehold · Bank Guaranteed
Construction Warranty · Aftersales Service

All properties are close to the beach and shops, within private landscaped gardens and with swimming pools

Information & Sale:—

CROWN EXECUTIVE VILLAS

Alicante & Murcia's Premier Real Estate Agents

TEL. 0602 484580
40 UPPER PARLIAMENT ST. NOTTINGHAM

NEW & RESALE

Properties in selected areas, on the coast and inland from Calpe to Gandia.

COSTA BLANCA

Apartments, Villas and Luxury Villas in all price ranges. We only deal with Registered Agents and reliable Developers.

PERSONAL SERVICE WITHOUT PRESSURE

7 Main Road, Hockley, Essex (Tel: 0702-206281)

deciding factors and with an equitable climate for almost the whole of the year, the Costa del Sol, between Nerja to the east of Málaga and the frontier with Gibraltar, is one of the most popular regions.

Costa del Sol. Much of this coastline has been heavily developed with high-rise hotel and apartment buildings during the past two decades and towns like Torremolinos, Marbella, Estepona and Fuengirola have been expanded almost beyond recognition.

The long stretches of sandy beach tend to be overcrowded in the summer with package tour holiday-makers, who patronise the many vacation attractions, such as the dozen golf courses, tennis clubs, swimming pools, nightspots, casino and an extensive range of bars and restaurants offering a worldwide choice of food. For permanent residence most expatriates prefer to seek out some of the small towns and villages largely unknown to the hordes of European tourists who descend on the coast in the peak holiday months between June and September.

Salobrina to the east of Málaga is an attractive town with white painted walls built on a hill, which is crowned by a fine castle overlooking the sea. A town house in one of the narrow streets leading to the summit could provide a retirement home for a couple prepared to mix with local people away from the tourist traps.

Calahonda is a fishing community of interest on the road beyond Motril, a little industrial town with a port.

In the hinterland, mountain villages include Algarrobo and Competa which are deep in the Sierra Almigara, while Velez-Málaga is an inland town hardly touched by tourism – it was founded by the Phoenicians about 600 BC.

All these locations are readily accessible to the coast, although some of the mountain roads are a little uneven.

West of Málaga, the province's capital which has a population of 400,000, the coast has been commandeered for the benefit of vacationists and there are few peaceful locations. Carvajal, near the fishing village of Los Boliches, still enjoys some serenity and Carteya, a small village with Roman ruins near San Roque, is favoured by some foreigners.

Mijas, a popular village 8 km from Fuengirola, was formerly a pretty centre of habitation but has recently been spoilt following exploitation by developers.

Mountain villages of note behind Spain's most popular coastline include Jimena de la Frontera and Casares where many old rural houses have been modernised for permanent living by for-

eigners. Other places to consider are Benahavís, Istán, Monda, Ojén and Coín which is now a market town serving the farming community in the neighbourhood.

Costa de la Luz. This little-known territory lies close to Gibraltar and stretches westwards beyond Cadiz to the boundary with Portugal.

Because of the distance from Málaga airport this coast has not really been discovered by the 'international set', although Spaniards from Madrid and elsewhere have enjoyed holidays here for many years. This beautiful coast, washed by the Atlantic, is expected to become more popular for permanent settlement and holidays, as the opening of the frontier with Gibraltar has led to further development.

Tarifa on the border of the Costa de la Luz is the southernmost town in Spain. This residential resort has a population of 21,000 and enjoys excellent views to Africa, just eight miles across the water.

The major city is Cadiz and within easy reach is the nature

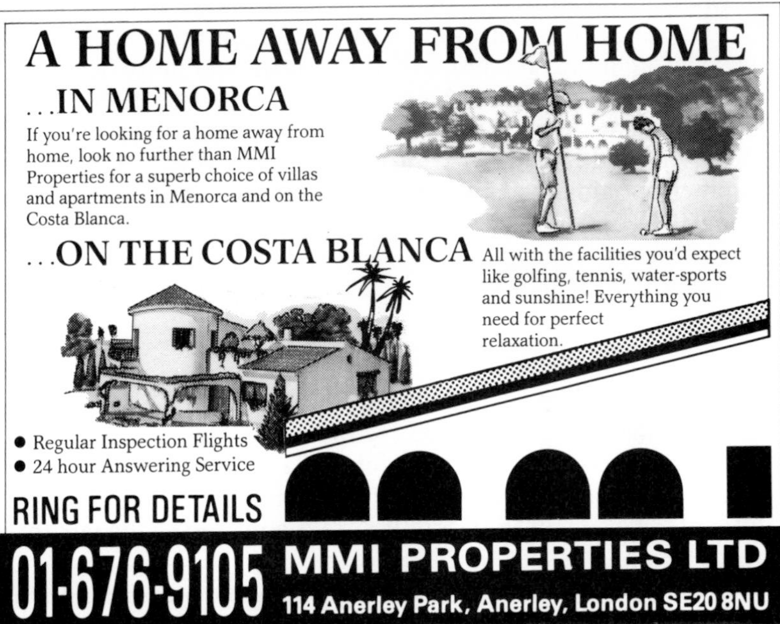

reserve of Donana by the mouth of the river Guadalquivir. Inland is the city of Seville (population 600,000) with its many cultural attractions. It is Spain's only inland port and ships of 15,000 tons can still navigate the Guadalquivir for some 100 km from the estuary to the city.

Costa Almería and Costa Calida. Almería is a large commercial town (population 200,000) adjacent to a stark hilly hinterland and extensive areas of open land which were formerly unproductive. Because of the warm climate it has recently been possible to produce profitable early vegetable and fruit crops, such as tomatoes, avocado and melon, under plastic sheeting. This produce is transported to England and parts of northern Europe in the winter when crops are not available from other sources.

This new-found prosperity, together with an expanding tourist trade, has attracted investment in residential property, particularly in places such as Mojácar, Adra, Almeriamar, Aguadulce and Roquetas de Mar.

The coast of Murcia province is known as the Costa Calida. The largest town is Cartagena which has important military and naval installations. It is also a manufacturing and shopping town.

The largest resort is La Manga, a strip of land with the Mediterranean on one side and the Mar Menor, a shallow inland sea, on the other. Highly geared to tourism, this town is very busy in the summer but almost empty for the rest of the year. Further east along the coast are Mazarrón and Aguillas which have many good beaches.

The town of Murcia is situated in the hills about 32 km from the sea.

Costa Blanca. The exact dimensions of the Costa Blanca are in dispute among experts. Some say the region starts at Denia and continues westwards 480 km as far as Cape Gata, beyond Cartagena. We describe Murcia and Almería under their own headings and information on the Costa Blanca is confined to the territory from Denia to east of the Mar Menor.

During 1986 this coastline was the most popular destination for purchasers from the UK seeking a home in the sun and many millions of pounds were invested in retirement and holiday homes.

The capital is Alicante, a fine city and harbour with an international airport on its perimeter. It has every possible residential amenity with a first-class shopping centre, some of Spain's best restaurants, an impressive cathedral, museums, sporting facilities, and a full range of schools; in fact, an ideal place to reside if you want to live amid the hustle and bustle of a big city.

To the east of Alicante the coast is littered with resorts, large and small, where Britons and many other Europeans have taken up residence in large numbers during the past 20 years.

There is still considerable building activity in towns such as Calpe, which has many multi-storey blocks of apartments, Moraira, a pleasant seaside town where private villas predominate and Jávea, where building activity has included both luxury villas and multi-storey blocks of apartments, but practically no new hotels have been constructed so the town is almost wholly residential. Water supplies in parts of Jávea are a bit uncertain in the high season and can be salty to the taste, but steps are being taken to rectify this problem.

Other small towns worth considering as the location for a permanent home include Villajoyosa, an ancient port, Altea, where the beaches are mainly pebbles and the old village is reached via

257 steps and Santa Pola, a small port where the restaurants are famed for serving some of the best seafood in the area.

Benidorm, the Blackpool of Spain's southern coast, should be avoided if you are seeking a quiet, peaceful life away from the masses, but it does have two fine sandy beaches and many essential daily living needs.

Inland Elche is renowned for its thousands of date palms which thrive throughout the city. These mainly grow in groves which are watered by a tenth-century irrigation system.

Locations away from the coast include Jijona, home of Spain's nougat manufacturing industry, Alcoy, where a variety of sweets are made, Guadalest, home of the 'eagle's nest' fortress built by the Moors over a thousand years ago, Jalón, a centre for the wine industry and Gata, best known for cane and basket work.

Costa del Azahar. Beyond Denia is the orange blossom coast, named thus because of the heavy concentration of orange groves. The hinterland is highly productive for agriculture and among the crops is rice, used in paella – the national dish.

The provinces of Castellón and Valencia are included in this region, which is not at all well known among foreigners.

Costa Dorado. The 'golden coast' includes the provinces of Barcelona and Tarragona. The two main cities after which the provinces were named are substantial industrial and commercial centres with large populations. Resorts include Sitges, Comarruga, Salou, Cambrils, Ampolla and San Carlos de Rapita.

Costa Brava. Just over the border with France the Costa Brava is the nearest coast for motorists from Britain. It can be reached via autoroutes all the way from Calais and is therefore popular with those who do not wish to fly to Spain.

The summer climate is not quite so warm as in the south and winters are generally cooler, but the average numbers of hours' sunshine in July exceeds 300.

Major resorts include Blanes, Lloret de Mar, Tossa de Mar, San Feliù, Palamos, Llafranch, Aiguablava, Estartit, La Escala, Rosas and Port Bou.

Gerona, the capital of the Costa Brava, is full of monuments to the past, for it was founded at the confluence of the rivers Ter and Onar several centuries BC. Ten bridges and an entire square cross the water and at the centre of the city is the old cathedral which dates back to the eleventh century.

Although there are a number of well-organised holiday resorts with high-rise buildings, the coastline has not been entirely spoilt by the ravages of summer visitors.

To the north of Palamos, there are pleasant small populated areas such as La Bisbal, Sa Riera, Sa Tuna and Aiguablava where villas can be found in small numbers, many with sea views.

Just inland, the town of Bagur is endowed with attractive small mansions huddled amid woodland and palm trees. These are mainly owned by wealthy Spanish families from Barcelona and other large cities, who prefer to nurture their families in country surroundings or near the sea rather than burden them with the problems of city living.

Occasionally this type of property comes on the open market to be snapped up by ambitious foreigners who delight in living in an aristocratic style. Prices are, of course, very high for this type of home.

Also away from the coast are Pals (not to be confused with the beach resort Playa de Pals – 6 km away) and Peratallada, once heavily fortified and where archaeologists unearthed in 1946 an entire Iberian city of the fifth to fourth centuries BC.

The Balearic Islands

Majorca. The largest island in this group is Majorca (in Spanish, Mallorca) with an area of 3640 sq km (1405 sq miles), about the size of Cornwall. Located in the Mediterranean over 150 km off the Valencia mainland, this island is heavily involved in mass tourism and attracts around 3 million visitors each year.

The majority of facilities and hotels for holiday-makers are located around the bay of Palma in places such as Magaluf, El Arenal, Illetas, Ca'n Pastilla, Palma Nova and Cala Mayor. Many high-rise apartments have been built overlooking the sea between Santa Ponsa and Paguera, while on the east coast much development has taken place at Cala Figuera, Cala d'Or, Porto Cristo, Cala Millor and Cala Bona.

Close to the north-west is a range of hills. The town of Soller is surrounded by citrus fruit groves and almond trees and Valldemosa is the home of a former Carthusian monastery.

The centre of the island is flat and fertile, with two main towns: Inca where there is a leather factory, and Manacor, centre of the island's artificial pearl industry.

Pollensa, Alcúdia and Ca'n Picafort in the north are favourite residential districts for foreigners who want to live well away from the centres of intense activity.

Minorca. The second largest island in the group is Minorca, which measures about 50 km by 20 and has a permanent population of 50,000. It is about 40 km from Majorca and is quite different in character. Occupied for long periods by the British in the eighteenth century, the island has many souvenirs of the former garrison including Georgian architecture and sash windows.

Far less dependent on tourists to earn a living, the islanders manufacture a wide range of leather goods, particularly shoes, distil gin to English recipes and produce fashion goods.

Mahón, the capital, is a tidy town with a main square, several principal streets and a host of narrow lanes. It adjoins a 6 km-long natural harbour, claimed to be the finest deep-water anchorage in the world after Pearl Harbour.

Many new estates have been built in recent years for local people and new residents from Britain and elsewhere. These are mainly located on the south and east coasts at Santo Tomas, Son Bou, Calan Porter, Binibeca, Villa Carlos and El Grao. On the north coast there are settlements at Fornells and Cala Morell.

The main town on the west coast is Ciudadela, the former capital. It has a picturesque harbour. Very little development has taken place in this region and deserted beaches are frequently discovered.

Minorca enjoys a temperate summer climate, but does suffer from cool winds at times during the winter.

Ibiza. The third largest of the Balearic Islands, with an area of 570 sq km, is located about 40 km west of Majorca. It is nearer to the coast of North Africa than to the Catalan city of Barcelona.

A relatively mild climate is enjoyed throughout the year with an average of 300 sunshine days per annum. In the peak summer month of August, temperatures reach 26°C and in the winter temperatures average 12°C.

Ibiza town, the capital, has a permanent population of 23,000 people. A modern town with shops exists near the harbour, but the fascinating part is Dalt Vila – the old town whose narrow cobbled thoroughfares climb steeply up to the summit, where the cathedral and fortress have superb views over the town and across the sea.

The other principal towns are quite small, with populations of around 10,000 people. These comprise San Antonio Abad and Santa Eulalia del Rio. They have both surrendered to tourism and are not ideal for residential purposes. Small resorts which attract prospective home owners include Cala Longa and Roca Lisa.

The Canary Islands

Tenerife. The largest island is Tenerife which is almost in the centre of this group of seven inhabited islands. A long-time favourite with northern Europeans keen to escape from the winter rigours of their homeland, Tenerife has the highest mountain (Teide) in Spain, a long coastline with sandy beaches in parts and a climate described by some as 'eternal spring'. Average air temperatures range from 16°C in February to 24°C in August. Most of the rain falls between November and February, but cloud can accumulate over Teide occasionally to hide the sun from towns in the north.

The capital is Santa Cruz, a busy commercial and industrial town, also a port, not much favoured for property ownership by foreigners.

Puerto de la Cruz on the opposite side of the island has all the facilities desired by vacationists. The lower part of the town adjoins the sea. Sandy beaches are rare but a huge lido has been

built on the promenade to accommodate the sun and sea enthusiasts. In the higher part of Puerto are some of the best hotels, also apartment blocks, a casino and the Botanical Gardens.

The expatriate community resides mainly on the outskirts and in the nearby Orotava valley where a considerable number of villas have been built among banana plantations and on hillsides.

Several years ago a new international airport was built in the south of the island and to make it accessible a fine new road was constructed.

The improved communications have been largely responsible for an entirely new holiday community built at Playa de las Americas and caused the expansion of Los Cristianos village. Huge new hotels and apartment blocks have already been completed, also some villas, and there are plans for more accommodation and a yacht marina.

The climate in this corner of Tenerife is warmer than elsewhere and the average number of sunshine hours is greater, hence the popularity with the international community.

Further north-west, on the coast, Los Gigantes and Puerto de Santiago are also expanding but the roads are not so modern.

Gran Canaria. Gran Canaria is well known world wide because of its capital Las Palmas, but it is in fact only the third largest of the islands.

Popular with British people in the first third of this century as a place for rest or retirement, the island has not maintained its attractions in post-war years compared with Tenerife. Although a number of holiday packages are offered by tour operators, there is almost a complete lack of organisations in Britain selling residential property in Gran Canaria.

With a population totalling over a quarter of a million people, Las Palmas is the largest city in the Canaries. It is a major commercial centre, a seaport and a cosmopolitan resort all at the same time. Major attractions include Santa Catalina Port described as a huge outdoor café, Las Canteras, a 4 km-long beach of fine sand, the Canary Village featuring local folklore and the Garden City with palatial residences and more modest houses all set in gardens with colourful blooms all year round.

Like Tenerife, Gran Canaria has some new resorts in the south, such as Playa de San Agustín and Playa del Ingles which are connected with the north by a good road. Tall hotels, blocks of flats, squat villas, pools and self-service food parlours are there in abundance.

A little further west beyond Maspalomas, some more modest urbanisations have been built around Puerto Rico.

Fuerteventura. The second largest island has an area of 2000 sq km. It is claimed that Fuerteventura has more beaches than hotels, but this may remain true for only a few more years, as expansion plans are afoot.

Of the total population which is around 20,000 people, over 7000 reside in the capital, Puerto del Rosario, a modest place with a harbour.

The nearest beach is Playa Blanca which is close to the airport. On the north coast Corraliejo was a small fishing port, but is growing in popularity because the bleached sand and the azure sea are so inviting for holiday-makers.

The southern strip of the island is known as Jandia. Along both sides of the peninsula are many more virgin beaches.

Property development is in its infancy at present.

Lanzarote. This island (area 800 sq km) has enjoyed boom conditions over the past decade, with many new developments both private and commercial.

The capital Arrecife has only modest attractions, but the shopping facilities are adequate and the international airport is nearby.

On the north-west coast, the Fire Mountains are spectacular and reminiscent of a lunar landscape. More than 300 extinct volcanic cones still exist and in parts volcanic fires glow a few feet below the surface.

In the north, land is sufficiently fertile to grow crops such as onions, tomatoes and vines with the aid of volcanic ash piled around the plants. This absorbs moisture from the night air and supplies water to the plants.

Costa Teguise, a few kilometres north-east of Arrecife, is a large urbanisation owned by an international company which installed all the necessary services and roads some years ago and the land is now being developed gradually, by a number of contractors, with apartments and villas. A nine-hole golf course is in operation and this is irrigated daily with part of the output from a desalination plant.

Small residential schemes have been completed or are under construction at Puerto del Carmen and Playa Blanca in the south.

The other islands. In order of size the remaining inhabited islands in the Canaries are as follows:

La Palma (725 sq km). A green island with a mountain peak nearly 8000 feet above sea level. Volcanic activity on the southern tip of the island occurred as recently as 1971. The capital and port, Santa Cruz de la Palma, is an attractive clean place with new offices and flats blending quite well with traditional architecture.

A small colony of foreigners have made La Palma their home, happy to be well divorced from the materialism of the late twentieth century.

Gomera (378 sq km). Located offshore from Los Cristianos, the port in the south of Tenerife, Gomera has a peak nearly 5000 feet above sea level in the centre of the island. The capital, San Sebastian, was the place where Christopher Colombus left the known world in September 1492 on his voyage of discovery to America.

Gomera's whistling language was used in former years for hilltop to hilltop communications. Now it attracts the attention of the day tourists who come on the car ferry from Tenerife, which takes about 1½ to 2 hours.

Occupation of residential property by foreigners is rare.

El Hierro (277 sq km). A wild island rarely visited by tourists because of the lack of hotels and facilities. The landscape varies from volcanic to verdant soil. The capital is Valverde which was built on a mountainside to counter attacks from pirates.

Inspection flights

Many of the organisations dealing in property in Spain have well-organised inspection flights on a regular basis. Specific details will be given by individual firms.

Recreation

Spain has been Europe's sunshine playground for many years and so it is hardly surprising that there is a vast range of leisure activities.

Sport is popular in Spain. As well as the traditional bullfight, football and cycling attract a large and enthusiastic following. For many, one of Spain's main attractions is golf. The many courses in such a perfect setting are hugely popular. Also, other facilities such as tennis courts and swimming pools are plentiful. Contrary to many people's image of Spain, there is a great deal of stunning countryside still left, and this encourages many to take up walking and camping.

In contrast, the main resorts and cities provide a large array of entertainment, varying from cinemas, theatres and nightclubs to shops. In many parts of the country, the traditional culture is very strong and can be observed in the form of crafts and dancers. Food is also taken very seriously and restaurants are plentiful and very good value.

The size and nature of the British expatriate community has encouraged the growth of clubs specifically for them. These include golf clubs, the film club in Marbella (Cine Club Bunuel), the Costa del Sol Garden Club, and also the British Society.

Communications

Air. Excellent selection of scheduled flights via Iberia, British Airways and other European airlines, plus a wide range of charter flights at competitive prices.

Rail. The nation is well served by an efficient rail service, and regular trains to and from France make for an adequate international service.

Road. Good trans-Pyrenean road communications have vastly improved the journey by road (via the cross-Channel ferries) from the UK.

Commuter services in Spain are frequent, if a little crowded.

Driving

There are some good roads in tourist areas and around the large cities, but some of the country and mountain roads are rather primitive. Traffic drives on the right-hand side of the road and passes on the left. All traffic approaching from the right has right of way. The wearing of seat belts outside towns is compulsory and those who do not comply will be fined heavily. Third party insurance is compulsory and a Spanish bail bond is advisable, as if you injure a pedestrian or damage another vehicle, you can be gaoled while the accident is being investigated. It is necessary to carry your driving licence always. An international driving licence is recommended, but is not compulsory.

Health services

In general, public hospitals and medical practices are good although perhaps not quite UK standard. Private health insurance may be worth while, to cover such things as post-operative or geriatric care. An agreement with BUPA exists also. Details of other welfare rights can be gained from the DSS.

Climate

Spain's climate varies from the temperate in the north to hot and dry in the south and inland. Those who can, desert Madrid in the hottest months.

	Madrid		*Barcelona*		*Palma*	
	Temperature (°C)	*Rainfall (mm)*	*Temperature (°C)*	*Rainfall (mm)*	*Temperature (°C)*	*Rainfall (mm)*
January	– 4-14	39	6-13	31	2-18	39
February	– 3-17	34	7-14	39	2-19	34
March	0-22	43	9-16	48	3-21	51
April	2-25	48	11-18	43	6-23	32
May	4-29	47	14-21	54	9-27	29
June	9-33	27	14-25	47	13-31	17
July	12-36	11	21-28	27	16-33	3
August	12-35	15	21-28	49	16-33	25
September	8-31	32	19-25	76	14-31	55
October	3-24	53	15-21	86	9-27	77
November	0-18	47	11-16	52	6-22	47
December	– 2-14	48	8-13	45	3-19	40

Switzerland

General information

Status. Confederation
Capital. Berne
Area. 41,288 sq km (15,945 sq miles)
Population. 6,437,300

Location

Longitude 46°N to 47.5°N; latitude 6°E to 10.5°E. Switzerland is situated in the central Alpine region of Europe and borders Italy to the south, Austria and Liechtenstein to the east, Germany to the north and France to the west. The south of the country is dominated by the Alps, which reach an altitude of more than 4000 m, and the north-west by the Jura range. In between this spectacular yet unproductive land lies the hilly 'middle land' where the majority of the towns and villages are situated.

Political stability

There can be little doubt that Switzerland is the most politically stable nation in Europe, if not the world. It is a federal state made up of 26 cantons, which in turn are split into some 3000 com-

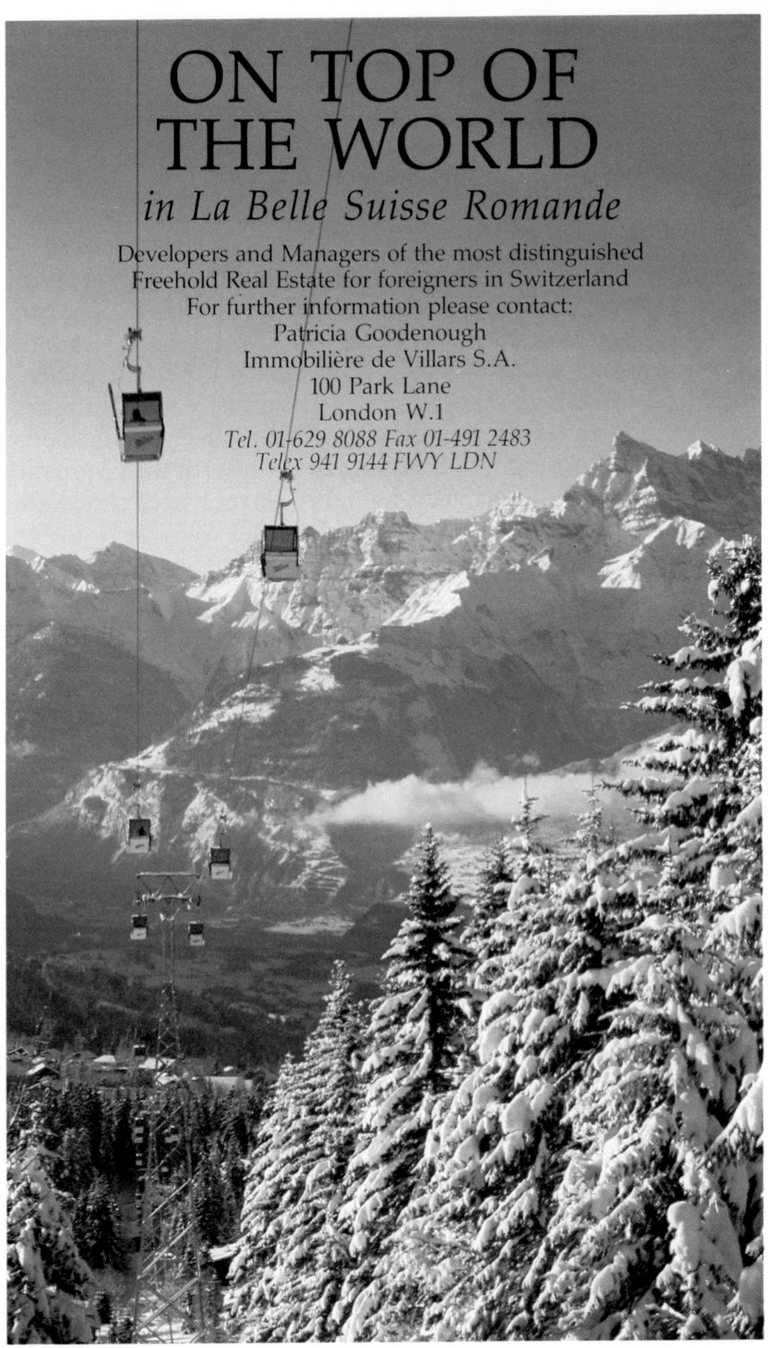
ON TOP OF
THE WORLD
in La Belle Suisse Romande
Developers and Managers of the most distinguished
Freehold Real Estate for foreigners in Switzerland
For further information please contact:
Patricia Goodenough
Immobilière de Villars S.A.
100 Park Lane
London W.1
Tel. 01-629 8088 Fax 01-491 2483
Telex 941 9144 FWY LDN

munes. This forms the basis of the unique political structure in which direct democracy is paramount. In terms of international relations, Switzerland has maintained its neutrality that was secured at the Congress of Vienna in 1815. In economic matters, non-alignment is the chosen course and this policy has been validated by the strength of the Swiss economy.

Economy

Cost of living. The Swiss economy is undoubtedly in a very buoyant state and so consequently living standards are high. The prosperity is also reflected in wage levels and when this is combined with the strength of the Swiss franc against other currencies, a move to Switzerland would appear to be a costly one. Necessities such as food and clothing appear especially expensive when compared with elsewhere. The Swiss are renowned for the production of certain luxury items such as music boxes, lace, chocolates, ladies' fashions and, of course, watches, and while these are very expensive, like most things in Switzerland, they are of the highest quality.

Taxation. Tax sovereignty is vested in the Swiss Confederation and in the 26 cantons, all of which grant taxing powers to their communes as well. This means that there are 26 different cantonal tax laws as well as federal tax legislation, and that taxes are levied by three separate authorities, federal, cantonal and communal.

There are no standard rates of income tax or capital tax, as these are normally levied at progressive rates. Federal Withholding Tax *(impôt anticipé)* and federal stamp duties are levied at flat rates. Taxes amounting to 1 per cent per annum of the value of any property owned are payable to the commune, canton and Swiss government. In the Swiss tax system, the accent is on cantonal and communal taxes which form the majority of the total tax revenue.

Exchange rate. Swiss francs 2.66 = £1.

Exchange control. There are no restrictions on the import and export of currency.

Language

There are four national languages in Switzerland: German, spoken by 65 per cent of the population in northern, eastern and central areas; French, spoken by about 18 per cent mainly in the west; Italian, spoken by about 10 per cent of the population in the southern Alps; Rhaeto-Romanic is spoken by less than 6 per cent in certain villages in the canton of Grisons. Knowledge of English is widespread, especially in the tourist areas.

Expatriate community

A cosmopolitan population is one of the hallmarks of Switzerland. About 15 per cent of the total population is made up of foreigners, and the country has been favoured by British expatriates for many years.

Security

All Swiss males are conscripted into the army for military training and so the country has a powerful militia, well able to defend the interests of the federation, should the need arise.

Residence permits

Recent years have seen entry regulations tightened up considerably and so the chances of obtaining a permit are much reduced. Generally, applications are only considered from those who are over 60 and are retired or of independent means. Non-residents can stay in Switzerland on a temporary visa for up to six months in one year, so long as any one visit does not last for more than three months.

Work permits

Before an alien can acquire a work permit, a valid passport, an assurance of a residential permit and an employment contract are required.

Personal effects

No duties are payable.

Housing

At first glance, it may appear that Swiss property prices are very much higher than comparable countries, but one must not forget that, to the Swiss, it is unthinkable that anything should be built that isn't up to the highest standards of quality and craftsmanship. This standard can be recognised in the new chalets and apartments which all have interior finishes, fitted kitchens, sanitary-ware, double glazing and joinery work of the best quality.

It is attention to detail that leaves nothing to chance. Usually separate laundry rooms and ski stores will be included in the price. The building may also contain a sauna or a swimming pool and will usually be managed by a highly efficient concierge.

Without taking into account the past strength of the Swiss franc against other international currencies, property prices in the past have on average risen by 3-5 per cent per annum.

Swiss laws require that a foreigner must obtain permission from the Swiss government prior to purchasing property in Switzerland. The number of permissions granted each year is severely restricted and in some major cities such as Geneva and Zurich it is virtually impossible to obtain approval. In the mountain resorts and on the lakesides, the possibilities are more generous and it is these locations which are in greatest demand from foreigners.

In order to prevent property speculation, foreigners are restricted to ownership of just one property per family. Non-dependent children over 20 may also purchase a single property. A foreign owner or member of the family is expected to spend at least three weeks per year in the property.

Buying property

A notary appointed by the government acts on behalf of the vendor and the purchaser. This official prepares the document and deeds for legal ownership, but his main duty is to protect the interests of the purchaser.

A notary with experience in local property is often recommended by the selling agent, or the developer in the case of new apartments and villas, but a buyer may use any notary he wishes.

A deposit is normally required to secure a nominated property and once purchase permission has been granted by Swiss authorities, the property deed is issued and registered. Then payment of the balance of the purchase price plus notarial and registration fees is required.

Notary fees are payable by the purchaser and, including the registration of ownership and tax, they amount to between 3 and 5 per cent, depending on the canton.

A notary can be granted power of attorney to sign all documents on behalf of the purchaser.

Where to live

See 'Housing' above.

Inspection flights

Scheduled flights only, not specifically for property inspection.

Recreation

The Swiss environment is ideally suited to the pursuit of a number of outdoor activities. Obviously, the Alpine regions have some of the finest winter sports facilities in the world, including skiing, skating and curling. The mountainous environment provides wonderful climbing, and hiking and camping are also very popular. The Swiss life-style necessitates quality facilities and so tennis courts, swimming pools and golf courses exist in abundance. The Swiss lakes provide plenty of opportunity for water sports and fishing.

Some of the most popular areas of Switzerland are the health resorts and spas. The clean air and pleasant climate make spas a blessing not only for the sick but for those merely seeking relaxation.

Nor is the cultural side of Swiss life lacking in any way. Music and theatre are thriving, the successes ranging from traditional yodelling to modern jazz concerts. Also, throughout the year, many festivals and celebrations occur, based primarily on old folk traditions. All this, combined with fine examples of art and architecture in the larger towns, make Switzerland an enjoyable and fulfilling place.

There is no lack of good restaurants offering exemplary cuisine of many different types. Traditional Swiss food is not of any distinct type, but eating houses do specialise in the local delicacy.

Communications

Air. Excellent services from Heathrow, Gatwick and Manchester to Basle, Berne, Geneva and Zurich international airports, via Swissair, British Airways and Dan-Air. Flying time is between 1½ and 2 hours.

Rail. The Swiss Federal Railway network is about 5000 km in all, having over 1800 stations and being fully electrified. The rail service is integrated closely with other modes of transport to provide a close-knit and efficient facility. This includes direct links to international airports, a wide range of postal, coach and boat services and mountain railways and cable cars. All this means the internal communications network in Switzerland is of the highest standard.

Road. The network is about 69,000 km long, with the national motorways stretching to about 1800 km.

Driving

The rules of the road differ little in Switzerland from elsewhere in mainland Europe. The minimum age for driving is 18 years. Drivers and front seat passengers must wear seat belts and children under 12 must travel in the rear of the car. Vehicle lights in heavy rain must be switched on and dipped headlights are compulsory in road tunnels. All laws concerning speed, lights and seat belts are strictly enforced by the police who are authorised to collect fines on the spot.

Health services

Health insurance is not compulsory but, as there is no national health scheme, it is advisable as treatment may be expensive. Such insurance is necessary for all members of the family and not just the breadwinner or head of the house.

A social security agreement does exist between the DSS and the Swiss authorities and details are given in DSS pamphlet SA6.

Climate

The climatic conditions of Switzerland vary considerably and perhaps no country in Europe combines within so small an area such marked climatic contrasts. In the northern plateau, surrounded by mountains, the climate is mild and refreshing. South of the Alps, the climate is warmer, coming as it does under the influence of Mediterranean weather. The Valais area is noted for its dryness. Summer brings warm weather but at high altitudes it is often quite cold at night.

	Geneva			*Zurich*		
	Average temp (°C)	*Average ppt (mm)*	*Sun (hours)*	*Average temp (°C)*	*Average ppt (mm)*	*Sun (hours)*
January	3	60	54	2	66	46
February	4	57	98	4	60	79
March	8	66	149	8	69	149
April	12	63	206	12	90	173
May	17	69	243	18	114	207
June	21	87	269	21	150	220
July	22	72	297	22	150	238
August	22	105	266	22	141	219
September	18	99	198	18	165	166
October	13	87	131	13	81	108
November	6	93	61	6	72	51
December	4	81	44	2	72	37

temp = temperature

ppt = precipitation

Turkey

General information

Status. Republic
Capital. Ankara
Area. 780,000 sq km (296,380 sq miles)
Population. 51 million

Location

Longitude 36°N to 42°N; latitude 26°E to 44°E. Turkey stands both in Europe and Asia, so it has two cultures. To the west of the Bosphorus which connects the Black Sea and the Mediterranean is the European part, and to the east, Asian Turkey comprises much high table land and mountains. Ankara is in the centre of the Anatolian peninsula in Asia, while Istanbul, the largest city, is in Europe and has suburbs in Asia.

Political stability

Surrounded by Russia, Iran, Iraq, Syria and Greece and having annexed the northern part of Cyprus following an invasion, Turkey is in a difficult position to ensure long-term political stability. Increasing links with the west through membership of NATO, OECD, the Council of Europe and associate membership of the EC, combined with expanding tourism and greater internal stability, will help.

Economy

Cost of living. It compares favourably with the west, especially in the goods that can be purchased in the markets (food and produce, crafts).

Taxation. There is a double taxation agreement with the UK. Income tax ranges between 25 and 55 per cent. VAT is 10 per cent.

Exchange rate. Turkish lira 3230 = £1.

Exchange control. In operation.

Language

The Turkish language belongs to the Ural-Altaic group and is spoken by about 150 million people in the world. It is written in Latin characters. More and more Turks, especially among the young generation, are studying foreign languages. Turks who have daily contact with foreigners (in shops, hotels, hospitals etc) know at least one of the major European languages.

Expatriate community

The expatriate community is very small and there are very few British citizens.

Security

Perhaps one of the less politically stable and secure countries dealt with in this book.

Residence permits

Application for residence permits should be made to the Turkish Foreign Office, where each case is studied on its individual merits. Personal income is a factor.

Work permits

The potential employee should apply to the Turkish Consulate-General for a work permit.

Personal effects

No duties are payable on personal effects.

Housing

There are some estate agents in the UK which are marketing homes in Turkey. Information is best gained from the Turkish Tourist Office or from a personal visit to Turkey.

Buying property

Foreigners are permitted to purchase real estate in Turkey provided the funds for the acquisition are transferred from abroad in a foreign currency. The purchase is subject to a registration fee of 0.5 per cent of the value of the property, but is exempt from VAT.

A land registry exists and transactions should be recorded when the regulations have been complied with.

Funds from the proceeds of the sale may be remitted abroad, provided evidence is available that the funds for the original property purchase emanated from abroad.

Where to live

Turkey has a wide variety of environments and cultures. Western Turkey, particularly Izmir, is Mediterranean in style.

Inspection flights

None.

Recreation

There is a wide variety of pursuits available in Turkey including yachting, hunting and fishing, skiing and mountaineering, as well as sampling the different cultures. The traditions (both religious and folk) and a rich heritage of monuments and museums are of interest. Shopping in the markets and bazaars is also very popular, where traditional crafts such as carpets, ceramics, copper and brassware can be purchased.

Communications

Air. Regular flights to Istanbul and Ankara by Turkish Airlines and British Airways, which take about 4 hours.

Sea. Passenger services from Italy and Cyprus.

Road. From London, Istanbul is about 3000 km. The journey can be made either all the way by road or part way by car ferry from Italy.

Telephone, postal and broadcasting facilities are adequate and western newspapers are available daily.

Driving

Vehicles can be brought into Turkey for up to three months by registering them on the owner's passport. After three months it is necessary to apply to the Turkish Touring and Automobile Club.

Speed limits are enforced at 50 kmh in built-up areas and 90 kmh elsewhere.

Health services

Many Turkish doctors and dentists have received training abroad and do command a foreign language. There are also some foreign operated hospitals in Istanbul.

A social security agreement between the UK and Turkey exists to protect entitlement to benefits.

Climate

	Temperature (°C)			
	January	*April*	*July*	*October*
Marmara region	7	16	28	19
Aegean region	9	20	30	21
Mediterranean	11	22	32	23
Black Sea region	8	16	27	18
Central Anatolia	4	15	30	18
Eastern Anatolia	–9	6	20	12

Chapter 26

Countries Across the Oceans

Australia

General information

Status. Independent state
Capital. Canberra
Area. 7,686,884 sq km (2,967,909 sq miles)
Population. 14,451,900

Location

Longitude 10°S to 43°S; latitude 113°E to 153°E. Australia is the only continent entirely occupied by one nation with one central government. It is the world's smallest continent in both population and size (except Antarctica) although it is 25 times larger than Great Britain. It is also the most remote continent, which has meant that the flora and fauna have developed in a unique way.

Political stability

Since 1984, when the moderate Labour government came to office, considerable political stability has been created. There have been some changes (notably the introduction of the Medicare scheme), but none so radical as to disturb the business sector. Although an independent nation, Australia retains close constitutional links with Britain and gives its allegiance to Queen Elizabeth II, who is formally the Queen of Australia.

Economy

Cost of living. This is marginally higher than in Britain, but is compensated for locally by the higher wages paid. Therefore, living standards are appreciably higher. Most goods in the shops originate in Australia, as imports are highly priced and difficult to obtain, because of the tariff levied on them.

Taxation. Taxes are levied at federal, state and local government levels. All areas of taxation, except customs and excise duties (which are exclusively the job of the federal government) are available to state and federal governments. Income tax is collected at national level and is a PAYE system, with instalments deducted from the weekly salary. Tax on income other than salary is collected in a lump sum by provisional tax. The basic rate begins at 24.2 per cent on income over £2200. There is no VAT although some non-essentials are subject to a sales tax. Finally, Australia does have a double taxation agreement with Britain.

Exchange rate. Australian dollars (A$) 2.10 = £1.

Exchange control. There are no restrictions on currency imports.

Language

English is spoken everywhere with some local variations on pronunciation and phrases.

Expatriate community

Since the Second World War, over 4 million migrants from over 120 countries have settled in Australia. Britain remains the largest source of immigrants (mainly because of the Commonwealth connection) but substantial communities from Malta, Cyprus, America and the Far East exist.

Security

In international relations, Australia's geographical position helps to make it one of the most secure of nations. Nevertheless, a powerful military is ready to repel any potential aggressors. Internally, Australia faces problems typical of an advanced capitalist nation, with one especially worrying aspect being the increasing menace of drugs.

Residence permits

Because of the demand in recent years to emigrate to Australia, a ceiling of about 84,000 immigrants per year is enforced. Application for entry should be made to the nearest Australian Consulate, each case being considered on merit. The immigration policy is non-discriminatory, allowing permanent residence especially for people with close family ties, or with capital and business expertise, skills, qualifications or other qualities needed in Australia, and others accepted under refugee or special humanitarian programmes.

Work permits

On applying to the Australian Consulate, details of work skills and professional experience are required so that it may be decided whether the immigrant's skill is of use to Australia.

Personal effects

Personal effects and household goods owned for at least one year may be imported free of duty.

Housing

The most popular dwelling unit in Australia is the detached brick-built bungalow with garden. Detached homes account for about 80 per cent of housing. Another outstanding feature of Australia is that about 75 per cent of householders own their own homes. Prices vary considerably both between and within cities. Property prices in Sydney have risen by about 20 per cent in the last 18 months and an average family home in a reasonable suburb may cost around £60,000. In Melbourne the rise has been less steep at approximately 14 per cent and basic prices tend to be lower at about £40,000. Perth is more expensive at around £54,000.

Buying property

The London office of the Commonwealth Bank of Australia, through their Financial and Migrant Information Service, publishes a regular Australian cost of living and housing survey.

Local building societies provide home loan finance with repayments spread over up to about 25 years. Interest rates vary but currently are around 14.5 per cent for loans under A$100,000. Banks also offer loans for house purchase at variable rates of interest. Government housing authorities are another source of long-term finance.

Stamp duty on house purchase transactions varies from state to state. In New South Wales the rate is 2 per cent of the purchase price. Legal fees generally amount to around 1 to 2 per cent.

Where to live

In such an enormous continent, the choice of residential zones is vast. The suburbs of cosmopolitan Sydney, New South Wales, are an excellent base for permanent residents, for the comprehensive facilities of the cosmopolitan city are close at hand. Brisbane's Gold Coast in Queensland is popular for retirement and holidays, while Melbourne, Victoria, has its devotees who seek a more traditional mode of life. The coastal cities in the south are popular with expatriates from Europe.

Inspection flights

None.

Communications

Transport and communications present enormous challenges for Australia because of the vastness of the country and the sparse population in most inland areas.

Air. Twenty-seven international airlines including Qantas, the national airline, operate to and from Australia. Domestic airlines carry about 10.4 million passengers a year with Trans Australian Airways being the largest operator.

Rail. The railways are mainly government owned and operated. Much of the 39,000 km of track is used by freight, but over 300 million passenger journeys are also made, mostly on the frequent and cheap commuter lines.

Road. Over 822,000 km of road for general use exist in Australia, used by more than 3.6 million motor vehicles. The trans-continental routes are used especially by the trucking industry but most towns and cities have excellent networks that are heavily used by commuters each morning.

Telecommunications. The long-established postal, telephone and telex systems make use of the most modern equipment and are generally very good for such a large country so isolated from the rest of the world.

Recreation

About 6 million Australians play sport, which includes tennis, cricket, surfing, the various forms of football and swimming, as well as a wide range of newer sports which are rapidly increasing in popularity. Recent Australian sporting successes, especially in sailing, golf, squash and marathon running, have prompted a surge in the popularity of these sports.

The climate lends itself to the pursuit of many outdoor activities including bushwalking, fishing and boating. The fine beaches, wondrous underwater scenery and ideal coastal waters are also a rich source of pleasure.

Club life, run by sporting or social organisations, forms the main source of nightlife. Membership entitles one to use the sports facilities too. Bars are usually male preserves, with heavy drinking taking precedence.

Entertainment and cultural pastimes are also strengthening. The theatre and especially the cinema have gained international reputations. Television is very American in style. Sydney Opera House and Australian opera singers are world famous.

Driving

Short-term visitors may drive on a British licence, but long-term or new residents must take another test soon after arrival. Regulations for the driving test vary slightly from state to state as do the regulations on vehicle safety and speed limits. Details are obtainable from the Agent General's Office.

Health services

Since 1984, a universal contributory health scheme (Medicare) has been in existence. This guarantees to all Australians 85 per cent of their medical costs, and access without charge of any nature to public hospital, inpatient and outpatient treatment. Short-term visitors will have to pay the full cost of treatment and so require private cover. Medicare is financed by a 1.25 per cent levy on taxable income.

Climate

Australia's climate ranges from the tropical in the north to the temperate in the south. The surrounding oceans moderate the extremes of climate giving the coastal areas a very pleasant weather pattern. It is important to remember that summer lasts from December to February and winter from June to August.

	Average daily sunshine (hrs)	*Annual ppt (mm)*	*Average temp for hottest month (°C)*	*Average temp for coolest month (°C)*
Adelaide	6.9	531	23.0	11.1
Brisbane	7.5	1,157	25.0	14.9
Canberra	7.2	639	20.3	5.4
Darwin	8.5	1,536	29.6	25.1
Hobart	5.9	633	16.7	7.9
Melbourne	5.7	661	19.9	9.5
Perth	7.9	879	23.7	13.2
Sydney	6.7	1,215	22.0	11.8

temp = temperature

ppt = precipitation

Canada

General information

Status. Commonwealth nation
Capital. Ottawa
Area. 10,010,000 sq km (3,850,000 sq miles)
Population. 25,354,064

Location

Longitude 48°N to 70°N; latitude 60°W to 140°W. Canada is about the same size as the whole of Europe and is the second largest country in the world. In this vast area are some of the world's largest lakes, huge prairies, massive mountain ranges and broad expanses of tundra. The north of the country is very cold as it stretches right up to and beyond the Arctic Circle. The majority of the population live within 500 km of the border with the United States.

Political stability

Canada is regarded by many observers as being the epitome of a stable and strong democracy. Internal conflict is rare and the party system, though well developed, is regarded as being more consensual than divisive. The country plays a leading role in foreign affairs and is a well-respected member of the Western Alliance.

Economy

Cost of living. Canada is considered to be one of the most financially stable countries in the world. High standards of living are enjoyed by most sectors of the population, because of the low level of inflation (around 4 per cent) and high wages. Generally, costs of living in all sectors of the economy are now lower than in the UK. Heavy winter fuel bills are to be expected. Petrol is much cheaper than in the UK. The long-term future for the economy looks bright as Canada is blessed with an incredibly large reservoir of natural resources.

Taxation. The Canadian government is making comprehensive reforms to the tax system which involve lowering tax rates and broadening the tax base. There will be changes to personal, corporate and sales taxes.

Tax reform will be implemented in two stages. The first stage, to be implemented in 1988, will include changes to the personal and corporate income tax systems. A number of interim changes to the existing federal sales tax will also be made, pending its replacement. In stage two of the tax reform, the current federal sales tax will be replaced by a multi-stage sales tax applied on a broad base of goods and services. When the current sales tax is replaced, further changes will be made to the personal income tax system.

Exchange rate. Canadian dollars (C$) 2.18 = £1.

Exchange control. There are no restrictions on the import and export of currency into Canada.

Language

The existence of two major linguistic groups is one of the features that helps to give Canada its unique character. English and French are both official languages and enjoy equal status. However, there has never been any national attempt to make the Canadian people bilingual and, apart from Quebec, the majority of Canadians use English.

Expatriate community

The population consists of people from a variety of cultures and traditions but many Canadians trace their origins back to French and Anglo-Saxon ancestors. Integration is encouraged but cultural traditions are still strong.

Security

Canada is rightly regarded as being free of any major internal problems that threaten security. In any case, the military and the police force are well trained and equipped. Therefore, apart from such common twentieth-century problems as are experienced throughout the western world, Canada can be said to be secure.

Residence permits

Older people are allowed to settle in Canada, provided they are at least 55 years old, have sufficient funds to live on and have no intention of joining the work force. Self-employed people and entrepreneurs are particularly welcome provided they are in possession of sufficient funds to establish a new business or purchase an existing one which provides employment for Canadian citizens or residents and contributes to economic development or cultural and artistic life. Such prospective immigrants are invited to submit their proposals to government officials. Families or individuals who wish to live and work in Canada should first apply to the Canadian government office in their home country for information on current requirements. The government sets a total number of immigrants that can be absorbed in any one period, but there is no quota restriction on those from any one country or area. Visitors who decide they want to live in Canada permanently cannot do so by applying from within the country as everyone has to apply from abroad.

Work permits

People who wish to work in Canada must obtain authorisation from a Canadian immigration office.

Personal effects

Most personal effects can be imported into Canada without incurring any duties provided they are kept for a minimum of 12 months after their arrival. The electricity supply is 110V, 60 cycles, and UK appliances are not suitable.

Housing

Canadian house prices rose by 15 per cent in 1988. The average price of a house on the Canadian resale market is expected to be around the £53,000 mark. It is predicted, however, that by the end of 1988 300,000 houses and condominiums will be sold, about 7 per cent more than in 1987. The huge demand for houses in Toronto and Vancouver has inflated the national average and together these two cities account for a quarter of the resale housing market. The average house in Toronto costs about £98,000, but average prices are lower in Vancouver.

Buying property

Legal fees charged by lawyers range from 0.75 to 1 per cent of the purchase price, but some lawyers who specialise in house conveyancing charge a flat fee of around £150, plus disbursements for title searches and other expenses.

A local transfer tax is assessed in most provinces when a property changes hands. This is usually less than 1 per cent of the purchase price.

Mortgages are generally arranged through banks, trust or insurance companies and credit unions. They normally require an up-to-date survey report on the property to be submitted with applications for home loans.

Newcomers who take up residence in Canada are not restricted from buying residential property, but most provinces apply a tax of around 20 per cent on the purchase of property by non-residents.

Where to live

The British will probably prefer the milder coastal climates. The bitter cold winters in the middle of the country make first-floor access to houses essential because of the deep snow. Therefore Vancouver is very popular in the east, and Toronto in the west.

Inspection flights

None.

Communications

Air. In such a vast country, effective air communications are vital. Therefore, the 61 airports in Canada are kept very busy by international flights, internal passenger flights and other varied services such as crop dusting, forest fire patrol, pipeline inspection and aerial surveying. Over 8 million people travel every year on international air services and over 20 million on domestic flights.

Rail. The railways have played an important role in the development of Canada. Today, two continent-wide lines, Canadian National and Canadian Pacific, span the country. They are used especially for the transportation of large quantities of goods. Smaller railway operations run on a provincial basis.

Road. Almost 14 million vehicles use Canada's excellent road network.

Water. As Canada has some of the world's largest lakes and is dominated in the east by the St Lawrence Seaway, communications on the water form an integral part of Canada's transport network.

Telecommunications. The Canadian telecommunications network is vast and is regarded as being one of the most efficient in the world.

Recreation

Canadians spend about 20 per cent of their income on leisure activities, so recreation obviously forms an important part of their life.

With four distinct seasons, the choice of outdoor activity is wide. In winter, there are opportunities for ice hockey, skating, tobogganing and skiing. The summer months can be occupied by playing tennis, swimming, golf, cycling and jogging. Spectator sports include hockey, ice hockey and baseball.

Canada's major cities have theatres, cinemas and concert halls. Smaller communities participate in amateur theatricals, annual fairs, folk music and handicraft exhibitions. In terms of history, Canada does not have many monuments of a glorious past, but the Indian cultures and 'gold rush' memorabilia provide a source of great interest.

The greatest single asset in Canada is the stunning environment. The vast countryside provides an idyllic setting for pursuits such as walking, cycling, hunting, fishing and camping.

Driving

Driving is on the right.

Health service

Responsibility for health and welfare is distributed between federal and provincial governments, who administer the services. The cost of medical and hospital treatment is high, but a government-sponsored insurance plan is available (details vary from province to province). However, dental and drug prescriptions are not normally covered by the schemes, and so private health insurance is an option and is tax deductible.

A wide range of social services and benefits is available (family allowance and pensions) and details of rights as an immigrant can be obtained from the DSS (pamphlet SA20).

Climate

Being such a vast country, it is impossible to categorise the climate as it varies greatly, from tundra to cool temperate, from snow-covered peaks to windy dry prairies, from climates that vary little during the year to ones susceptible to great extremes without warning. Between November and April the temperature can fall as low as minus 30°C.

Average mid-summer temperatures (°C)

Quebec City (Quebec)	18.1-25.8
Ottawa (Ontario)	12.6-25.3
Vancouver (BC)	20.9-22.5
Montreal (Quebec)	20.9-26.4
Toronto (Ontario)	23.6-28.1
Calgary (Alberta)	19.8-25.8

The Caribbean

ANTIGUA AND BARBUDA

General information

Status. Independent state
Capital. St Johns
Area. 442 sq km (179 sq miles)
Population. 76,500

Location

Longitude 17°N; latitude 62°W. Antigua and Barbuda together form part of the Leeward Island chain. The larger of the two, in terms of population and size, is Antigua. The islands, being only 400 km south of Puerto Rico, are regarded as the gateway to the Caribbean.

Political stability

Despite the fact that Antigua and Barbuda is a relatively young nation (having only gained full independence from Britain in 1981), it does have a long history of political stability. The system of government is modelled on the British parliamentary system. There is a strong regard for democracy and the rule of law, illustrated by the fact that there has never been any political violence in the islands' history. The country is a member of the Commonwealth and the United Nations.

Economy

Cost of living. As Antigua and Barbuda are small islands, the cost of imported goods (especially consumer durables) is high, and they are sometimes a little hard to obtain. Signs of a strengthening economy with increasing emphasis on agriculture and light industry may, in the long term, bring down the cost of living as the economy diversifies. However, local produce, especially fish and vegetables, is cheap and other special purchases include straw goods, pottery and jewellery made from semi-precious Antiguan stones. English bone china, French perfumes and Swiss watches are also cheap.

Taxation. There is no capital gains tax but a property tax amounting to 10 per cent of the purchase price of any property is due. There is also a small annual land tax of about 70 pence for every acre owned.

Income tax is nil. For the past four years Antigua has been an offshore financial centre.

Exchange rate. Eastern Caribbean dollars (EC$) 4.96 = £1.

Exchange control. There is free import and export of local and foreign currency.

Language

English is the official language. Local variations and dialects do exist, though.

Expatriate community

Antigua has, for a number of years, attracted expatriates from Europe and the USA in large numbers.

Security

The country suffers from no special security problems.

Residence permits

Those wishing to live on the islands must apply to the Ministry of Agriculture in St Johns. A local solicitor will usually deal with this. Consent is usually granted, so long as the authorities are satisfied that the applicant is of good character and has adequate means of financial support.

Work permits

Any application for a work permit must be made by the potential employer to the Ministry of Labour. To set up one's own company, permission from the Ministry of Finance is necessary.

Personal effects

Duties are payable on some large items (it is especially high on cars), but most personal effects can be imported free of duty.

Housing

There are some interesting small developments on the islands which are marketed in the UK and the USA, including one- and two-bedroom bungalows. A substantial villa on a good plot can be bought for under £60,000.

Buying property

The procedure is fairly simple, although it is necessary to employ a local solicitor to deal with the formalities.

Inspection flights

Properties are marketed in the UK, but no flights are chartered specifically for property inspection.

Communications

Air. Several international airlines including British Airways and VC Bird International fly to Antigua's international airport. Regular services also link Antigua with other Caribbean islands. A regular service links Antigua with Barbuda in just 10 minutes.

Sea. St Johns has a deep harbour and is served by cruise liners. Local boats link Antigua with Barbuda.

Road. There are nearly 1000 km of roads in the country, about 140 km of which are all-weather.

Recreation

As Antigua and Barbuda are havens for tourism, it is not surprising that the islands are geared towards that industry. Consequently, excellent facilities are available. The most popular activities are water-based sports such as sailing, swimming, diving, windsurfing, waterskiing and, of course, fishing, and cricket. Facilities for golf and tennis are also available.

There are a number of places of interest on the island, including museums, historical monuments and fortifications, as well as some idyllic countryside to explore.

The islands' cuisine is based on fish dishes and is highly regarded and reasonably priced. Locally produced red and white rum is a speciality.

Driving

Traffic moves on the left and international road signs are observed. A valid British licence is adequate to secure an Antiguan equivalent for a small fee.

Health services

Private health insurance is recommended.

Climate

The islands enjoy a very pleasing climate which is tropical in character and remains warm and fairly dry throughout the year.

	Temperature (°C)	*Rainfall (mm)*
January	18-25	234
February	17-24	155
March	17-25	206
April	18-26	185
May	19-27	292
June	21-28	358
July	20-27	447
August	21-28	389
September	21-28	417
October	20-27	315
November	19-27	123
December	14-26	257

THE BAHAMAS

General information

Status. Independent state
Capital. Nassau
Area. 11,406 sq km (4404 sq miles)
Population. 238,500

Location

Longitude 21°N; latitude 72°W. The island group has two main centres of population, namely Nassau (New Providence) and Freeport (Grand Bahama). In addition, there are more than 700 out-islands scattered across some 100,000 square miles of sea off the Florida coast, southwards towards Cuba. Many of these islands are uninhabited.

Political stability

The Bahamas gained independence in 1973, adopted a new constitution and became a sovereign nation within the Commonwealth. The parliamentary system is secure, having celebrated its 250th anniversary, and has the additional presence of the Queen's representative, the Bahamian Governor General. The current government came to power in 1967 and is generally regarded as socially forward looking.

Economy

Cost of living. Living in the Bahamas is not cheap (except for some local produce and crafts). The economy tends to be very reliant on the US economy, and so living costs are roughly comparable.

Taxation. There are considerable tax advantages for those living in the Bahamas. No taxes on capital, income, profits, inheritance or dividends exist. The main source of revenue for the government comes from import duties.

Exchange rate. Bahamian dollars (Bahama $) 1.83 = £1.

Exchange control. The Bahamas is an important financial market, with over 300 banks and the second largest Eurodollar market, so freedom to move capital with little restriction is necessary. Thus, exchange controls are nominal.

Language

English is spoken universally.

Expatriate community

About 2 million tourists, mainly from North America, visit the Bahamas every year. The two main islands both have significant communities from Britain, the USA and elsewhere. The attitude of the Bahamians to foreigners is very friendly, due in part to the 'people to people' programme organised by the Ministry of Tourism, which encourages local people to meet visitors and new residents, and offer them hospitality and show them around the island.

Residence permits

Residence on a permanent basis can be arranged, especially for individuals wishing to invest in property or a business. A fee of $5000 is charged. Those who wish to reside for more than eight months without working locally are required to submit references, have sufficient money to support themselves, provide a medical certificate and have no criminal record. The annual fee is $1000 plus $20 for each dependent living with them.

Work permits

Work permits are required and expatriates are not permitted to accept work where there is a similarly qualified local person. Permits cost between $25 and $5000. A permit will not be issued to anybody who entered the country as a visitor.

Personal effects

Duties are payable on some larger items. Details can be obtained from the Bahamas High Commission.

Housing

About 20 years ago, a considerable housing campaign was mounted to market individual plots of land on some of the largest out-islands such as Andros, Exhuma and Abaco for sums as little as £295 and £395. Unfortunately, few of these schemes ever came to fruition and purchasers had only dreams of living on a tropical island to compensate them.

However, Freeport on Grand Bahama was extensively developed with tourist and industrial facilities, and became a very prosperous area. Nassau, the capital, also expanded and many new holiday facilities, beach-side apartments and luxury villas were built over a 10-year span, with prices increasing in leaps and bounds. Currently, parity with Florida prices should be expected.

Buying property

Bahamian law is based largely on British common law and so procedures hardly differ. Initially, however, it is necessary to make an application to the Foreign Investment Board in Nassau, as a formality.

Where to live

With over 700 islands to choose from, the decision is entirely personal, although most properties are available on the larger developed islands.

Inspection flights

None.

Communications

Air. British Airways have direct flights from Heathrow several times a week to Nassau, and connecting flights from provincial airports (flying time about 8 hours). The domestic airline is Bahamasair which undertakes numerous internal flights. Other major airlines offer flights to the USA, Canada, Bermuda and Jamaica.

Sea. As the Bahamas is an island group, communications between the islands by boat is important. Also, the Bahamas is a favourite port of call for the Caribbean cruises.

Telecommunications. Being an important financial market, the Bahamas offers excellent telecommunications and telex services for an island of its size.

Recreation

In line with many Caribbean islands, the Bahamas offers a variety of leisure activities. Not surprisingly, the surrounding waters provide a rich source of pleasure ranging from fishing, sailing, cruising and windsurfing to swimming and diving. Other sporting facilities include 15 golf courses and over 150 tennis courts.

As it is orientated so much towards the tourist, facilities, especially around the main centres, are excellent. Restaurants, casinos and clubs provide a lively nightlife.

Driving

The Bahamas, in line with the traditional links with Britain, drive on the left of the road. Speed limits are low, reaching a maximum of 55 kph.

Health services

Private health insurance is advisable, as the best hospitals in Nassau and Freeport are private. However, the services offered, including general and maternity care, and a wide range of specialist care, are very good. Serious problems are sometimes dealt with on the US mainland in Miami.

Climate

A sub-tropical climate produces high humidity in the peak summer months of July and August when the maximum temperature range falls between 24° and 32°C. The wettest month is September when about 175 mm of rain falls in short but heavy cloud bursts. None the less, the rainfall does help to keep the land green all year round. December is the driest month, and February the coolest, when the maximum temperature ranges between 18° and 25°C.

BARBADOS

General information

Status. Independent state
Capital. Bridgetown
Area. 430 sq km (166 sq miles)
Population. 260,000 (approx)

Location

Longitude 13°N; latitude 59°W. Barbados is considered to be

one of the most British islands and is the most easterly of the West Indies. It is about 35 km long and 23 km wide. This coral island is endowed with many white sandy beaches and the capital has a population of 100,000.

Political stability

Barbados is the Caribbean's most politically stable nation, being the third oldest democracy in the Commonwealth with its first parliament in 1639.

Economy

Cost of living. Being a small island reliant on tourism and sugar cane production, the need to import most goods is great and this means that consumer goods are expensive and a little hard to acquire. However, locally produced goods and produce are cheap.

Taxation. Unlike many similar islands, Barbados is no tax haven. Tax on income and profits is levied.

Exchange rate. Barbados dollars (Barbados $) 3.69 = £1.

Exchange control. There are no restrictions on bringing capital into the country and many prices are quoted in US dollars. Repatriation of funds from the sale of property may be subject to delays. You are allowed to take out what you brought in plus a 'reasonable profit'.

Language

English is spoken by all.

Expatriate community

Despite its popularity with Americans, Barbados still maintains its British atmosphere, and this is compounded by the presence on the island of Britons whose families have resided there for generations. The local people are very friendly towards foreigners and refer to themselves as Bajans.

Security

Barbados is not subject to any major threats to its internal or external security.

Residence permits

No visas are required for stays of up to three months. Those who wish to stay longer or reside permanently, to work or to establish a profession, should apply to the Chief Immigration Officer in Bridgetown.

Work permits

These are necessary before you may seek a job.

Personal effects

Some duties are payable on some items. Details can be obtained by contacting the Barbados High Commission.

Housing

A wide selection of housing is normally available for sale. These are mainly individual villas that have been built to order. Recent offerings have included a three-bedroom home in over an acre of land with a swimming pool for £72,500, while a large three-bedroom house on the beach costs £150,000. Recent years have seen a stagnation of prices on the island leading to what may be described as a buyers' market.

Buying property

There are no restrictions on British people buying property in Barbados. The purchase incurs a tax of 10 per cent plus any legal fees.

Where to live

Villas are available all over the island but one of the more popular developments is at Glitter Bay.

Inspection flights

None.

Communications

The flight time from London to Grantley Adams Airport, Barbados, is about 8 hours. British Airways have daily services (except Mondays) and many other airlines fly to the island.

Recreation

Plenty of opportunities exist for outdoor sport including swimming, scuba diving, fishing, windsurfing, tennis, golf, horse racing and equestrian facilities. There are also many attractive walks on the island and places to explore.

Driving

Driving is on the left. Roads are relatively well signposted, but surfaces are often narrow and of poor quality, with potholes.

Health services

Private health insurance is strongly advisable.

Climate

Often described as perfect, the climate is comfortably tropical with hot sunshine and cooling trade winds. In January, the average minimum temperature is 20°C and this is the peak season. In July, it rises to 24°C. The annual rainfall is about 1200mm and the wettest months are July to September.

BRITISH VIRGIN ISLANDS

General information

Status. British Dependent Territory
Capital. Road Town
Area. 153 sq km (50 sq miles)
Population. 11,558

Location

Longitude 18°N; latitude 64°W. The British Virgin Islands comprise about 50 islands, many of which are uninhabited, and are located about 100km east of Puerto Rico. The largest island is Tortola, where the capital Road Town is situated. This is the financial and administrative centre of the island group and the location of the main shops, banks, the hospital and Government House. Many of the islands are quite mountainous. The vegetation varies with the rainfall pattern, ranging from palm trees and mangoes to cactus and frangipani.

Political stability

Politics on the islands is not viewed with any great interest by most of the population. The task of administering such an island group is delegated to the individual islands in many instances. Also, as the islands are still a colony, links with Britain are strong, adding further to the stability.

Economy

Currency. The local currency is the US dollar but the Barbados dollar is also used.

Cost of living. Because the majority of goods have to be imported, prices are likely to be high. Locally produced crops and fish are, however, available in abundance.

Taxation. There is no sales tax or VAT but a 7 per cent tax is added to any hotel bills. Tax on land for non-islanders is about \$20 per year on the first acre and \$10 thereafter. A property tax of 1½ per cent is charged on all privately owned buildings based on an assessment of the rentable value. A tax holiday of up to 10 years is offered for businesses which are specially needed in the islands and capital equipment may be imported duty free for these enterprises.

Exchange rate. As for US dollar.

Exchange control. There are some restrictions.

Language

English is spoken by all, with certain local variations.

Expatriate community

Because of its proximity to the United States, the expatriates are mainly from North America. The status of British colony has, for years, also attracted many Britons.

Residence permits

Non-islanders are permitted to land without restrictions and may be granted certificates of residence. Those who wish to take up residence or invest should contact the Chief Immigration Officer on the islands. Visitors from the UK may stay for up to six months provided that they can produce evidence of adequate means of support, have return tickets and pre-arranged accommodation.

Work permits

Non-islanders can only gain a permit to work on the islands if the post cannot be filled by a local person.

Personal effects

No duties are payable.

Housing

Several modest sized developments are being built, comprising houses on plots of one acre or more and some apartments on the water's edge at Tortola. Crown land is available for leasing on favourable terms where the developer can justify investment potential for the benefit of the territory. Private land can be leased or bought for development by obtaining a landholding licence. Modern homes generally exceed £120,000 in price.

Buying property

To prevent speculation, if you purchase land, you must build on it within two years.

Inspection flights

None direct from the UK.

Communications

Air. As the two main airports on Beef Island, Tortola and Virgini Garda are so small, there are no direct services from Europe. However, there are services from Miami and Puerto Rico.

Sea. The islands are reliant on the sea for their internal communication network so boats exist in abundance to ferry people and goods to the main centres.

Recreation

Plenty of opportunities exist for water sports including boating, swimming, scuba diving and snorkelling. Fishermen can also enjoy excellent sport. Well-kept tennis courts are provided by some hotels and clubs but golf is not so popular, with only two small practice courses.

Not unnaturally, the cultural facilities are somewhat limited, but there are some fascinating ruins to explore.

Driving

Valid British driving licences are required by all seeking to drive. For a fee of US$5, an island licence can be obtained. Cars drive on the left and there is a strict speed limit of 50 kph. All bicycles must be registered (cost US$5) and have a licence plate fitted.

Health services

There are hospital and medical facilities on Tortola, and also dentists and visiting eye specialists. International vaccination certificates are not required. Facilities are regarded as good, but insurance is advised. On Tortola, there is a small private hospital specialising in plastic surgery.

Climate

The islands have a fine sub-tropical climate thanks to the trade winds which moderate the extremes of heat and humidity. Rainfall is erratic and droughts are not uncommon (annual rainfall about 1000 mm).

	Average air temperature (°C)	*Average sea temperature (°C)*
January	25	26
February	25	26
March	25	26
April	25	27
May	26	27
June	27	28
July	28	28
August	28	28
September	27	28
October	27	28
November	25	28
December	24	27

THE CAYMAN ISLANDS

General information

Status. British Dependent Territory
Capital. George Town
Area. 259 sq km (100 sq miles)
Population. 22,000

Location

Longitude 19°N; latitude 81°W. The Cayman Islands of Grand Cayman, Cayman Brac and Little Cayman are about 770 km south of Miami. Unlike most of the Caribbean islands, they are not mountainous and volcanic, but flat. The capital, George Town, is situated on the largest island, Grand Cayman.

Political stability

The island group is a British colony and has a British governor who represents the Queen. He presides over a 12-man elected assembly. Stability and peace have been maintained.

Economy

Cost of living. The cost of living for those who wish to live in some degree of comfort is high compared with Europe. Consumer goods are especially costly as they have to be imported and so incur heavy freight charges.

Taxation. No income tax, corporation tax, inheritance tax, capital gains tax, wealth tax or sales tax is imposed.

Exchange rate. Cayman Islands dollars (Cayman Islands $) 1.52 = £1.

Exchange controls. None.

Language

English is spoken by all, with a soft Caribbean accent.

Expatriate community

The population of the islands is only small and consequently there are not huge numbers of expatriates living there. However, a number of Britons have been attracted because of the two countries' links.

Security

The Cayman Islands are one of the more secure island groups in the Caribbean, the only major problem being drug traffic. There are tough penalties for possession of hard or soft drugs.

Residence permits

Prospective permanent residents need to apply to the Chief Immigration Officer on Grand Cayman on a form which has to be accompanied by a deposit of about CI$1000. Applicants are required to prove they have sufficient capital and income to support themselves in retirement and to invest at least CI$150,000. Permission is granted only if applicants do not take up any work on the islands. Permanent residential status requires a minimum of six months' residence in the country.

Work permits

A permit must be acquired before work of any nature can be undertaken.

Personal effects

No duty is payable.

Housing

The Cayman Islands are one of the fastest growing property and real estate markets in the world. A number of developments have been built for the purpose of attracting expatriates. The houses are of the highest specification and there are a number of estate agents on the island. Property is, however, expensive, and a detached villa is likely to exceed £150,000.

Buying property

It is advisable to use an attorney as he will know the details of the buying procedure. Stamp duty on property purchase is 7½ per cent.

Where to live

There are developments at Snug Harbour, Cayman Kai, Rum Point and Seven Mile Beach.

Inspection flights

None.

Communications

Air. Cayman Airways run regular services to the American coast, twice daily from Miami and three times a week from Houston, Atlanta and Tampa. Air Jamaica also flies to the island three times a week.

Road. The island's roads are good. Speed limits are strictly enforced.

Telecommunications. Links with the US and beyond are excellent for a country of its size. Cable and Wireless is responsible for communications.

Recreation

Like most small Caribbean islands with a perfect climate, the most popular pursuits are linked to the surrounding sea. Fishing is very popular and the beaches are an excellent base for sunbathing, swimming and sailing. The most spectacular feature is undoubtedly the underwater scenery and so tours on a privately owned submarine are available, as are opportunities for scuba diving.

Driving

The single most important fact is that they drive on the left, as in Britain. The road signs and rules of the road also have much in common with the UK. Import duty on vehicles is 27½ per cent. New and second-hand cars are readily available – mostly American and Japanese makes.

Health services

Full private health insurance is a must.

Climate

The climate is typical of a Caribbean island with an average temperature of 27°C and little distinction between seasons. The idyllic setting is occasionally disturbed by hurricanes.

New Zealand

General information

Status. Commonwealth nation
Capital. Wellington
Area. 269,800 sq km (103,736 sq miles)
Population. 3.3 million

Location

Longitude 35°S to 46°S; latitude 167°E to 178°E. New Zealand is located in the southern Pacific, 2200 km east of Australia across the Tasman Sea. The two main islands (North and South Islands) differ greatly in character (climate, vegetation and geology). Nearly three-quarters of the inhabitants live in the North Island, especially on the fertile coast or plains. Generally, New Zealand has much in common with Britain except for a better climate, arguably better scenery, a more egalitarian society and a higher standard of living.

Political stability

The move from left to right influences in government over recent years has not introduced any violent changes of policy. New Zealand is a leading nation in the anti-nuclear campaign.

Economy

Cost of living. The actual cost of living is roughly the same as the UK but salaries are higher and so therefore are living standards (somewhere between the UK and Canada). Certain goods are expensive to buy including cars, clothes and some electrical goods. The best buys are foodstuffs, especially dairy produce.

Taxation. Income tax on worldwide income ranges from 24 per cent up to NZ$30,875 and 33 per cent above that level. A double taxation agreement does exist between New Zealand and the UK.

Exchange rate. New Zealand dollars (NZ$) 2.80 = £1.

Exchange control. There are no restrictions on the import and export of money.

Language

The language is English but Maori is still spoken by survivors (and many others) of that race who were the original settlers, but now form 12 per cent of the population.

Expatriate community

The vast majority of the population have their family origins elsewhere, mainly Britain.

Security

New Zealand is situated well away from known trouble spots and is a nuclear-free zone.

Residence permits

The entry rules for new residents are very strict and in effect only provide for family reunification in the case of anyone wanting to retire to the country. Under the 1964 Immigration Act, non-New Zealand citizens need permits to enter the country and if they intend to remain for more than one year, an application for permanent entry has to be made, but is unlikely to be granted unless their children are already residing in the country.

Work permits

These are not easy to obtain unless a firm offer of accommodation and employment has been obtained in a category that is considered by the Department of Labour to be in high demand. The high demand list varies from time to time and can be consulted at the New Zealand High Commission in London.

Personal effects

No duties are payable provided that the goods have been owned for at least 12 months. New goods over a certain value and goods sold or given as gifts have duties to pay.

Housing

Single-storey houses on quite large plots of land form the majority of modern homes in the towns and cities. They are often built of timber and brick with sheet iron roofing which is generally preformed into shapes which look like tiles and then coated with an insulating product to add colour and texture to the finished product. Prices of homes are higher in the North Island where they range from upwards of £27,000. In the South Island costs commence at about £16,000. Local building societies provide home loans with interest rates at about 14 per cent. Town houses and low rise flats are being built in heavily populated areas.

Buying property

A deposit of at least 20 per cent is required and so most people need a second mortgage to cover this expense.

Where to live

The cities of Auckland, Wellington and Hamilton in the North Island are most heavily populated. Sheep farming is widespread in South Island around Christchurch. Outside the cities one can be 80 km from the nearest neighbour. The choice depends on one's personal requirements.

Inspection flights

None.

Communications

British Airways and New Zealand Airways have regular scheduled flights to Auckland with an actual travelling time of about 26 hours, with two short refuelling stops en route. Other airlines have frequent flights via Australia. There are domestic flights to 24 centres. Road and rail services are good and public transport is especially efficient and well run.

Recreation

New Zealanders are very fond of life outdoors and during the summer spend weekends and holidays by the sea or in the country and enjoy fishing, sailing, horse racing, walking and active sports such as horse riding, rugby, cricket and golf. In the winter on South Island, skiing and skating are popular.

Clubs form an important part of New Zealand's life-style and there are also theatres and cinemas in the big cities. Television has a reputation for being unexciting. The legislation to allow restaurants to be licensed has seen a growth in their popularity too.

Driving

Short-term visitors can drive on their British licences, but permanent residents need to take a New Zealand test shortly after arrival.

Health services

A highly organised health and welfare service is provided by the government and is available under a reciprocal plan to new residents from the UK who have made appropriate contributions in the past. Details of this agreement can be obtained from DSS pamphlet SA8.

Climate

The country has a temperate climate, warmer in the North Island because it is nearer the equator. There are glaciers and ice fields in the cooler South Island dominated by the Southern Alps. Gusting winds are not uncommon.

	Average temperatures (°C)		*Average annual rainfall*
	Max	*Min*	*(mm)*
Auckland	28	3	1289
Christchurch	34	-5	668
Wellington	27	1	1305

The United States of America (Florida)

General information (USA)

Status. Federal Republic
Capital. Washington
Area. 9,399,300 sq km (3,615,125 sq miles)
Population. 233 million (approx)

General information (Florida)

Status. State
Capital. Tallahassee
Area. 151,670 sq km (58,560 sq miles)
Population. 10,416,000

Location

Longitude 24°N; latitude 80°W. The state of Florida is in the far south-east of the United States, jutting out as a huge peninsula separating the Atlantic from the Gulf of Mexico. It is a land of rich vegetation (including the Everglades) and a warm temperate climate.

Political stability

The USA is the richest and most powerful country in the world. US politics tend not to reflect the huge divide between rich and poor and recent years have seen growing stability and success. The country is also regarded as the leader of the Western Alliance. Since the US is a federation, Florida is run with a certain degree of autonomy with regard to local issues. At national level, Florida is represented in both Congress and the Senate.

Economy

Cost of living. The cost of living is roughly 60 per cent higher in the US than in the UK, but this is compensated for by much higher wages (two and a half times higher). Thus, when all factors are taken into account, living costs in real terms are reasonable. Inflation is running at a very low level (about 3.5 per cent), and the economy is generally regarded as being in a very healthy condition.

Taxation. Those living in the US for over 183 days in a fiscal year are required to complete a tax form. This is a complicated document (as with all US tax procedures) and assistance is often required from a tax expert. The system is under review at present. A double taxation agreement does exist between the UK and the US. There is no VAT levied but sales taxes exist on a regional basis. When a property is sold at a profit, a capital gains tax of 20 per cent is levied.

Exchange rate. US dollars 1.83 = £1.

Exchange control. No exchange controls are in operation.

Language

It is often said that the UK and the US are two nations divided by a common language. Nevertheless, the transition from British English to 'American' English is a necessary requirement for all immigrants.

Expatriate community

US society is very cosmopolitan, and includes many Britons (or descendants of) who have made a successful life. Americans are, on the whole, very friendly.

Security

Despite being the most powerful nation in the world, the US is surprisingly devoid of large-scale destabilisation – there are no active terrorist groups in the US and no war has been fought on American soil since the American Civil War.

Far greater are the problems associated with crime. The police forces are over-stretched in some areas and faced with huge problems, especially in the impoverished inner cities. Organised crime and the drugs threat are especially problematic. However, the expatriates tend to move to the more affluent and stable areas, where such problems are not so evident.

Residence permits

Very strict immigration laws are imposed on those wishing to settle in the US, because of the immense number of applicants. There are two categories of prospective immigrants: preference and non-preference. Those with the latter status who are retired stand little chance of gaining admission unless they have close relatives, such as an adult son or daughter, already living in the USA, in which case their application may be successfully processed in under six months.

All immigrants have to undergo a thorough medical examination and elderly applicants are sometimes refused admission on health grounds.

It is worth while employing a specialist lawyer to handle applications for residential status, because of the many complexities. Because of the favourable climate many elderly couples decide to buy a home in Florida and maintain a permanent residence in the UK so that they can spend six months a year in each location. Visas are no longer required for visits of up to six months by UK citizens.

Work permits

A work permit is a necessary requirement and the potential employer must apply for one on your behalf.

Personal effects

Goods that have been in your possession for more than one year may be imported free of duty, but may not be sold within three years of entry unless duty is paid. UK electrical appliances need transformers and new plugs within the US, where the supply is 110-115 volts at 60 cycles AC, and a two-pin plug is used.

Housing

Most Americans buy their homes with the aid of federal or commercial finance from banks, savings and loans and also mortgage companies. In expanding states such as Florida, an immense amount of new building is still in progress and developers become involved in many enterprising marketing schemes in order to achieve sales in a very competitive market. Among popular promotion schemes are 'Parades of Homes' which are held in many important house building centres.

Generally, the supply of housing is adequate, including new estates by well-known British companies such as the 1300-acre Taylor Woodrow site at Sarasota. Single family homes and garden apartments cost from £49,950.

Buying property

Under the Real Estate Settlement Procedures Act, a federal statute, every individual who submits an application for a house purchase loan must be provided with a copy of the informative 36-page booklet entitled 'A Buyer's Guide to Settlement Costs'. Settlement is the formal process by which ownership is transferred from the seller to the buyer. The book was prepared by the Office of Consumer Affairs and Regulatory Functions of the US Department of Housing and Urban Development. The first part describes the settlement process, negotiating a sales contract, selecting an attorney, selecting a lender, home buyers' rights and obligations, protection against unfair practices and title insurance. The second part is devoted to an item-by-item discussion of possible conveyance charges, together with some worksheets which enable comparison of costs levied by the various companies providing the services. The publication is distributed by the Mortgage Bankers Association of America, 1125 Fifteenth Street NW, Washington DC 20005, USA.

Where to live

Miami and Palm Beach are the traditional resorts on the east coast for holiday and retirement property, but these have tended to become overcrowded and expensive.

The west coast, with its seaboard on the Gulf of Mexico,

between St Petersburg, Sarasota and Fort Myers, has grown in popularity because numerous new resorts have been created for permanent living. Hurricanes are also less of a problem on the west coast.

Inspection flights

None.

Communications

In general, communication links with both the USA and the state of Florida are excellent. Flights from all over the world jet into Miami and Tampa International Airports. From here it is possible to travel by plane, train, car or bus.

Driving

The roads that link the various centres in Florida are generally regarded as good. The Americans drive on the right of the road; speed limits are lower than in most countries and are quite strictly enforced.

Recreation

Being one of the main tourist areas, Florida is geared very much towards the pursuit of leisure. Sporting facilities such as swimming pools, tennis courts and golf courses are plentiful, although they are mostly associated with membership of private clubs. The sea is also a source of recreation, with fishing and sailing popular. All of the many facilities are surpassed, however, by the incredible Disney World, which alone attracts millions of tourists every year.

Florida may be a little lacking in cultural and historical heritage, but there are plenty of other things to do, including a lively nightlife and numerous excellent restaurants.

Health services

There is no equivalent to the UK National Health Service in the USA, so all medical expenses have to be paid by the patient or the family. Consequently, medical costs are often very high.

Details of social security rights within the US can be obtained from the DSS.

Climate

Florida is part of the temperate southern climatic zone known as the 'sun belt'.

American terms

Some words in American English have different meanings from British English. A few examples in connection with property are listed below.

British English	*American English*
Boundary	Lot line
Bath	Tub
Cloakroom	Half bathroom
Curtains	Drapes
Cooker	Stove
Electric point	Wall plug/outlet
Estate agent	Realtor
Exchange of contracts	Closing
First floor	Second floor
Fitted cupboard	Closet
Garden	Yard
Ground floor	First floor
Housing estate	Apartment complex/public housing (if council estate)
Lavatory/wc	Commode/toilet/bathroom
Lift	Elevator
Outside garden tap	Spigot
Property	Real estate
Rates	City taxes
Semi-detached	Duplex
Skirting board	Base board
Tap (inside)	Faucet
Verandah	Screen porch
Work surface	Counter top

Part 5
Appendices

1. Telephoning Home

Subscriber trunk dialling is now available in many countries, and the codes for dialling the UK are given below, together with the time differences. The 0 which prefixes all UK numbers is omitted.

On new developments, in busy towns and in many rural locations it may take several months to have a telephone installed and the cost can be high. In some new apartment complexes enlightened builders arrange for the initial wiring to be installed prior to occupation by owners, so connections to individual flats are quite simple.

Do not delay in the payment of telephone accounts when they are rendered or you may find your line disconnected and it may take weeks to have it reactivated. If you occupy your accommodation for only part of the year, it is a wise precaution to arrange for accounts to be sent to your local bank and instruct them to pay accounts on presentation.

	Code for UK	*Code from UK*	*Time difference Hours +/− GMT*
Australia	001 144	010 61	+ 8 to 10
Austria	00 44	010 43	+ 1
Bahamas	011 44	010 1 809	− 5
Barbados	011 44	010 1 809	− 4
Canada	011 44	010 1	− 3½ to −9
Cyprus	00 44	010 357	+ 2
France	19 44	010 33	+ 1
Germany (West)	00 44	010 49	+ 1
Gibraltar	00 44	010 350	+ 2
Greece	00 44	010 30	+ 2
Israel	00 44	010 972	+ 2
Italy	00 44	010 39	+ 1
Malta	0 44	010 356	+ 1
New Zealand	00 44	010 64	+12
Portugal	00 44	010 351	Nil
South Africa	09 44	010 27	+ 2
Spain	07 44	010 34	+ 1
Switzerland	00 44	010 41	+ 1
Turkey	00 44	010 90	+ 3
USA	011 44	010 1	− 5 to −11

2. Radio and Television

For many years the BBC World Service has been a valued and much appreciated source of reliable information about world affairs for British expatriates in almost every corner of the world. It still broadcasts for 24 hours a day throughout the year with news bulletins on the hour every hour, plus many informative and entertaining programmes in between.

London Calling is a monthly magazine which discloses much information about programmes on the BBC World Service. It can often be studied at British Consulates or an annual postal subscription can be ordered from *London Calling*, BBC, Bush House, Strand, London WC2B 4PH.

Forces' broadcasting in English is heard in Europe, from either British or American networks.

Another source of English language radio programmes is Voice of America. This powerful station can be received on a number of frequencies and broadcasts news and feature items with an American bias. Frequency charts and programmes can be obtained from Voice of America, 300 C Street SW, Washington, DC 20847, USA.

Modern technology is having a considerable effect on radio and television transmissions and with the aid of satellites British TV programmes can be received over a wide area of the globe. BBC programmes are often available in Western Europe, and in south-west Spain, for instance, it is possible to receive British transmissions from Gibraltar TV.

Watching foreign television can be a considerable aid to learning the local language. Constant repetition of certain words in the advertisements finally lodges vocabulary in the memory of even the worst linguist. Watching the numerous British or American films with sub-titles can also help.

3. International Lawyers

There are a number of lawyers with experience in handling the sale of overseas properties who have offices in London and other cities. They can help to ensure that a proper, unencumbered title is obtained to villas and apartments purchased overseas, and help with foreign legal matters generally.

Their fees tend to be higher than for similar transactions in the UK, because of the technical work involved, but are normally a worthwhile expenditure.

A number of these firms are:

Amhurst Brown Colm Botti, 2 Duke Street,
St James's, London SW1Y 6BJ; 01-930 2366.

Anthony Bertin & Associates, Tontine House,
Tontine Street, Folkestone, Kent; 0303 46000.
(Specialists in Spain)

Blackstone Franks, Barbican House,
26-34 Old Street, London EC4V 9HL;
01-250 3300.

Antonio de Fortuny, 16 Rex Place,
London W1Y 5PP; 01-629 2673.
(Specialists in Spain)

Frank Charlesly & Co., 161 Fleet Street,
London EC4A 2DY; 01-353 1588.

Glaisyers, 1 Rowchester Court,
Whittall Street, Birmingham B4 6DZ;
021-233 2971.

Hedleys, 15 St Helen's Place, Bishopsgate,
London EC3A 6DJ; 01-638 1001.
(Specialists in Portugal)

John Howell & Co, 427-431 London Road,
Sheffield S2 4HJ; 0742 501000.
(Specialists in Spain)

Leathes Prior, International Department,
Holland Court, The Close, Norwich NR1 4DR;
0603 610911.
(Specialists in France, Holland, Portugal and Spain)

McKenzie & Chester, 89a Queen Street,
Exeter, Devon EX4 3RP; 0392 218218.
(Specialists in France, Spain and Portugal)

Jose Medio & Co, 14 Dover Street,
London W1X 3PH; 01-409 2355.
(Specialists in Spain; no UK qualification)

J Richardson, Spanish Consul Bureau,
40 Upper Parliament Street, Nottingham NG1 2AG;
0602 470501.
(Specialist in Spain)

Rosemary de Rougemont, Abreu and Marques,
Imperial House, 15-19 Kingsway, London WC2B 6UU;
01-240 9107.
(Specialist in Portugal)

Russell & Russell, 9-13 Wood Street,
Bolton BL1 1ER; 0204 34051.
(Specialists in Portugal)

Dr Salvatore Sammarco, 2 Duke Street,
St James's, London SW1Y 6BJ; 01-930 2366.
(Specialist in Italy)

Saville Associates, 2 Richmond Hill,
Bournemouth, Dorset BH2 6HU; 0202 298585.
(Specialists in Spain)

Michael Soul Associates, 20 Essex Street,
London WC2R 3AL; 01-242 0848.
(Specialists in Spain)

Sparrow & Sparrow, 38 Sudley Road,
Bognor Regis, West Sussex PO21 1ET;
0243 864589.
(Timeshare solicitors)

Stoneham Langton & Passmore, 8 Bolton Street,
Piccadilly, London W1Y 8AU; 01-499 8000.

John Venn & Sons, Imperial House, 15-19 Kingsway,
London WC2B 6UU; 01-836 9522.
(Specialists in Spain, Portugal, Italy and France)

4. Further Reading

A good selection of specialised books and magazines is now available through the retail trade and some can be consulted at public reference libraries. A few of these publications are listed below.

General

Buying Overseas Property, published by Homefinders, 387 City Road, London EC1V 1NA. A digest of informative articles about buying property in a variety of European countries and elsewhere. Price £3.

Daily Telegraph Overseas Property Guide by David Hoppit, the property correspondent of the *Daily Telegraph,* covering over 20 countries. Available from Daily Telegraph Publications, 83 Clerkenwell Road, London EC1R 5AR.

Retiring Abroad, Financial Times Business Information, 7th floor, 50-64 Broadway, London SW1H 0DB.

Sun, Sand and Cement by Cheryl Taylor. Rosters, 60 Welbeck Street, London W1M 7HB.

Villa Guide, published by Private Villas, 52 High Street, Henley in Arden, Solihull, West Midlands.

Working Abroad, the Daily Telegraph Guide to Working and Living Overseas by Godfrey Golzen. Annual. Kogan Page, London.

France

France – Information Handbook by Frank Rutherford, Sprucehurst Ltd, PO Box 388, London W8 5AX. A slim handbook full of useful information for those planning to buy a home in France.

Living in France Today by Philip Holland, New edition 1989. Robert Hale, London.

Setting Up in France by L de Warren and C Nollet. 1988. Merehurst Ltd, London.

Italy

Living in Italy by Y M Menzies. 1987. Hale, London.

Portugal

Buying Property in Portugal published by the Portuguese Chamber of Commerce, London. 1987.

Guide to Buying Property in Portugal, free from Glaisyers, 1 Rowchester Court, Whittall Street, Birmingham B4 6DZ.

Living in Portugal by Susan Thackery. Second edition 1988. Hale, London.

Your Home in Portugal by Rosemary de Rougemont. An Allied Dunbar Money Guide 1988. Longman, London.

Spain

The Blackstone Franks Guide to Living in Spain. 1988. Kogan Page, London.

Guide to Buying Property in Spain, free from Glaisyers, 1 Rowchester Court, Whittall Street, Birmingham B4 6DZ.

Living in Spain by John Reay Smith. New edition 1988. Robert Hale, London.

Spain, Costa del Sol. A guide to shops, sports facilities and restaurants between Marbella and Estepona. 1988. Sunshine Holiday Publications, Ashtead, Surrey.

You and the Law in Spain by David Searl. Published by *Lookout* Magazine, Pueblo Lucia, 29640 Fuengirola, Málaga, Spain. Lookout Publications.

Your Home in Spain published by the Institute of Foreign Property Owners. An Allied Dunbar Money Guide 1988. Longman, London.

Timesharing

International Timesharing by James Edmonds. 2nd edition 1986. Publisher Services to Lawyers, London.

Timesharing – A Buyer's Guide by James Edmunds. 1988. Kogan Page, London.

Timesharing – All You Need to Know by Burt Mason. 1988. Hale, London.

Timesharing – A Practical Guide by Brian L Wates. 1987. David & Charles, Newton Abbot, Devon.

Periodicals

Algarve Magazine, published monthly, price 100 escudos. An English language tourist magazine with property reports. Annual subscription £12 from Algarve Magazine, Rua 25 Abril, 8400 Lagoa, Algarve, Portugal.

Algarve News, An English language newspaper published monthly by Travelpress Europe Ltd, Douglas, Isle of Man. Algarve office: Rua 25 Abril, 8400 Lagoa, Portugal. Annual subscription £6 including postage.

The American, a newspaper published in Britain for Americans living in the UK. Fortnightly, price 20p; subscription £8.50 per year, from The American, 114-15 West Street, Farnham, Surrey.

Costa Blanca Post, a weekly newspaper in English; Apartado 2071, Benidorm, Alicante, Spain.

Costagolf, a monthly magazine devoted to golf topics and property on Spain's Costa del Sol; Apartado 358, Torremolinos, Málaga, Spain.

Cyprus Daily and *Cyprus Weekly,* English language newspapers. PO Box 1992, Nicosia, Cyprus.

The Entertainer, weeekly, a British publication for the coast of Spain. Subscription £20 from *The Entertainer,* Apartado 414, Garrucha, Almería, Spain.

Homes Overseas, a monthly illustrated magazine dealing with residential property in Europe and elsewhere, also includes a section on timesharing. Established 23 years. Annual subscription £12 including postage from Homefinders, 387 City Road, London EC1V 1NA.

Homes & Travel Abroad, a monthly periodical available on subscription from Homefinders, 387 City Road, London EC1V 1NA, or newsagents.

Iberian Daily Sun, an English language daily newspaper; San Felia 25, Palma, Majorca, Spain.

The Island Gazette, a monthly English language magazine with news about the Canary Islands, particularly Tenerife. Other islands covered include Lanzarote, La Palma and Gran Canaria; Calle Iriarte 43, Puerto de la Cruz, Tenerife.

London Calling, the monthly journal of the BBC World Radio Service, published from Bush House, Strand, London WC2B 4PH.

Lookout, a general interest English language monthly magazine with regular features on property and procedures for living in Spain. Publisher's address: Pueblo Lucia, 29640 Fuengirola, Málaga, Spain.

Mallorca Daily Bulletin, address as for *Iberian Daily Sun.*

Marbella Times, monthly social magazine in English. Address: Alonso de Ojeda 2.1°, Km. 188, Carretera de Cadiz, Marbella, Málaga, Spain.

New York Herald Tribune, an English language edition is produced in Paris and is available in many European countries, mainly at airports or railway bookshops. It tends to relate an American version of world news.

The Riviera Reporter, published alternate months.
35 Avenue Howarth, 06110 Le Cannet, France.

Tenerife Property Scene, a monthly magazine devoted to new property development being offered in Tenerife, plus property buying procedures. Subscription £15 per annum from Tenerife Property Scene, Carretera General a Guaza-Toscales s/n, Valle San Lorenzo 38627, Arona, Tenerife.

Timeshare News, A journal for the industry. UK subscription £45 per year. Tourism Advisory Publications Ltd, Freepost, Sudbury, Suffolk.

5. Useful Addresses

American Embassy
Grosvenor Square, London W1A 2JB; 01-499 3443
Andorran Delegation
63 Westover Road, London SW18 2RF; 01-874 4806
Association of British Overseas Property Agents (ABOPA)
16 Jacobs Well Mews, London W1H 6BD
Association of Malta Estate Agents
7 Whispers, Ross Street, Paceville, Malta; (010 356) 337 373
Antigua and Barbuda High Commission
15 Thayer Street, London W1M 5DL; 01-486 7073
Australian High Commission
Australia House, Strand, London WC2B 4LA; 01-379 4334
Austrian Embassy and Consular Section
18 Belgrave Mews West, London SW1X 8HU; 01-235 3731
Bahamas High Commission
10 Chesterfield Street, London W1X 8AH; 01-408 4488
Bank of England
Threadneedle Street, London EC2R 8AH
Barbados High Commission
1 Great Russell Street, London WC1B 3NH; 01-631 4975
Blackstone Franks
Barbican House, 26-34 Old Street, London EC1V 9HL; 01-250 3300
British Association of Removers & Federation of International Removers
3 Churchill Court, 58 Station Road, North Harrow
HA2 7SA; 01-861 3331
British Embassy in France
35 Rue du Faubourg St Honoré, 75008 Paris
British Embassy in Portugal
Rua S Domingos à Lapa 35-37, Lisbon, Portugal.
British Embassy in Spain
Fernando El Santo 16, Madrid 4, Spain.
British Virgin Islands Tourist Bureau and Information Centre
48 Albemarle Street, London W1X 3FE; 01-629 6353
BUPA International
Equity & Law House, 102 Queens Road, Brighton BN1 3XT
Canada Immigration & Visa Enquiries
38 Grosvenor Street, London W1X 0AA; 01-409 2071

Cayman Islands Government Office
Trevor House, 100 Brompton Road, London SW3 1EX; 01-581 9418
Department of Tourism; 01-581 9960
Channel Islands
Guernsey States Office, St Peter Port, Guernsey
Jersey States Office, Royal Square, St Helier, Jersey
Cyprus High Commission
93 Park Street, London W1Y 4ET; 01-499 8272
Department of Social Security
Overseas Branch, Benton Park Road,
Newcastle upon Tyne NE98 1YX; 091-285 7111
Department of Social Security
Information Division, Leaflets Unit, Block 4 Government Building,
Honeypot Lane, Stanmore, Middlesex HA7 1AY
Federation of Overseas Property Developers, Agents and Consultants (FOPDAC)
Imperial House, 15-19 Kingsway, London WC2B 6UU;
Administration 0273 690919
French Embassy
Consulate General, 24 Rutland Gate, London SW7 1BB;
01-581 5292
German Embassy
23 Belgrave Square, London SW1X 8PZ; 01-235 5033
Gibraltar Tourist Office
4 Arundel Great Court, Strand, London WC2R 1EH;
01-836 0777
Greek Consulate General
1a Holland Park, London W11 3TP; 01-727 8040
Inland Revenue
for payments of pensions or dividends overseas: Inspector of Foreign Dividends, Inland Revenue, Lynwood Road, Thames Ditton, Surrey KT7 0DP
Inland Revenue
for booklets: Public Enquiry Room, Inland Revenue, West Wing, Somerset House, London WC2R 1LB
Interval International
57-61 Mortimer Street, London W1N 7TD; 01-631 1765
Irish Embassy
17 Grosvenor Place, London SW1X 7HR; 01-235 2171
Isle of Man Government
Government House, Bucks Road, Douglas, Isle of Man
Israel, Embassy of
2 Palace Green, London W8 4QB; 01-937 8050
Italian Consulate
38 Eaton Place, London SW1X 1AN; 01-235 9371
Law Society
113 Chancery Lane, London WC2A 1PZ; 01-242 1222

Malta High Commission
16 Kensington Square, London W8 5HH; 01-938 1712
New Zealand High Commission
New Zealand House, Haymarket, London SW1Y 4TQ; 01-930 8422
Portuguese Consulate General
62 Brompton Road, London SW3 1BJ; 01-581 8722
Private Patients Plan
Eynsham House, Tunbridge Wells, Kent TN1 2PL
Resort Condominiums International (RCI)
Parnell House, 19-28 Witton Road, London SW1V 1LW; 01-821 6622
Royal Institution of Chartered Surveyors
12 Great George Street, London SW1P 3AE; 01-222 7000
Spanish Consulate General
20 Draycott Place, London SW3 2RZ; 01-581 5921
Spanish National Tourist Office
57 St James's Street, London SW1A 1LD; 01-499 0901
Swiss Embassy
16-18 Montagu Place, London W1H 2BQ; 01-723 0701
Timeshare Developers Association
23 Buckingham Gate, London SW1E 6LB; 01-821 8845
Turkish Consulate General
Rutland Lodge, Rutland Gardens, London SW7 1BW; 01-589 0949
Turkish Embassy
43 Belgrave Square, London SW1X 8PA; 01-235 5252
Villa Owners Club Ltd
HPB House, Newmarket, Suffolk CB8 8LX
Women's Corona Society
Minster House, 274 Vauxhall Bridge Road, London SW1V 1BB; 01-828 1652. Runs one-day courses for emigrants; has overseas branches in many countries and provides a welcome link for newcomers.

[illegible]

[illegible]

Queen Elizabeth [illegible]

[illegible]

Y

[illegible]

[illegible]

Index